W9-CAD-006

Southern Living® Cookbook Library

The Poultry Cookbook

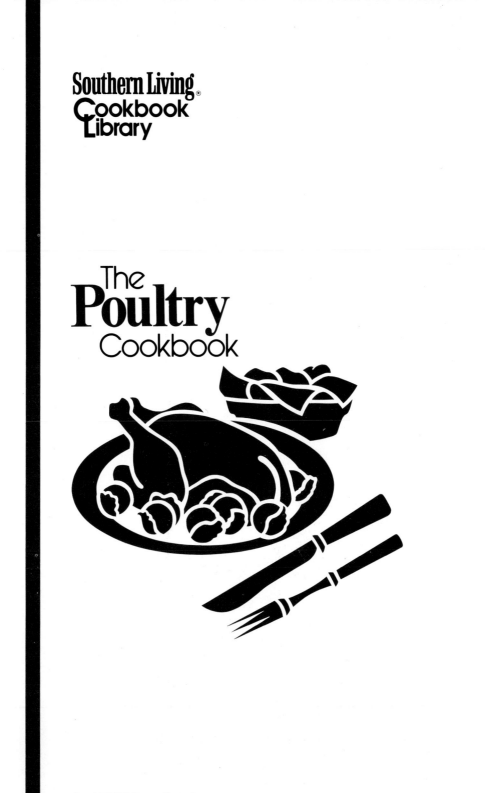

Copyright© 1977 Oxmoor House, Inc.
All rights reserved.
Library of Congress Catalog Number: 76-42088
ISBN: 0-8487-0347-2

Cover: Outdoor Charcoal-Barbecued Turkey (page 160)
Left: Conversation Curry (page 86)

contents

preface

"That's as southern as fried chicken."

This old saying captures the love Southerners have not just for chicken but for every kind of poultry. History tells us that Jamestown's earliest settlers brought chickens with them from England to provide needed food values in an unknown land. Clever cooks soon adapted their chicken recipes to accommodate the fowl they found in the teeming woods and waters of the New World — turkey, quail, ducks, and geese. For untold generations, the very best of these poultry recipes were carefully handed down from mother to daughter. Each generation added its own touch. The result: poultry recipes unmatched anywhere in our country.

Now, the readers of *Southern Living* magazine proudly share these recipes with you. Here, in the *Southern Living Poultry Cookbook,* you'll discover the secret of incomparable southern fried chicken, mouth-watering recipes for rich pies of turkey and chicken, and gourmet-pleasing ways to prepare game birds. To browse through the pages of this book is to share a priceless treasury of recipes.

Every recipe you find has been family-approved and proudly signed by a southern homemaker. These are the very finest recipes from the kitchens of some of America's most creative women, and they are yours in this unique book. From our kitchens to yours, welcome to the wonderful world of poultry — southern style.

COOKING AIDS

ABBREVIATIONS USED IN THIS BOOK

Cup	c.	Large	lge.
Teaspoon	tsp.	Small	sm.
Tablespoon	tbsp.	Package	pkg.
Pound	lb.	Pint	pt.
Ounce	oz.	Quart	qt.
Gallon	gal.	Square	sq.
Minutes	min.	Slice	sl.

EQUIVALENTS

3 tsp. = 1 tbsp.

2 tbsp. = 1/8 c.

4 tbsp. = 1/4 c.

8 tbsp. = 1/2 c.

16 tbsp. = 1 c.

5 tbsp. + 1 tsp. = 1/3 c.

12 tbsp. = 3/4 c.

4 oz. = 1/2 c.

8 oz. = 1 c.

1 oz. = 2 tbsp. fat or liquid

2 c. fat = 1 lb.

2 c. = 1 pt.

2 c. sugar = 1 lb.

5/8 c. = 1/2 c. + 2 tbsp.

7/8 c. = 3/4 c. + 2 tbsp.

1 lb. butter = 2 c. or 4 sticks

2 pt. = 1 qt.

1 qt. = 4 c.

A few grains = less than 1/8 tsp.

Pinch = as much as can be taken between tip of finger and thumb

Dash = less than 1/8 tsp.

OVEN TEMPERATURE

Temperature (°F)	Term
250-300	Slow
325	Moderately slow
350	Moderate
375-400	Moderately hot
425-450	Hot
475-500	Extremely hot

ROASTING CHARTS

GAME BIRDS

GAME BIRDS	READY-TO-COOK WEIGHT	OVEN TEMP.	ROASTING TIME	AMOUNT PER SERVING
Wild Duck	1-2 lbs.	350°	20-50 min.	1-1 1/2 lbs.
Wild Goose	2-4 lbs. 4-6 lbs.	325°	1-1 1/2 hrs. 1 1/2-2 1/2 hrs.	1-1 1/2 lbs.
Partridge	1/2-1 lb.	350°	30-45 min.	1/2-1 lb.
Pheasant	1-3 lbs.	400°	1-2 1/2 hrs.	1-1 1/2 lbs.
Quail	4-6 oz.	375°	15-20 min.	1/2-1 lb.
Squab	12-14 oz.	350°	30-50 min.	12-14 oz.

DOMESTIC BIRDS

DOMESTIC BIRDS	READY-TO-COOK WEIGHT	OVEN TEMP.	ROASTING TIME	
			UNSTUFFED	STUFFED
Chicken	1 1/2-2 lbs. 2-2 1/2 lbs. 2 1/2-3 lbs. 3-4 lbs.	375° 375° 375° 375°	3/4 hr. 1 hr. 1 1/4 hrs. 1 1/2 hrs.	1 hr. 1 1/4 hrs. 1 1/2 hrs. 2 hrs.
Capon	4-7 lbs.	375°	2 hrs.	3 hrs.
Turkey	6-8 lbs. 8-12 lbs. 12-16 lbs. 16-20 lbs. 20-24 lbs.	325° 325° 325° 325° 325°	3 1/2 hrs. 4 hrs. 4 1/2 hrs. 5 1/2 hrs. 6 1/2 hrs.	4 hrs. 4 1/2 hrs. 5 1/2 hrs. 6 1/2 hrs. 7 1/2 hrs.
Foil-Wrapped Turkey	8-10 lbs. 10-12 lbs. 14-16 lbs. 18-20 lbs. 22-24 lbs.	450° 450° 450° 450° 450°	2 1/4 hrs. 2 1/2 hrs. 3 hrs. 3 1/4 hrs. 3 1/2 hrs.	2 1/2 hrs. 3 hrs. 3 1/4 hrs. 3 1/2 hrs. 3 3/4 hrs.
Domestic Duck	3-5 lbs.	375° then 425°	1 1/2 hrs. 15 min.	2 hrs. 15 min.
Domestic Goose	4-6 lbs. 6-8 lbs. 8-10 lbs. 10-12 lbs. 12-14 lbs.	325° 325° 325° 325° 325°	2 3/4 hrs. 3 hrs. 3 1/2 hrs. 3 3/4 hrs. 4 1/4 hrs.	3 hrs. 3 1/2 hrs. 3 3/4 hrs. 4 1/4 hrs. 4 3/4 hrs.
Cornish Game Hen	1-1 1/2 lbs.	400°	1 1/2 hrs.	1 1/2 hrs.
Guinea Hen	1 1/2-2 lbs. 2-2 1/2 lbs.	375° 375°	3/4 hr. 1 hr.	1 hr. 1 1/2 hrs.

Basil can be chopped and added to cold poultry salads. If your recipe calls for tomatoes or tomato sauce, add a touch of basil to bring out a rich flavor.

Bay leaf, the basis of French seasonings, is nice added to soups, stews, marinades, or stuffings.

Bouquet garni, a must in many Creole cuisine recipes, is a bundle of thyme, parsley, and bay leaf tied together and added to soups, stews, or sauces.

Celery seed, from wild celery rather than our domestic celery, adds pleasant flavor to bouillon or stock.

A LIGHT TOUCH OF

herbs & spices

Chervil is one of the traditional *fines herbes* in French-derived cooking. (The others are tarragon, parsley, and chive.) It is particularly good in omelets or soups.

Chive, available fresh, dried, or frozen, can be substituted for raw onion in any poultry recipe.

Garlic, one of the oldest herbs in the world, must be carefully handled. When cooking, don't simmer until black or it will create an offensive odor. For best results, press the garlic clove against the kitchen table and half crush, then cook. If your recipe calls for sliced garlic, substitute grated or pressed garlic. The flavor will improve noticeably.

Marjoram is an aromatic herb from the mint family. It is good in soups, sauces, stuffings, and stews.

Mustard (dry) brings a sharp bite to sauces. Sprinkle just a touch over roast chicken for a delightful flavor treat.

Oregano is a staple in Italian, Spanish, and Mexican cuisines. It is very good in savory dishes with a tomato foundation.

Paprika, a mild pepper, adds color to poultry dishes. The very best paprika is imported from Hungary — there is a world of difference between it and the supermarket variety.

Rosemary, a tasty herb, is an important part of poultry stuffing for duck, partridge, and capon.

Sage, the perennial favorite with all kinds of poultry, adds flavor to stuffings. It is particularly good with goose.

Tarragon, one of the *fines herbes,* has wonderful flavor and goes well with all poultry dishes except one: it is too pungent for poultry soups.

Thyme is used in combination with bay leaf in soups and stews.

SPICES

Allspice, a pungent, aromatic spice, comes in whole or powdered form. It is excellent in marinades or curries and goes particularly well in game marinades.

Cinnamon, ground from the bark of the cinnamon tree, is important in preparing savory, flavorful dishes.

Coriander adds an unusual flavor to soups, stews, chili dishes, and curries.

Cumin is a staple spice in Mexican cooking. To use, rub seeds together and let them fall into the dish just before serving.

HERB AND SPICE CHART

This chart was designed to help you buy fresh herbs and spices . . . the very best kind to use in cooking poultry or any other food. If you cannot find fresh herbs and spices, use dried ones and crush them just before adding. Allow one-fourth as much dried herb or spice when using it in place of fresh.

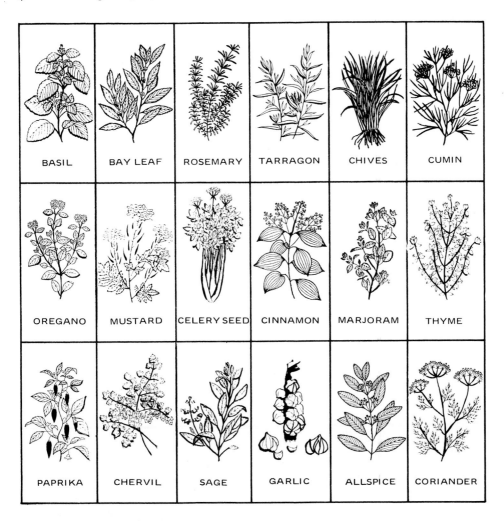

BASIL	BAY LEAF	ROSEMARY	TARRAGON	CHIVES	CUMIN
OREGANO	MUSTARD	CELERY SEED	CINNAMON	MARJORAM	THYME
PAPRIKA	CHERVIL	SAGE	GARLIC	ALLSPICE	CORIANDER

BUYING CHICKEN

Chicken is popular with homemakers not only because it has a delicious, mild flavor but because it also is one of today's best buys. Although low in price, chicken is high in protein, niacin, and iron . . . an important consideration for nutrition-minded women.

In choosing chicken, look for birds with short legs, plump bodies, and unbruised skins. They should have a good fatty layer. If pre-packaged, the packages should be unbroken. Almost all poultry sold is inspected and is rated Grade A. Under the latest legislation, chicken-packing plants are continuously inspected for your family's protection.

BUYING AND STORING
poultry

Broiler-fryers are the most popular type of chicken. They are an excellent buy from May until September. These young, tender chickens weigh between 1 1/2 to 3 1/2 pounds and come ready to cook. They are perfect for roasting, simmering, baking, frying, grilling, or broiling.

Capons are large chickens, usually weighing from four to seven pounds. They yield a large amount of white, flavorful meat. They are most often roasted, although they may be baked, fried, or broiled.

Roasters are large – 3 1/2 to 5 pounds – tender birds and are an excellent buy from September to January. Usually sold ready to cook, they are delicious when stuffed and baked in the oven.

Stewing chickens are mature, less tender birds weighing from 2 1/2 to 5 pounds. They are priced lowest from October to January. These fatty birds are cooked in a large amount of liquid. One stewing chicken will usually yield enough meat for a chicken pie plus a salad, with plenty of rich broth left over.

Cornish game hens are the smallest and youngest members of the chicken family. Weighing 1 1/2 pounds or less, they are excellent for roasting, broiling, or frying. They are also the most expensive of all chickens.

Chicken roasts generally come in two-pound sizes. They are made of uncooked chicken boned, rolled, and covered with skin. They are just right for small family meals, luncheons, or in buffet service when you want pieces of uniform size.

The amount of chicken you buy will depend on how many people you are serving. In general, allow 1/4 to 1/2 a bird per person for broiling or frying.

If roasting or stewing, allow 1/2 pound per person (3/4 pound for hearty eaters). Allow one Cornish hen per person. If you are serving chicken roasts, plan on 1/3 pound per serving.

BUYING TURKEY

The same general rules for buying chicken apply in buying turkey. Your best buy in turkeys is the 16- to 24-pound birds – they yield more meat per pound. If this size is too big for your family, ask the butcher to split it: freeze half and use it later.

Like chicken, turkey is available in boned and rolled roasts. These roasts come in 2 1/2 to 10-pound sizes. Also available are rolls – three to ten pounds of fully cooked turkey not covered with skin. These rolls are perfect for sandwiches or casseroles.

In buying turkey, you'll want to calculate how many people you can serve per pound. For a 5- to 12-pound turkey, allow 3/4 to 1 pound per person. A 12- to 24-pound turkey will give you 1/2 to 3/4 a pound per serving. For uncooked boneless roasts, allow 1/3 pound per person.

STORING CHICKEN AND TURKEY

Chicken and turkey you are going to use within a day or two can be safely kept in the refrigerator. Giblets and liver should be used within 24 hours. Ready-to-cook, whole chicken will keep in the refrigerator for two to three days; cut-up chicken will keep two days. Whole turkey will keep for four to five days. To prepare for refrigeration, remove any wrapping around the poultry as soon as you get home from the store, wash the bird, separate the giblets and liver (usually wrapped separately), and wrap both bird and giblets and liver loosely in transparent paper or foil.

Turkey and chicken may be kept in the refrigerator's freezing compartment or your home freezer. All poultry should be frozen at zero degrees or less. To prepare for freezing, remove all wrapping and rinse the bird thoroughly under cold running water. Pat dry and wrap tightly in transparent wrap, foil, or freezer paper. Try to squeeze out as much air as possible. Whole chickens can be kept frozen for 12 months, cut-up chicken and whole turkeys for 6 months. Never freeze stuffed poultry – the dressing will sour.

To store cooked poultry, remove the stuffing and cooked meat from the bones as soon as possible. Chill both the stuffing and the meat thoroughly. Both may be frozen or kept in the refrigerator. Cooked poultry with liquid will keep in the refrigerator for two days or in the freezer for six months. Poultry without liquid keeps in the refrigerator for two days and in the freezer for one month. Gravy and stuffing may be kept in the refrigerator for three to four days or in the freezer for two months.

Roasting takes place in an oven preheated to 325 degrees. Poultry to be roasted should be rubbed thoroughly with softened butter and placed on a rack in a shallow roasting pan. Turn the bird breast-side up for the last 15 minutes of cooking time for added color and a crisper skin. Covering the roasting pan with a tent of foil will not only ensure good color and crispness but will keep grease from spattering your oven surfaces. When the drumstick moves easily, the bird is cooked.

methods
of preparation

Barbecuing is a traditional southern way of preparing poultry. Place broiler-fryer quarters or halves, skin-side up, on a grate about six inches away from glowing coals. Brush with your favorite barbecue sauce — you'll find many delicious sauces in the following pages. Turn frequently and brush often with sauce. The meat will cook in 45 minutes to one hour depending on the size of your pieces.

Broiling is a dry-heat cooking method. Preheat your broiler with the oven temperature set at 350 degrees. (Hotter than this and the poultry will singe.) Brush your broiler halves or quarters with melted butter — you may want to try seasoning the butter for added flavor. Place broiler pan as far away from the heat as possible and broil for 20 minutes on each side, brushing with melted butter frequently. After 40 minutes, prick the chicken with a skewer. If the juices run red, additional cooking time is needed.

Of all the cooking methods of poultry, none is more southern than *frying*. Cover the cut-up pieces of your fryer with seasoned or plain flour. Meanwhile, heat 1/2 inch oil or shortening in a skillet. Beginning with the larger pieces, place chicken skin-side down in the pan of oil over moderate heat. Turn and brown other side. Reduce heat and cook for 15 to 25 minutes on each side.

Braising is much like frying, but the cooking is done in oil plus another liquid. To braise, season cut-up pieces of chicken and place them, skin-side down, in a skillet with 1/4 cup oil. Brown over high heat to seal in all the juices. Reduce heat and add 1/2 cup broth, consomme, vegetable juice, or other liquid and cook, covered, for 30 minutes or until tender.

Stewing is a good method to use with older poultry. Place chicken in a large kettle with water to cover. Add your favorite seasonings — celery, onion, peppercorns, salt, and parsley are nice. Cover and simmer for one to three

Clockwise from left: Chicken with Mushrooms (page 67), Chicken Stew (page 86), Glazed Roast Chicken (page 54), Lemon-Fried Chicken (page 106)

hours, or until the meat comes away from the bones easily. Cooking time will depend on the age and size of your bird.

SPECIAL METHODS FOR GAME

Both waterfowl – ducks and geese – and upland birds – grouse, pheasant, quail, pigeons, doves, woodcock, snipe, and wild turkey – should be well larded before cooking. Larding is the process of adding fat to the poultry by placing strips of bacon over it or by inserting fat into the flesh with a larding needle. Roasting is the preferred cooking method for most game birds.

Quail is the notable exception. It is almost all white meat and can be cooked like domestic chicken. It may be sauteed, broiled, stewed, or roasted. Whatever the cooking method, quail should be thoroughly larded.

chicken salads & appetizers

When hot weather has taken away your appetite . . . when you're looking for a light luncheon or supper dish . . . or when you want to get a special meal off to a great start . . . you naturally think of salads and appetizers.

Southern homemakers are experts at transforming chicken into elegant, eye-pleasing salads and appetizers. Just look at the recipes you'll find in the following pages, from the kitchens of *Southern Living* readers.

Chicken Almond Salad, for example, combines the smoothness of chicken with the crisp crunchiness of almonds for a superlative salad. Chicken Salad with Cranberry Topping brings two traditional favorites together in a colorful taste treat. And elegant Chicken Mousse shows what wonderful things can happen when a woman decides to develop a new dish.

You'll find favorite recipes for outstanding appetizers as well. Think how guests at your next party will enjoy smoothly delicious Bacon-Wrapped Chicken Livers . . . creamy Chicken in Canape Shells . . . or light-as-a-feather Chicken Cream Puffs. Even the names sound like a party!

The recipes you'll discover in this section have been home-developed and tested on family and friends alike. They are the favorites of the southern homemakers who share them with you.

15

CHICKEN-ALMOND SALAD

3 c. diced cooked chicken	1 c. seedless green grapes (opt.)
1 1/2 c. diced celery	1 1/2 tsp. salt
3 tbsp. lemon juice	1 tsp. dry mustard
1/2 unpeeled apple, diced	Pinch of pepper
1/2 c. drained pineapple chunks	1/4 c. light cream
1 c. toasted slivered almonds	1 c. mayonnaise

Combine the chicken, celery and lemon juice in a bowl and chill for 1 hour. Add the apple, pineapple, almonds and grapes. Mix remaining ingredients and toss lightly with chicken mixture. Place on lettuce leaves, if desired. 8 servings.

Mrs. M. C. Chandler, Shreveport, Louisiana

APPLE-CHICKEN SALAD

2 lge. apples, cut in cubes	1/4 c. cream
1 ripe avocado, cut in cubes	1 tsp. minced onion
2 tbsp. lemon juice	1/4 c. crumbled bleu cheese
1/2 c. mayonnaise	2 c. cubed cooked chicken

Place the apples and avocado in a bowl and sprinkle with lemon juice. Combine the mayonnaise, cream and onion and mix well. Add the cheese and chicken to avocado mixture. Pour the cream mixture over top and toss well. Serve on lettuce leaves.

Mrs. Katherine S. Hunter, Irving, Texas

Golden Salad Ceylon (page 17)

BANANA-CHICKEN SALAD

1 c. sliced bananas	1/4 c. sliced olives
1/2 c. diced pineapple	1 1/2 tsp. salt
1 1/2 c. diced cooked chicken	2 tbsp. mayonnaise
1/2 c. diced celery	Lettuce

Combine the bananas and pineapple in a bowl. Add the chicken, celery, olives, salt and mayonnaise and mix lightly. Serve in lettuce cups. 4-6 servings.

Mrs. G. S. Tramn, Orlando, Florida

CHICKEN-AVOCADO-RICE SALAD

1 1/2 c. cubed avocados	1/2 tsp. chopped green onion
2 tbsp. lemon juice	1 tsp. salt
1 c. cubed cooked chicken	2 tbsp. sour cream
1 c. cooked rice	2 tbsp. mayonnaise
1/2 c. finely chopped celery	

Place the avocados in a bowl and sprinkle with lemon juice. Add remaining ingredients and toss lightly. Chill. Serve on lettuce leaves. 6 servings.

Mrs. Hubert Adami, Alice, Texas

GOLDEN SALAD CEYLON

4 Delicious apples	2 tbsp. mayonnaise
2 oranges	1 tsp. lemon juice
1 c. diced cooked chicken, white meat	Salt to taste
3 or 4 pieces of candied ginger, chopped fine	Pepper to taste
	Watercress or spinach leaves

Quarter, core and slice the apples, then cut slices in half. Place in a mixing bowl. Peel and segment the oranges and combine with apples. Add the chicken and ginger and mix well. Thin the mayonnaise with lemon juice and fold into the apple mixture gently. Add salt and pepper. Refrigerate for at least 1 hour to blend flavors. Drain and spoon onto serving plates lined with watercress.

Chutney Dressing

1/2 c. mayonnaise	1/2 tsp. salt
1/2 c. sour cream	1/8 tsp. hot sauce
1/2 c. chutney and syrup	2 tbsp. salad oil
1/4 tsp. curry powder	1 tbsp. white wine vinegar

Place all ingredients in a blender container and blend until smooth. Serve with chicken salad.

CHICKEN SALAD WITH CRANBERRY TOPPING

1/2 c. heavy cream, whipped
1/2 c. mayonnaise
1/3 c. cranberry sauce
1 5-lb. hen
1 lge. onion, chopped
3 stalks celery, chopped
1/4 c. chopped pickle
4 hard-cooked eggs, chopped

3 c. mayonnaise
4 tbsp. Durkee's dressing
2 c. halved white grapes
1/2 lb. sliced almonds
1 tsp. salt
Pepper to taste
15 pineapple slices

Combine the whipped cream, mayonnaise and cranberry sauce in a bowl and mix well. Chill. Cook the hen in boiling, salted water until tender. Drain and cool. Remove chicken from bones and chop. Place in a bowl. Add the onion, celery, pickle, eggs, mayonnaise, Durkee's dressing, grapes, almonds, salt and pepper and mix well. Place the pineapple slices on individual salad plates and mound the chicken salad on pineapple. Top with cranberry mixture.

Mrs. Ernest S. Gibson, Centenary, South Carolina

CHICKEN AND FRUIT SALAD

1 5-lb. hen
3/4 c. diced celery
1 c. seedless white grapes
1 c. mandarin orange sections
1/2 c. mayonnaise
1/2 c. sour cream
2 tbsp. finely minced onion
Chopped parsley to taste

1 tbsp. lemon juice
1/2 tsp. salt
1/2 tsp. pepper
1/2 tsp. herb salad dressing
   mix
Lettuce
1/4 c. toasted slivered almonds

Cook the hen in simmering, salted water until tender. Drain and cool. Remove skin. Remove chicken from bones and cut in large pieces. Place in a bowl and add the celery. Cut the grapes in half and add to chicken mixture. Drain the orange sections and add to chicken mixture. Chill. Mix the mayonnaise, sour cream, onion, parsley, lemon juice, salt, pepper and dressing mix and pour over chicken mixture. Mix well and cover. Chill for several hours. Serve on lettuce and sprinkle with almonds.

Mrs. Maude Pomine, Tempe, Arizona

BIRD OF PARADISE

3 c. cubed cooked chicken
1 1/2 c. diced celery
1 tsp. salt
3 hard-cooked eggs, chopped
3 sweet pickles, chopped
Mayonnaise

1 fresh pineapple
1 apple
4 maraschino cherries
Lettuce
1 tomato, sliced

Combine the chicken, celery, salt, eggs and pickles in a bowl. Add enough mayonnaise to moisten and mix well. Slice the pineapple in half. Scoop out pineapple pulp and cut in cubes. Place back in pineapple shells. Place the chicken salad on pineapple cubes to form body of birds. Slice the apple in half and attach an apple half to each pineapple half with toothpick to form head of birds. Attach cherries to apple for eyes. Form tail of birds with straws. Place on a platter of lettuce and garnish with tomato slices and additional hard-cooked eggs. 2 servings.

Mrs. Richard L. Smith, Tucson, Arizona

CHICKEN COCKTAIL

3/4 c. walnuts	1 1/2 tsp. prepared
2 tsp. butter	horseradish
1/8 tsp. sweet basil or dill	2 drops of hot sauce
1 tsp. seasoned salt	1 red apple
1/2 c. mayonnaise	1 1/2 c. diced cooked chicken
1/4 c. white dinner wine	3 tbsp. sliced stuffed olives
1 tbsp. chili sauce	Parsley sprigs
1 tsp. onion powder	

Reserve several large walnut pieces or halves for garnish and chop remaining walnuts coarsely. Melt the butter in a skillet with sweet basil and 1/4 teaspoon seasoned salt. Add all the walnuts and cook over moderate heat, stirring constantly, for about 5 minutes or until walnuts are crisp and lightly toasted. Cool. Combine the mayonnaise, wine, remaining seasoned salt, chili sauce, onion powder, horseradish and hot sauce in a bowl and chill. Core the apple and cut 8 or 10 thin slices for garnish. Dice remaining apple and toss with the chopped walnuts, chicken and olives. Spoon into serving glasses and top with creamy cocktail sauce. Garnish each serving with 2 apple slices and reserved walnuts and top with parsley sprig. 4-5 servings.

Chicken Cocktail (above)

CURRIED CHICKEN SALAD

1 tbsp. salt	1 tbsp. curry powder
4 qt. boiling water	1 tbsp. salt
1 16-oz. package rice	1/2 tsp. pepper
6 c. chopped cooked chicken	1/2 c. milk
1 c. sliced cauliflower	1 c. green pepper strips
8 oz. creamy French dressing	1 c. diced celery
1 c. mayonnaise or salad	1 c. thinly sliced red onions
dressing	1 head romaine

Add salt to boiling water in a saucepan. Add the rice and cover. Cook over low heat until rice is tender, then drain. Place in a bowl and cool. Cover and refrigerate until chilled. Chill the chicken. Toss rice with cauliflower and French dressing. Cover and refrigerate for at least 2 hours. Combine the mayonnaise, curry powder, salt and pepper and stir in milk slowly. Add the chicken and toss. Cover and refrigerate for at least 2 hours. Combine rice and chicken mixtures and add green pepper, celery and onions. Place on romaine leaves. Serve with flaked coconut, salted peanuts, canned pineapple cubes, tomato wedges, chutney, crisp bacon bits, sliced avocados and grated orange rind as accompaniments. 12 servings.

Mrs. B. J. Tourville, Ft. McPherson, Georgia

MUSHROOM CREOLE SALAD

1 lb. fresh mushrooms	1/2 c. salad oil
2 c. cherry tomatoes, halved	2 tbsp. wine vinegar
2 c. cubed cooked chicken	2 tbsp. lemon juice
2 sm. zucchini, thinly sliced	1 tsp. salt
1 green pepper, diced	1/2 tsp. ground pepper
1 scallion, sliced	1/2 tsp. sugar

Rinse, pat dry and slice the mushrooms. Arrange the mushrooms, tomatoes, chicken, zucchini, green pepper and scallion in desired pattern in a large lettuce-lined salad bowl. Refrigerate until ready to serve. Mix the oil, vinegar, lemon juice, salt, pepper and sugar. Pour over salad and toss gently. 6-8 servings.

Photograph for this recipe on page 14.

BEANS-BACON AND CHICKEN

4 tbsp. catsup	4 tomatoes, diced
1/2 c. mayonnaise	1 head lettuce, cut in chunks
2 tbsp. vinegar	2 c. cubed cooked chicken
1/2 tsp. salt	5 slices fried bacon, crumbled
1/8 tsp. pepper	1 c. grated Swiss cheese
2 c. cooked green beans	

Combine the catsup, mayonnaise, vinegar, salt and pepper and mix. Mix the beans, tomatoes, lettuce and chicken in a large salad bowl. Add the catsup mixture and toss lightly. Chill. Garnish with bacon and cheese. 4 servings.

Mrs. W. M. Sawyer, Hot Springs, Arkansas

CHICKEN AND ARTICHOKE DELIGHT

2 c. cubed cooked chicken	12 pitted ripe olives
1 qt. (lightly packed) torn	Olive oil
romaine	Wine vinegar
1 6-oz. jar marinated	Seasoned salt to taste
artichoke hearts	Pepper to taste

Mix the chicken with romaine, undrained artichoke hearts and olives in a salad bowl. Add desired amounts of oil and vinegar. Add the salt and pepper and toss lightly. 4 servings.

Mrs. G. T. Olson, Nashville, Tennessee

POTATO-CHICKEN SALAD SUPREME

6 lge. potatoes	1/2 c. minced dill or parsley
6 eggs	1 c. chopped celery
1 tsp. salt	1 c. grated carrots
1/2 tsp. pepper	2 c. cubed cooked chicken
4 slices bacon, diced	Lettuce
1 c. salad dressing	Tomato slices

Cook the potatoes in jackets in boiling, salted water until tender. Drain and cool. Peel and cut in chunks. Cook the eggs in boiling water for 10 minutes, then drain and cool. Peel and cut in chunks. Mix the eggs, potatoes, salt and pepper in a bowl. Fry the bacon in a skillet until crisp and add to potato mixture with drippings. Add the salad dressing, dill, celery and carrots and mix. Fold in chicken and place in a salad bowl. Surround with lettuce and tomato slices and garnish with parsley sprigs.

Mrs. Ed Steinke, Birmingham, Alabama

POTATO SALAD A LA CHICKEN

2 cooked chicken breasts	1/4 c. chopped onion
4 slices boiled ham, 1/2 in.	1/2 c. chopped celery
thick	3 hard-cooked eggs, diced
2 tbsp. salad oil	Mayonnaise
2 tbsp. lemon juice	12 lettuce leaves
8 med. boiled potatoes, diced	

Cut twenty-four 3 x 1/2-inch strips from both chicken and ham and reserve. Chop remaining chicken and ham. Pour salad oil and lemon juice over reserved chicken and ham strips and toss lightly. Cover and refrigerate overnight. Combine chopped chicken and ham, potatoes, onion, celery and eggs in a bowl. Add enough mayonnaise to moisten and mix well. Place lettuce leaves on individual salad plates and place chicken salad on lettuce. Top each salad with 2 chicken and 2 ham strips and garnish with mayonnaise and stuffed olives. 12 servings.

Mrs. E. G. Rice, Covington, Kentucky

SPANISH CHICKEN SALAD

5 c. diced cooked chicken	1/2 c. red wine vinegar
6 scallions, thinly sliced	Salt and pepper to taste
2 heads lettuce, shredded	6 pitted ripe olives, sliced
5 tomatoes, cut in wedges	6 stuffed olives, sliced
3/4 c. olive oil	

Combine the chicken, scallions, lettuce and tomatoes in a large salad bowl. Add the oil, vinegar, salt and pepper and toss lightly. Garnish with olives. 12 servings.

Mrs. Dan M. Parker, Marietta, Georgia

COBB SALAD

1/2 head lettuce, shredded	3/4 c. crumbled Roquefort
2 cooked chicken breasts, diced	cheese
2 tomatoes, diced	2 med. avocados, cut in wedges
3 hard-cooked eggs, chopped	1 tbsp. cut chives
6 slices cooked bacon, crumbled	1/2 c. Brown Derby Dressing

Place the lettuce in a salad bowl and place chicken, tomatoes, eggs, bacon and cheese over lettuce. Add the avocado wedges and sprinkle with chives. Toss with Brown Derby Dressing. 6-8 servings.

Brown Derby Dressing

1/2 c. wine vinegar	1/2 tsp. sugar
1/2 c. water	1/2 tsp. dry mustard
1 tbsp. lemon juice	1 clove of garlic
1 1/2 tsp. Worcestershire sauce	1 1/2 c. salad oil
1 tsp. salt	1/2 c. olive oil
1 1/2 tsp. pepper	

Place all ingredients except salad oil and olive oil in a saucepan and mix. Bring to a boil. Reduce heat and simmer for 15 minutes. Cool. Pour into a jar and add oil. Cover and shake well. 2 cups.

Mrs. R. E. Goggin, Key West, Florida

CHICKEN SALAD DELUXE

1/4 c. chicken broth	1/4 c. sliced stuffed olives
3/4 c. mayonnaise	3/4 tsp. salt
2 1/2 c. diced cooked chicken	1/4 tsp. pepper
1/4 c. broken pecans	4 lge. tomatoes
1 1/2 c. diced celery	4 lettuce leaves

Mix the chicken broth and mayonnaise in a large bowl. Add the chicken, pecans, celery, olives and seasonings and toss well. Peel the tomatoes and cut in 5 sections almost to stem end. Press sections apart and fill with chicken salad. Place on lettuce and garnish with mayonnaise. 4 servings.

Mrs. George McCullough, Tulsa, Oklahoma

TALK-OF-THE-TOWN SALAD

1 sm. head lettuce, torn	8 stuffed olives, sliced
2 tomatoes, cut in wedges	1/2 tsp. onion salt
1/4 c. diced celery	Dash of garlic salt
1 4-oz. can mushrooms, drained	1 1/2 c. chopped cooked chicken
1/8 c. diced Velveeta cheese	French dressing to taste
2 tbsp. diced bleu cheese	Salt and pepper to taste
2/3 c. canned peas	1 c. cooked macaroni (opt.)

Place all ingredients in a large salad bowl and toss well. 4 servings.

Mrs. O. H. Parsons, Johnson City, Tennessee

TOMATO STUFFED WITH CHICKEN SALAD

1 c. diced cooked chicken	6 stuffed olives, sliced (opt.)
2/3 c. diced celery	3 tbsp. French dressing
3 tbsp. diced cucumber	Mayonnaise
3 hard-cooked eggs, chopped (opt.)	8 med. tomatoes
1 c. cooked peas (opt.)	Salt to taste

Mix all ingredients except tomatoes and salt in a bowl, adding enough mayonnaise to moisten and chill for 30 minutes. Wash and peel tomatoes and cut out blossom end. Cut tomatoes from top to within 1/4 inch of bottom in 6 sections and add salt. Chill. Pull tomato sections apart and fill with chicken salad.

Mrs. T. F. Sherman, Richmond, Virginia

STUFFED ARTICHOKE SALAD

1 6-oz. can water chestnuts	2 tbsp. salad oil
2 c. cubed cooked chicken	1/2 lemon, sliced
1/4 c. finely diced celery	1 clove of garlic
3/4 c. mayonnaise	12 stuffed olives
4 artichokes	1 tbsp. capers
1 tbsp. salt	

Drain the water chestnuts and chop. Mix the chicken, celery, water chestnuts and mayonnaise in a bowl and refrigerate for several hours. Cut the stems from artichokes and place artichokes in a saucepan. Add boiling water to cover, salt, oil, lemon and garlic and cook for 1 hour. Drain and cool. Refrigerate until chilled. Spread leafy spines of artichokes from tip carefully and remove inner leaves. Remove the heart with a spoon and fill cavity with chicken salad. Garnish with olives and sprinkle with capers. 4 servings.

Margaret Lopp, Chandler, Arizona

CHICKEN AND RICE SALAD

1 1/2 c. diced cooked chicken	2/3 c. mayonnaise
1 c. cold cooked rice	2/3 c. whipped cream
3/4 c. chopped celery	1 tbsp. unflavored gelatin
2 tbsp. chopped green pepper	1/2 tsp. salt
1 tbsp. chopped sour pickle	Dash of pepper
6 stuffed olives, chopped	Dash of red pepper
1/3 c. chopped pecans	Dash of paprika
1/2 tbsp. chopped parsley	

Combine the chicken, rice, celery, green pepper, sour pickle, olives, pecans, parsley, mayonnaise and whipped cream in a bowl and mix well. Soften the gelatin in 1/4 cup cold water. Add 3/4 cup boiling water and stir until gelatin is dissolved. Stir into chicken mixture and cool. Add the salt, pepper, red pepper and paprika. Pour into a mold and chill until firm. 8 servings.

Mrs. P. D. Abner, High Point, North Carolina

CHICKEN AND TONGUE IN ASPIC

1 4-lb. stewing chicken	2 hard-cooked eggs, sliced
3 env. unflavored gelatin	2 tomatoes, cut in wedges
1/2 c. cold water	1 c. mayonnaise
1 can tongue, thinly sliced	1/2 c. chili sauce or cream

Cook the chicken in boiling, salted water until tender. Drain and reserve 4 cups broth. Chill reserved broth. Cool the chicken and slice. Soften the gelatin in cold water for 5 minutes. Skim off fat from broth and heat in a saucepan to boiling point. Add the gelatin and stir until dissolved. Pour 1 cup gelatin into a 6-cup mold. Place mold in ice water and tilt until inside surface is covered with a layer of congealed gelatin. Arrange slices of tongue and chicken alternately around sides and bottom of mold and place egg slices near top all around mold. Combine remaining gelatin with remaining chicken, tongue and egg and spoon into mold. Press down to displace air bubbles. Chill until firm. Unmold on serving dish and garnish with tomato wedges. Mix the mayonnaise with chili sauce and serve with salad.

James T. Harris, South Hill, Virginia

CHICKEN BUFFET MOLDS

1 env. unflavored gelatin	3 tbsp. chopped green olives
1 c. mayonnaise or salad dressing	1 tbsp. chopped pimento
1 1/2 c. diced cooked chicken	2 tbsp. lemon juice
1/2 c. chopped cucumber	1/2 tsp. salt
1/3 c. diced celery	1/4 tsp. paprika
3 tbsp. minced onion	1 c. heavy cream, whipped

Soften the gelatin in 1/2 cup cold water and dissolve over hot water. Add remaining ingredients except whipped cream and mix well. Fold in the whipped cream and pour into individual molds. Chill until firm. 8 servings.

Mrs. L. M. Dawson, Tampa, Florida

CHICKEN-COTTAGE CHEESE SALAD

1 sm. package lime gelatin	1/2 c. mayonnaise
1 c. hot water	1 c. cream-style cottage cheese
1/2 c. cold water	1/2 c. diced celery
2 tbsp. lemon juice	1 c. diced cooked chicken
1/2 tsp. salt	1/2 c. finely chopped pickles

Dissolve the gelatin in hot water in a bowl. Add the cold water, lemon juice, salt and mayonnaise and blend well. Chill until partially set. Beat with a rotary beater until light and fluffy, then fold in remaining ingredients. Place in a mold and chill until firm. Unmold and serve on lettuce leaves, if desired. 6-8 servings.

Patricia Jones, Jackson, Mississippi

CHICKEN-CRANBERRY MOLD

1 sm. package lemon gelatin	1/4 c. chopped celery
1 1/2 c. hot water	1/3 c. salad dressing
2 c. cubed cooked chicken	1 can jellied cranberry sauce
1 hard-cooked egg, chopped	2 tbsp. orange juice

Dissolve the gelatin in hot water in a bowl. Combine the chicken, egg, celery and salad dressing with 1/2 cup gelatin and pour into 8-inch square pan. Beat the cranberry sauce until smooth and stir in the orange juice and remaining gelatin. Pour over the chicken mixture and chill until firm. Cut into squares and serve on lettuce. 9 servings.

Mrs. M. L. Hostetter, Huntington, West Virginia

CHICKEN MAYONNAISE

2 env. gelatin	1 No. 2 can English peas,
1/2 c. cold water	drained
2 c. hot chicken broth	2 c. diced celery
1 cooked chicken, chopped	3 hard-cooked eggs, sliced
1 c. chopped nuts	Salt and pepper to taste
1 pt. salad dressing	

Soften the gelatin in cold water. Add the chicken broth and stir until dissolved. Cool, then add remaining ingredients. Mix well. Pour into a mold and chill overnight. Serve on lettuce leaves.

Essie L. Stanley, Saltillo, Texas

CHICKEN-CRANBERRY SALAD

2 c. whole cranberry sauce
2 c. crushed pineapple
1/3 c. chopped pecans or
   walnuts
4 env. unflavored gelatin
2 1/2 c. chopped cooked chicken
3/4 c. finely chopped celery

3 tbsp. chopped parsley
1 1/2 c. mayonnaise
3/4 c. evaporated milk
Monosodium glutamate and salt
   to taste
Rosemary and lemon juice to
   taste

Mix the cranberry sauce, pineapple and pecans in a bowl. Soften 2 envelopes gelatin in 1/2 cup water and dissolve over hot water. Add to cranberry mixture and mix well. Pour into a mold and chill until set. Combine the chicken, celery and parsley in a bowl. Soften remaining gelatin in 1/2 cup water and dissolve over hot water. Combine the mayonnaise, milk and seasonings and stir in gelatin. Mix with chicken mixture and pour over the cranberry layer. Chill until firm. 8 servings.

Mrs. Curtis E. Conner, Daingerfield, Texas

CHICKEN MOUSSE

2 tbsp. gelatin
1 c. mayonnaise
2 c. chopped cooked chicken
4 hard-cooked eggs, mashed
1/2 c. celery
8 pickle chips, cut fine

Salt and pepper to taste
Dash of Worcestershire sauce
Dash of red pepper
1 sm. pimento, cut up
Juice of 1/2 lemon

Soften gelatin in 1/4 cup cold water. Add 1/2 cup boiling water and stir until gelatin is dissolved. Cool. Add the mayonnaise and remaining ingredients and pour into a loaf pan. Chill until firm, then slice. 8 servings.

Elizabeth Heard, Jackson, Mississippi

MOLDED CHICKEN SALAD

1 5-oz. can water chestnuts
1 env. unflavored gelatin
1 c. cold water
1 can cream of chicken soup
Hot sauce to taste
2 tbsp. lemon juice

1/4 c. mayonnaise
1 5-oz. can chicken, diced
1/3 c. chopped toasted almonds
1 1-lb. can jellied cranberry
   sauce

Drain and chop the water chestnuts. Soften the gelatin in 1/2 cup cold water. Place over low heat and stir until dissolved. Remove from heat. Mix remaining water and soup and stir in gelatin, hot sauce, lemon juice and mayonnaise. Chill until partially set. Fold in water chestnuts and remaining ingredients except cranberry sauce and turn into 4 individual molds. Chill until firm. Cut the cranberry sauce in 4 slices and place the chicken salad on cranberry sauce. 4 servings.

Jean A. Cary, Burkesville, Kentucky

GLAZED CHICKEN

1/3 c. pine nuts	1 c. chicken stock
2 tbsp. olive oil	2 env. unflavored gelatin
2/3 c. finely chopped shallots or scallions	1 c. heavy cream
3/4 c. chopped stuffed olives	Whole stuffed olives
3 tbsp. chopped parsley	Parsley sprigs
1/2 tsp. grated lemon peel	Cooked asparagus tips
4 lge. chicken breasts	Boston lettuce
	3/4 c. mayonnaise

Saute the pine nuts in oil in a large skillet until lightly browned. Add 1/3 cup shallots and saute until tender but not browned. Stir in 1/2 cup chopped olives, chopped parsley and lemon peel. Remove skin and bones from chicken breasts and discard. Cut the chicken breasts in half. Place each piece of chicken between 2 pieces of waxed paper and flatten with a rolling pin. Place about 1 1/2 tablespoons olive mixture in center of each chicken piece and roll up. Secure with wooden picks. Place in a large skillet and add remaining shallots and the chicken stock. Cover. Simmer for 15 minutes, turning chicken once. Remove chicken from skillet and cool. Cover and chill. Strain the chicken stock and pour back into skillet. Boil until stock is reduced to 1/2 cup. Soften 1 envelope gelatin in cream. Add to stock and heat until gelatin is dissolved. Remove wooden picks and place chicken on rack over a pan. Place cream mixture over bowl of ice and stir until thickened to consistency of unbeaten egg white. Spoon over chicken and chill chicken until glaze sets. Repeat glazing and chilling until all glaze is used. Any glaze left in pan under rack may be reheated and chilled to proper consistency for glazing. Slice several whole olives for garnish. Soften remaining gelatin in 1/2 cup water and heat until dissolved. Cool. Dip olive slices and parsley sprigs in the clear gelatin and arrange on chicken. Spoon remaining gelatin over chicken and chill until firm. Arrange chicken, asparagus and whole olives in lettuce-lined dish. Mix remaining chopped olives with the mayonnaise and serve with chicken mixture. 4-6 servings.

Glazed Chicken (above)

Walnut-Chicken Condiment Salad (below)

WALNUT-CHICKEN CONDIMENT SALAD

2/3 c. chopped toasted walnuts
2 c. cubed cooked chicken
1/4 c. finely chopped celery
2 tbsp. chopped green onion
2 tbsp. chopped raisins
2 tbsp. chopped chutney
1/4 c. mayonnaise

1/4 tsp. salt
2 tsp. lemon juice
Crisp lettuce
4 slices tomato
4 slices pineapple, drained
Toasted walnut halves

Combine the chopped walnuts, chicken, celery and onion in a bowl. Mix the raisins, chutney, mayonnaise, salt and lemon juice and fold into chicken mixture. Arrange lettuce on 4 chilled salad plates. Center each serving of lettuce with a tomato slice and top with a pineapple slice. Divide chicken salad into 4 equal portions and pile or scoop on top of each pineapple slice. Garnish with walnut halves. Serve with additional mayonnaise, if desired.

BAKED CHICKEN SALAD

2 c. diced cooked chicken
1 c. cream of chicken soup
1 c. diced celery
3 tbsp. minced onion
1/2 tsp. salt

1/4 tsp. pepper
1 tbsp. lemon juice
1 c. mayonnaise
3 hard-boiled eggs, sliced
Crumbled potato chips

Combine all ingredients except potato chips and mix well. Place in a casserole and cover with potato chips. Bake at 350 degrees for 15 to 20 minutes. 4-6 servings.

Mrs. Thomas Hudson, Roanoke Rapids, North Carolina

CHICKEN SALAD

1 lge. hen	1 tsp. salt
3 lb. lean pork	3 tsp. melted butter
12 hard-cooked eggs, chopped	3 tsp. flour
2 bunches celery, chopped	Dash of cayenne pepper
12 sweet pickles, chopped	2 c. hot milk
1/2 lb. chopped blanched almonds (opt.)	1 c. vinegar
4 egg yolks	1 tsp. dry mustard
1 c. sugar	Juice of 1 lemon

Cook the chicken and pork together in boiling water until tender. Drain and cool. Remove chicken from bones. Grind the chicken and pork and place in a large bowl. Add the eggs, celery, pickles and almonds and mix. Beat the egg yolks in a bowl until thick and add sugar and salt. Mix the butter, flour and pepper in top of a double boiler. Add the milk and egg mixture and mix well. Place over hot water and cook until hot. Mix the vinegar and mustard and stir into milk mixture. Cook until thick. Remove from hot water and beat well. Cool and add lemon juice. Add to the chicken mixture and mix well. 20 servings.

Mrs. Raymond Combs, Bradenton, Florida

CHICKEN-MACARONI SALAD

6 oz. macaroni	6 hard-cooked eggs, diced
1 pkg. frozen peas and carrots	3/4 c. heavy cream, whipped
1 cooked chicken, chopped	1 1/2 c. salad dressing
1/4 c. chopped green pepper	2 tsp. chopped parsley
1 c. chopped celery	Salt and pepper to taste
1 tbsp. chopped dill pickle	Garlic salt to taste

Cook the macaroni and peas and carrots according to package directions. Drain and cool. Combine the chicken, peas and carrots, green pepper, celery, pickle, eggs and macaroni and mix well. Combine the whipped cream and salad dressing and fold into chicken mixture. Add the parsley and seasonings and mix. Garnish with tomato slices, olives and parsley, if desired. 12-15 servings.

Mrs. C. A. Davis, Charleston, South Carolina

CUCUMBER AND CHICKEN SALAD

4 c. diced cooked chicken	3 hard-cooked eggs, sliced
1 1/2 c. chopped celery	1 tbsp. minced pimento
1/2 c. sliced cucumbers	1 tsp. salt
1/4 c. French dressing	1/4 c. chopped parsley

Mix the chicken, celery and cucumbers in a bowl. Pour French dressing over all and chill. Add remaining ingredients and mix well. Place on lettuce and serve with boiled dressing.

Mrs. Mary A. Walters, Bonnieville, Kentucky

CHICKEN SALAD IN CORNUCOPIAS

1 10-oz. package frozen puff pastry shells, thawed	1/3 c. mayonnaise
2 c. diced cooked chicken	1 tsp. chicken base
2 tbsp. lemon juice	1/4 tsp. salt
1/2 c. chopped celery	1/4 tsp. pepper
2 hard-cooked eggs, chopped	2 to 3 drops of hot sauce

Roll each puff pastry shell on a floured board into a 6-inch circle and trim edges evenly. Start at outer edge and cut each circle into a continuous strip 3/4 inch wide. Wind strip over outside of an aluminum foil cone, starting at pointed end, and seal by dampening and overlapping edges of strip. Place on ungreased cookie sheet. Bake at 425 degrees for 20 minutes. Cool on a wire rack and remove aluminum cones carefully. Place the chicken in a medium bowl. Add the lemon juice and toss well. Add the celery and eggs. Combine the mayonnaise, chicken base, salt, pepper and hot sauce and mix until smooth. Add to chicken mixture and toss well. Chill for at least 1 hour. Fill pastry shells with chicken mixture. 6 servings.

Mrs. Gertrude Lacy, Tampa, Florida

CHICKEN LIVER SPREAD

1/2 c. shortening or oil	2 hard-cooked eggs
2 onions, sliced	1 1/2 tsp. salt
1 lb. chicken livers	1/2 tsp. pepper

Melt 1/4 cup shortening in a skillet. Add the onions and cook for 10 minutes, stirring frequently. Remove the onions from skillet and set aside. Melt remaining shortening in the same skillet and cook the livers for 10 minutes, stirring occasionally. Grind the onions, liver and eggs. Add the salt and pepper and mix well. Chill. Spread on crackers or small slices of rye bread. 6 servings.

Shirley Goldberg, Lakeland, Florida

RUMAKI

1/2 lb. chicken livers	1 sm. can pineapple chunks
2 tbsp. soy sauce	8 slices bacon, halved
1 sm. can water chestnuts	

Place the livers in a bowl and pour soy sauce over livers. Let stand for 30 minutes, then cut into pieces. Drain the water chestnuts and cut into pieces. Place a piece of water chestnut, a pineapple chunk and a piece of chicken liver in each bacon strip. Roll up and secure with toothpicks. Place in a baking pan. Broil, turning frequently, until bacon is crisp. 16 servings.

Mrs. G. L. Lawson, Durham, North Carolina

BACON-WRAPPED CHICKEN LIVERS

1 lb. chicken livers   **1 lb. bacon**

Cut the chicken livers in half. Cut the bacon strips in half. Wrap bacon around chicken livers and secure with toothpicks. Place in a baking pan. Broil until brown and crisp and drain on paper towels. 6 servings.

Jeanette LeBlanc, Chalmette, Louisiana

APPETIZER CHICKEN-CURRY MOLD

2 env. unflavored gelatin   **2 tbsp. lemon juice**
1 c. milk   **2 c. finely chopped cooked**
2 chicken bouillon cubes   **chicken**
2 eggs, separated   **1/4 c. finely chopped chutney**
1/4 tsp. salt   **1/4 c. diced pimento**
2 tsp. curry powder   **2 tbsp. minced onion**
3 c. creamed cottage cheese   **1 c. heavy cream, whipped**

Sprinkle the gelatin over milk in a saucepan. Add the bouillon cubes and beaten egg yolks and mix well. Place over low heat and stir constantly for about 5 minutes or until gelatin and bouillon cubes are dissolved and mixture is slightly thickened. Remove from heat and stir in the salt and curry powder. Sieve or beat the cottage cheese with an electric mixer at high speed until smooth, then stir into gelatin mixture. Stir in the lemon juice, chicken, chutney, pimento and onion. Chill until mixture mounds slightly when dropped from a spoon. Beat the egg whites until stiff, but not dry, and fold into gelatin mixture. Fold in the whipped cream and turn into an 8-inch springform pan. Chill until firm. Loosen side of pan with tip of knife and remove side of pan. Garnish with ring of toasted, slivered almonds and white grapes on lemon leaves. 24 appetizer servings.

Appetizer Chicken-Curry Mold (above)

CHICKEN IN CANAPE SHELLS

1 recipe pastry for 2-crust pie	1 tsp. grated onion
1 6-oz. can broiled mushrooms	1/2 tsp. curry powder
2 5-oz. cans boned chicken	1/2 tsp. salt
1/2 c. diced celery	Sliced cherry tomatoes
2/3 c. sour cream	Parsley sprigs

Divide the pastry and roll each half on lightly floured board into 12-inch circle. Cut with 1 3/4-inch round scalloped cutter. Fit into tiny muffin pan cups and prick with a fork. Bake at 425 degrees for 7 minutes, then cool on wire racks. Drain the mushrooms and chop fine. Chop the chicken fine. Combine the mushrooms with chicken and celery in a bowl. Mix the sour cream, onion, curry powder and salt in a bowl. Add to the chicken mixture and toss to mix. Chill. Place 1 rounded teaspoon in each canape shell just before serving and garnish each canape with a tomato slice and parsley.

Mrs. Thomas G. Fulton, Aberdeen, Maryland

CREPES A LA REINE

3 tbsp. butter	Salt
1 4-oz. can sliced	Pepper and nutmeg to taste
mushrooms	2 tsp. chopped chives
1 tsp. instant minced onion	3 tbsp. dry sherry
Flour	2 c. diced cooked chicken
1 2/3 c. evaporated milk	1/2 c. water
1/3 c. chicken broth	3 eggs, well beaten

Melt the butter in a medium saucepan. Drain the mushrooms and add to butter. Add the onion and saute until mushrooms are lightly browned. Blend in 3 tablespoons flour, then stir in 2/3 cup evaporated milk and chicken broth slowly. Cook and stir over medium heat until thickened and season with salt to taste, pepper and nutmeg. Blend in the chives, sherry and chicken and cover. Chill. Mix 3/4 cup flour with 1/2 teaspoon salt. Mix remaining milk and water. Add flour mixture to eggs alternately with milk mixture and beat until smooth. Pour 1/4 cup batter onto a lightly greased hot griddle and brown on one side only, removing from griddle when upper surface is bubbly and slightly dry. Place, browned side down, on a towel to cool. Repeat with remaining batter, making 12 crepes. Divide the chicken mixture into 12 portions and place a portion on the uncooked side of each crepe. Roll as for jelly roll and place, seam side down, in a greased baking dish. Cover tightly. Bake in 350-degree oven for 20 minutes or until heated through. Transfer to a chafing dish, if desired.

Sauce Supreme

2 tbsp. butter	1 c. evaporated milk
2 tbsp. flour	Salt and pepper to taste
1/2 c. chicken broth	

Melt the butter in a small saucepan. Blend in the flour, then the chicken broth and milk. Cook and stir over medium heat until thickened. Season with salt and pepper and serve with crepes.

CHICKEN CREAM PUFFS

1/2 c. water
1/4 c. butter or margarine
1/8 tsp. salt
1/2 c. all-purpose flour
2 lge. eggs
1 c. diced cooked chicken

1/4 c. chopped sweet pickles
1/4 c. chopped celery
Grated onion to taste
Salt and pepper to taste
Mayonnaise

Preheat oven to 400 degrees. Combine the water, butter and salt in a saucepan and bring to a boil over medium heat. Remove from heat and beat in flour with a spoon. Place over low heat and stir for 1 to 2 minutes or until mixture leaves side of pan and forms a ball. Remove from heat. Add 1 egg and beat until well blended. Add remaining egg and beat for about 1 minute or until satiny. Drop from teaspoon 2 inches apart on an ungreased cookie sheet. Bake for 20 to 25 minutes. Remove puffs from cookie sheet carefully and cool on a wire rack. Cut off tops with sharp knife. Combine the chicken, pickles, celery, onion, salt and pepper in a bowl. Add enough mayonnaise to moisten and mix well. Fill puffs and replace tops.

Mrs. Alvin Stewart, Nashville, Tennessee

PICK-UP CHICKEN STICKS

3 lb. chicken wings
3/4 c. melted butter
1 1/2 c. flour
1/3 c. sesame seed

1 tbsp. salt
1/2 tsp. ginger
Juice of 1/2 lemon

Cut the chicken wings in 3 sections and discard the wing tips. Dip remaining sections in butter. Mix the flour, sesame seed, salt and ginger and roll chicken sections in flour mixture. Place in a foil-lined baking pan. Bake at 350 degrees for 1 hour, then sprinkle with lemon juice. 6-8 servings.

Mrs. Jack McKain, Sarasota, Florida

Crepes a la Reine (page 32)

barbecued chicken

Throughout the Southland — from the coast of Georgia to the vast expanses of Texas — barbecuing is a way of cooking particularly enjoyed by southerners. Part of this joy comes from the gentle southern climate, so conducive to year-round outdoor cooking. But the biggest part comes from the delicious recipes developed by generations of southern women and carefully handed down from mother to daughter.

Now, in the following section, proud cooks share with you their finest recipes for barbecued chicken. You'll discover that each section of the vast South has a way of cooking uniquely its own. Explore the wonderfully varied world of Alabama-Style Barbecued Chicken . . . Tennessee Barbecued Chicken . . . Texas Barbecued Chicken . . . and many more. Each is as delightfully different as the state for which it is named!

Your family and guests will share your excitement over Marvelous Backyard Barbecue. And for those occasions when you've planned an outdoor barbecue but the weather doesn't cooperate, try Oven Barbecued Broilers . . . you'll never know they didn't come off a grill!

Some especially delicious refinements in the art of barbecuing are yours in this section. Think how you'll enjoy Sweet and Smoky Barbecued Chicken, Ginger Chicken, or Barbecued Lemon Chicken. In fact, for every occasion, you'll find a just-right barbecued chicken recipe.

CHICKEN IN BARBECUE SAUCE

1/3 c. minced onion	1/8 tsp. salt
3 tbsp. butter	3 tbsp. brown sugar
1 c. catsup	1/2 c. water
1/3 c. vinegar	1 fryer, disjointed
2 tsp. dry mustard	

Saute the onion in butter in a skillet until tender. Add remaining ingredients except chicken and simmer for 5 minutes. Add the chicken and cover skillet. Cook over medium heat for 30 to 45 minutes, turning once. 4 servings.

Mrs. Curtis Avery, Columbus, Georgia

BARBECUED CHICKEN IN PAPER BAG

1 tsp. mustard	1 tsp. salt
4 tbsp. catsup	5 tbsp. water
3 tbsp. vinegar	1/2 tsp. cayenne
2 tbsp. Worcestershire sauce	1 tsp. chili powder
3 tbsp. brown sugar	1 tsp. paprika
3 tbsp. butter	1 lge. chicken, disjointed

Place all ingredients except chicken in a saucepan and bring to a boil. Remove from heat. Grease the inside of a medium-sized heavy paper bag and place in a baking pan. Season the chicken with additional salt. Dip each piece in sauce and place in the bag. Pour remaining sauce into bag and tie top of bag tightly. Bake at 500 degrees for 15 minutes. Reduce temperature to 350 degrees and bake for 1 hour and 15 minutes longer. Do not open bag while baking. 4 servings.

Mrs. Harry K. Wilson, Springdale, Arkansas

CHICKEN AND SAUCE

1 chicken, disjointed	2 tbsp. prepared mustard
1 bottle chili sauce	Minced gingerroot to taste
1 bell pepper, chopped	1 sm. can mushrooms, chopped
1 med. onion, chopped	2 c. water
Dash of pepper sauce	

Fry the chicken in a skillet in small amount of fat until browned, then place in a baking dish. Mix remaining ingredients and pour over chicken. Bake at 350 degrees for 1 hour.

Mrs. W. H. Neel, Grand Ridge, Florida

COLA-BARBECUED CHICKEN

1 lge. fryer, disjointed	1 king-sized cola beverage
Salt and pepper to taste	1/2 bottle catsup

Season the chicken with salt and pepper and place in a frying pan. Pour cola beverage and catsup over chicken and cover. Cook over medium heat for 30 to 45 minutes or until tender.

Mrs. McKinley Holmes, Westville, Florida

PAPER SACK BARBECUED CHICKEN

3 cloves of garlic, crushed	1 catsup bottle water
1 tbsp. salt	1 bottle chili sauce
1/5 bottle liquid smoke	1 chili sauce bottle water
1/5 bottle hot sauce	1 tbsp. Worcestershire sauce
Juice of 3 lemons	1 tbsp. garlic salt
Grated rind of 1 lemon	1 tsp. celery salt
1 can tomato paste	1 stick margarine
1 tomato paste can water	1 lge. fryer, disjointed
1 bottle catsup	

Preheat oven to 325 degrees. Mix the garlic and salt in a saucepan and let stand for 15 to 20 minutes. Add remaining ingredients except chicken and heat until the margarine is melted. Grease the inside of a large brown paper sack well and place on a cookie pan. Season the fryer with additional salt and dip into barbecue sauce, coating all sides. Place in a single layer in the sack and close sack tightly. Bake for 1 hour.

Mrs. James Pizzotti, Fairhope, Alabama

RED PEPPER CHICKEN

1 3-lb. fryer, disjointed	1 c. vinegar
Salt to taste	1 tsp. ground red pepper
3 tbsp. flour	1/4 c. catsup
1 stick margarine	1/4 tsp. paprika
1 c. water	

Sprinkle the chicken with salt and flour and place in single layer in a large baking pan. Melt the margarine in a saucepan and stir in the water. Add remaining ingredients and heat through. Pour over chicken. Bake at 350 degrees for 1 hour and 30 minutes.

Mrs. Ashley Hall, Fuquay-Varina, North Carolina

CRUSTY BARBECUED CHICKEN

1 2 1/2-lb. fryer, disjointed	4 c. crushed corn flakes
2/3 c. barbecue sauce	

Dip the chicken in barbecue sauce and roll in corn flake crumbs until well coated. Place, skin side up, in a shallow baking pan lined with aluminum foil. Bake in 350-degree oven for about 1 hour or until tender.

Mrs. W. C. Lindsey, Ferris, Texas

DELICIOUS BARBECUED CHICKEN

2 tbsp. butter	3 tbsp. vinegar
1/4 c. chopped green pepper	2 tbsp. lemon juice
1/4 c. chopped onion	1/4 tsp. chili powder
1/4 c. chopped celery	1/8 tsp. pepper
1 8-oz. can tomato sauce	1 tsp. salt
3 tbsp. molasses	3 c. chopped cooked chicken

Melt the butter in a saucepan. Add the green pepper, onion and celery and cook until tender. Add remaining ingredients except chicken and simmer for 10 to 15 minutes. Add the chicken and simmer for 15 minutes longer.

Mrs. George F. Turner, Timberville, Virginia

ALABAMA-STYLE BARBECUED CHICKEN

1 2 1/2 to 3-lb. chicken, halved	Juice of 2 lemons
Salt to taste	3 tbsp. sugar
1 c. evaporated milk	1/2 tsp. salt
1 c. mayonnaise	1/2 tsp. pepper
1/2 stick margarine	1/3 c. white vinegar

Season the chicken with salt and place in aluminum foil-lined baking pan. Combine remaining ingredients in a saucepan and bring to a boil, stirring frequently. Pour over chicken and cover with foil. Bake at 350 degrees for 1 hour.

Wilma H. Pearce, Danville, Alabama

CHIP-BARBECUED CHICKEN

1 2 to 3-lb. fryer, disjointed	1 lge. bag barbecue potato chips
1 stick margarine, melted	

Dip the chicken into margarine. Crush the potato chips and roll chicken in potato chips. Place in a single layer in a shallow baking pan. Bake at 350 degrees for 1 hour.

Mrs. Henry Henagan, Baton Rouge, Louisiana

TEMPTING CHICKEN BREASTS

5 chicken breasts with wings	1/2 c. lemon juice
1/2 c. Worcestershire sauce	1/4 c. sugar

Place the chicken breasts in a baking pan, wing side up. Combine remaining ingredients in a saucepan and heat through. Pour over chicken and cover tightly. Bake in 350-degree oven for about 1 hour or until tender, basting occasionally.

Mrs. Annie Maude Nichols, Selma, Alabama

BARBECUED CHICKEN WITH A TWIST

1 2 1/2-lb. fryer, disjointed	1/2 c. chopped green pepper
Salt to taste	1 c. catsup
Pepper	1 c. water
Flour	2 tbsp. Worcestershire sauce
1 lge. onion, sliced	2 tbsp. brown sugar
1/2 c. chopped celery	1 No. 2 can yellow corn

Season the chicken with salt and pepper to taste and dredge with flour. Fry in hot, deep fat until golden brown. Drain and cool. Remove chicken from bones and cut in small pieces. Place in a greased 2-quart casserole. Fry the onion in small amount of fat in a saucepan until tender. Add 1/8 teaspoon pepper and remaining ingredients except corn and mix well. Pour over chicken and cover the casserole. Refrigerate for at least 6 hours. Bake at 350 degrees for 45 minutes. Remove cover. Add the corn and stir. Bake for 25 minutes longer. 6-8 servings.

Mrs. R. D. Cox, Raleigh, North Carolina

CHICKEN BARBECUE

2 2 1/2-lb. broilers, halved	1/4 c. Worcestershire sauce
1/4 c. salad oil	1/4 c. finely chopped onion
1/2 c. sugar	2 cloves of garlic, minced
1/2 c. catsup	1/4 tsp. dry mustard
1/2 c. lemon juice	1/4 tsp. hot sauce

Cook the chickens in hot oil in a skillet until golden brown. Remove to a shallow baking pan. Mix remaining ingredients in a bowl and brush over chickens liberally. Bake at 350 degrees for about 1 hour, basting frequently with sauce. Serve remaining sauce with chickens.

Chicken Barbecue (above)

Angostura Chicken Barbecue (below)

ANGOSTURA CHICKEN BARBECUE

1/2 c. salad oil	2 tbsp. angostura aromatic
2/3 c. cider vinegar	bitters
1 c. chili sauce	1/2 tsp. crumbled oregano
1 c. orange juice	1 tsp. hot sauce
1 tbsp. salt	3 2-lb. broilers, halved
2 tsp. onion powder	

Combine all ingredients except chickens in a saucepan and simmer for 5 minutes. Place the chickens in a large, shallow baking pan in a single layer and brush with barbecue sauce. Bake at 350 degrees for about 1 hour and 15 minutes or until tender, brushing frequently with sauce. Serve remaining sauce with chickens.

DIXIE-BARBECUED CHICKEN PLATE

1 2 1/2-lb. chicken	1/4 c. minced onion
1 lge. can tomato sauce	2 c. self-rising cornmeal
1/2 c. catsup	2 tbsp. flour
1 tbsp. white vinegar	1 egg
1 tbsp. Worcestershire sauce	1 2/3 c. milk
1/4 c. brown sugar	1/4 c. bacon drippings
Salt and pepper to taste	

Cook the chicken in boiling water until tender. Drain and cool. Remove chicken from bones and cut in large pieces. Combine the tomato sauce, catsup, vinegar, Worcestershire sauce, brown sugar, salt, pepper and onion in top of a double boiler and mix well. Add the chicken and cook over hot water for 1 hour. Mix the cornmeal and flour in a bowl. Add the egg and milk and mix well. Stir in the bacon drippings and pour into a greased 8 x 12-inch baking pan. Bake for 15 minutes at 400 degrees. Cut in 4-inch squares and split in half. Cover bottom half with chicken mixture and top with remaining half. Spoon additional chicken mixture over top, if desired. 6 servings.

Mrs. P. C. Peeler, Decatur, Georgia

DEEP SOUTH-BARBECUED CHICKEN

2 tsp. catsup	2 tsp. butter
2 tsp. Worcestershire sauce	1 tsp. paprika
1/2 tsp. cayenne pepper	2 tbsp. water
1 tsp. prepared mustard	1 tsp. salt
2 tsp. vinegar	1 tsp. chili powder
2 tsp. lemon juice	1 chicken, disjointed

Mix all ingredients except chicken in a saucepan and heat until butter is melted. Dip chicken into barbecue sauce until well coated and place in a baking pan. Cover. Bake at 350 degrees for 1 hour. 4 servings.

Mrs. Raymond Reneau, Albany, Kentucky

MARVELOUS BACKYARD BARBECUE

1 c. catsup	1 tsp. celery seed
1/4 c. brown sugar	2 tbsp. lemon juice
1/4 c. vinegar	2 tbsp. minced onion
1/4 c. A-1 sauce	2 c. boiling water
1 tsp. chili powder	2 2-lb. broilers, quartered

Mix all ingredients except broilers in a saucepan and bring to a boil. Place the chicken on rack in a broiling pan. Broil until chicken is tender and brown, turning once and basting frequently with barbecue sauce. May be cooked on grill over charcoal.

Mrs. Frank S. Hewitt, Georgetown, Delaware

JUICY BARBECUED CHICKEN

2 fryers, halved	1/2 c. catsup
1 c. melted butter	Juice of 1 lemon
Salt and pepper to taste	2 tbsp. sugar
1/2 c. vinegar	

Place the fryers in a baking pan, skin side down, and pour 1/2 cup butter over fryers. Add salt and pepper and cover bottom of pan with water. Combine the vinegar, catsup, lemon juice, sugar and remaining butter in a saucepan and bring to a boil. Pour half the sauce over fryers. Bake at 350 degrees for 45 minutes. Turn fryers and add remaining sauce. Bake for 45 minutes longer or until done, basting occasionally.

Mrs. F. E. Thurmond, Modoc, South Carolina

NAPA VALLEY-BARBECUED CHICKEN

1 chicken, disjointed	1 minced med. onion
1 c. catsup	1 tbsp. Worcestershire sauce
1/2 c. sherry	2 tbsp. melted butter
1/3 c. water	1 tbsp. brown sugar
2 tbsp. lemon juice	

Preheat oven to 325 degrees. Brown the chicken in small amount of fat in a frying pan, then place in a 2-quart casserole. Combine remaining ingredients in a saucepan and bring to a boil. Pour over chicken and cover the casserole. Bake for 1 hour and 15 minutes or until chicken is tender.

Mrs. O. M. Harrison, Greensboro, North Carolina

EASY BARBECUED CHICKEN

1/4 c. butter	1/4 c. steak sauce
1/4 c. shortening	1/4 c. Worcestershire sauce
1/4 c. vinegar	Dash of hot sauce
1 c. catsup	1 lge. onion, chopped fine
1/2 c. water	1/4 c. sugar
3 cloves of garlic, minced	2 fryers, disjointed

Combine all ingredients except fryers and mix well. Place the fryers in a baking pan and pour the sauce over fryers. Bake at 375 degrees for 1 hour and 30 minutes, basting occasionally.

Mrs. Fred P. Simmons, Owensboro, Kentucky

OVEN-BARBECUED CHICKEN

2 c. diced onions	2 tbsp. Worcestershire sauce
1 c. diced celery	1 tbsp. prepared mustard
4 tbsp. bacon drippings	1 green pepper, chopped
3/4 c. molasses	1/4 tsp. minced garlic
3 sm. cans tomato sauce	Salt and pepper to taste
1 c. (packed) brown sugar	Dash of nutmeg and cinnamon
1/2 c. vinegar	1/2 tsp. soda
3/4 c. catsup	4 sm. fryers, cut in half

Cook the onions and celery in drippings in a saucepan until tender. Add remaining ingredients except fryers and simmer for about 1 hour, stirring frequently. Place the fryers in a large baking pan, skin side up, and add enough water to cover bottom of pan. Bake at 350 degrees for 1 hour. Pour barbecue sauce over fryers and bake for 30 minutes longer or until fryers are tender, basting frequently.

Martha G. Dicus, Michie, Tennessee

TENNESSEE CHICKEN

1 fryer, disjointed	3/4 c. catsup
1 tsp. salt	2 tbsp. lemon juice
1/2 tsp. pepper	1 tsp. prepared mustard
Flour	2 tbsp. light brown sugar
1 med. onion, chopped fine	1/2 tsp. Worcestershire sauce
1 tbsp. margarine	1/2 c. water

Season the fryer with salt and pepper and dredge with flour. Brown in small amount of fat in a skillet. Place large pieces on bottom of a baking dish and place small pieces on top. Cook the onion in margarine in a saucepan until brown. Add remaining ingredients and simmer for 15 minutes. Pour over chicken. Bake in 400-degree oven for 40 minutes.

Mrs. Grady Southern, Chattanooga, Tennessee

HERB-BARBECUED CHICKEN

2/3 c. corn oil	1/4 tsp. marjoram
1/3 c. vinegar	1 clove of garlic, sliced
1 tsp. salt	1 1 1/2 to 2 1/2-lb. chicken,
1/4 tsp. pepper	quartered
1/4 tsp. thyme	

Mix the corn oil, vinegar, salt, pepper, thyme, marjoram and garlic in a shallow dish. Add the chicken and cover. Refrigerate for at least 3 hours, turning frequently. Line inside of a baking pan with aluminum foil and place a greased rack on the foil. Remove chicken from marinade and place, skin side down, on rack. Bake at 350 degrees for about 1 hour or until tender and brown, basting frequently with marinade and turning chicken once.

Herb-Barbecued Chicken (above)

OVEN-BARBECUED BROILERS

1/4 c. unsulphured molasses	1 8-oz. can tomato sauce
1/4 c. butter or oil	1/4 tsp. hot sauce
1 tbsp. prepared mustard	1/2 tsp. monosodium glutamate
1 tbsp. vinegar	4 broilers, halved

Combine all ingredients except broilers in a saucepan and heat until butter is melted. Sprinkle broiler halves on both sides with additional monosodium gluta-mate and place, skin side down, in a single layer in aluminum foil-lined baking pan. Brush with barbecue sauce. Bake at 350 degrees for 30 minutes. Turn broilers and brush with sauce. Bake for 30 minutes. Brush with sauce and bake for 15 minutes longer. 8 servings.

Mary Guerrero, Shallowater, Texas

SWEET AND SMOKY BARBECUED CHICKEN

1 3-lb. broiler, disjointed	2 tbsp. prepared mustard
1 lge. onion, sliced	1/2 c. salad oil
1 tsp. hickory smoked salt	1/4 c. vinegar
1/4 tsp. pepper	1/2 c. maple syrup
1/2 c. catsup	

Place the chicken in a baking pan and add enough water to cover bottom of the pan. Place onion slices around chicken and sprinkle chicken with smoked salt and pepper. Bake in 375-degree oven for 30 minutes. Mix the catsup, mustard, oil, vinegar and syrup and pour over chicken. Bake for 30 minutes longer, basting with sauce every 10 minutes. 6 servings.

Mrs. Gertrude P. Hill, Buckhannon, West Virginia

TEXAS-STYLE BARBECUED CHICKEN

1 tbsp. salt	1 tsp. hickory smoked salt
1/2 tsp. pepper	1 c. hot water
4 tbsp. honey	1/2 c. vinegar
1/2 c. catsup or chili sauce	1 c. salad oil
2 tbsp. brown mustard	1 clove of garlic, split
2 tbsp. Worcestershire sauce	1 fryer, disjointed

Combine the salt, pepper, honey, catsup, mustard, Worcestershire sauce, smoked salt, water and vinegar in a saucepan and mix with a rotary beater. Beat in oil gradually. Cook, stirring, until thickened. Rub sides of a greased shallow casserole with garlic. Place the chicken in the casserole in a single layer and brush with sauce. Bake in 350-degree oven until tender, basting with sauce occasionally.

Mrs. Pearl Nichols, Houston, Texas

DELICIOUS BARBECUED CHICKEN

1 1/2 c. tomato juice	1 tsp. sugar
1/4 tsp. cayenne pepper	3/4 c. cider vinegar
Salt	1/4 tsp. garlic juice
Pepper	3 tbsp. margarine
1/4 tsp. powdered mustard	2 lge. fryers, cut in half
4 1/2 tsp. Worcestershire sauce	3 onions, sliced
1 bay leaf	

Mix the tomato juice, cayenne pepper, 2 teaspoons salt, 1/4 teaspoon pepper, mustard, Worcestershire sauce, bay leaf, sugar, vinegar, garlic juice and margarine in a saucepan and simmer for 10 minutes. Place the fryers, skin side down, in large baking pan and cover bottom of the pan with hot water. Season the fryers with salt and pepper to taste and place onion slices under wings and legs. Bake in 350-degree oven for 1 hour. Pour off all but 3/4 cup liquid and turn fryers. Pour sauce over all and bake for 35 to 45 minutes longer, or until tender.

Mrs. Leo Bales, Lampasas, Texas

PEACHY BARBECUED CHICKEN

1 3-lb. chicken, disjointed	1 1-lb. can peach halves
1/2 tsp. salt	1 can tomato sauce
Flour	1 tbsp. lemon juice
3 tbsp. butter	1 med. onion, chopped

Sprinkle the chicken with salt and roll in flour. Brown in butter in a skillet, then place in a baking dish. Drain the peaches and reserve syrup. Mix reserved syrup with tomato sauce and lemon juice and pour over chicken. Sprinkle onion over top. Bake at 350 degrees for 30 minutes. Place peaches over chicken and bake for 30 minutes longer. 4-6 servings.

Mary Ann Pickett, Annapolis, Maryland

PRESIDENT'S CHOICE CHICKEN

1 tbsp. salad oil	1/4 c. lemon juice
1 tbsp. butter or margarine	3 tbsp. Worcestershire sauce
1 fryer, disjointed	2 tbsp. vinegar
1 med. onion, chopped	1 1/2 tsp. prepared mustard
2 tbsp. brown sugar	1/2 c. chopped celery
1 c. water	Salt to taste
1 c. catsup	Dash of pepper sauce

Heat the oil and butter in a skillet. Add the chicken and brown on both sides. Remove from skillet and place in a casserole. Saute the onion in the skillet until tender. Add remaining ingredients and simmer for 30 minutes. Pour over chicken and cover. Bake in 350-degree oven for 1 hour. 4 servings.

Mrs. Noyce W. Burt, Montgomery, Alabama

Chicken Barbecue for a Crowd (below)

CHICKEN BARBECUE FOR A CROWD

12 fryers, halved
Salt to taste
3/4 c. salad oil
2 8-oz. cans seasoned tomato
  sauce

2/3 c. lemon juice
1/4 c. Worcestershire sauce
2 tbsp. prepared mustard
1 garlic clove, minced

Sprinkle the chickens on both sides with salt and place, skin side up, on a grill 3 to 6 inches from heat. Combine remaining ingredients in a large bowl and blend well. Brush on chickens. Cook chickens for 45 minutes to 1 hour and 15 minutes or until tender, turning and brushing occasionally with sauce. Leg should twist easily out of thigh joint and pieces should feel tender when probed by fork when chicken is done.

BARBECUED LEMON CHICKEN

3 broilers
1 c. salad oil
3/4 c. lemon juice
1 tbsp. salt
2 tsp. paprika

2 tsp. onion powder
1 tsp. garlic powder
2 tsp. crushed sweet basil
2 tsp. crushed thyme

Split chickens and remove wings, backbone and tail. Place in a shallow pan. Combine remaining ingredients in a jar. Cover and shake well to blend. Pour over chicken and cover. Refrigerate overnight, turning chicken occasionally. Bring to room temperature. Drain chicken and reserve marinade. Place chicken on grill over hot coals. Cook for about 20 minutes on each side, basting frequently with reserved marinade. 6 servings.

Mrs. Albert Walker, Macon, Georgia

GINGER CHICKEN

1/2 c. salad oil	1/3 c. soy sauce
3/4 c. pineapple juice	1 tsp. ginger
1/4 c. molasses	1 fryer, halved or quartered
1/4 c. lemon juice	

Combine all ingredients except chicken. Place chicken on grill 3 to 6 inches from coals and brush with sauce. Cook over low coals for about 1 hour or until tender, turning and brushing with sauce frequently.

Esther McConnell, Charleston, West Virginia

CHICKEN WITH SPANISH BARBECUE SAUCE

2 3-lb. fryers	1/3 c. seedless raisins
Salad oil	6 tbsp. water
Salt and pepper to taste	6 tbsp. honey
3 8-oz. cans tomato sauce	1 1/2 tbsp. vinegar
with onions	2 tsp. soy sauce
1 c. chopped stuffed olives	2 cloves of garlic, crushed

Tie the legs of each chicken together and fold wings under back. Brush with oil and sprinkle with salt and pepper. Balance chickens on rotisserie spit and secure with skewers. Place a pan under chickens to catch drippings. Combine remaining ingredients in a saucepan and cook over low heat for 20 minutes, stirring occasionally. Roast chickens 9 inches from heat for about 1 hour and 30 minutes or to 190 degrees on a meat thermometer, brushing with sauce during last 15 minutes of roasting time. Heat remaining sauce and serve with chickens. 8 servings.

Photograph for this recipe on page 34.

BARBECUED CHICKEN

3 2-lb. chickens, halved	2 tsp. sugar
2/3 c. melted butter	1 tsp. salt
2/3 c. hot water	2 tsp. flour
2 tsp. A-1 sauce	Dash of cayenne (opt.)
1 1/2 tbsp. lemon juice	2 cloves of garlic, minced
1/4 tsp. hot sauce	(opt.)

Place the chickens on grill over coals, cavity side down. Mix the butter, water, A-1 sauce, lemon juice and hot sauce in a saucepan. Add remaining ingredients and stir well. Cook for 2 to 3 minutes or until thickened. Cook chicken until tender, basting with sauce frequently. May use bunch of celery with leaves for an aromatic basting broom. 6 servings.

Mrs. Sarah West, Asheville, North Carolina

HOME-STYLE BARBECUED CHICKEN

1 egg, beaten	1/4 tsp. white pepper
1/2 c. salad oil	1 1/2 tsp. poultry seasoning
2 tbsp. salt	5 broiler halves

Mix the egg and oil and beat until thick and creamy. Add the salt, pepper and poultry seasoning and stir. Dip broiler halves into sauce. Place on grill about 6 inches from coals. Cook for about 45 minutes or until tender, turning and basting with sauce every 10 minutes. 5 servings.

Mrs. Davis Clay, Dover, Delaware

BARBECUE SAUCE FOR CHICKEN

2 eggs, beaten	2 tbsp. poultry seasoning
1 1/2 c. salad oil	1 tsp. pepper
1 qt. vinegar	20 chicken halves
1/4 c. salt	

Mix the eggs and oil and beat well. Add vinegar, salt, poultry seasoning and pepper and mix thoroughly. Place the chicken on outdoor grill 6 inches from coals. Cook for 30 minutes on each side, basting frequently with sauce. 20 servings.

Mrs. Edgar Bennett, Santa Fe, New Mexico

GRILLED BARBECUED CHICKEN

1 c. water	2 tbsp. salt
2 c. vinegar	4 fryers, halved
1 c. margarine or butter	

Combine the water, vinegar, margarine and salt in a saucepan and heat until margarine is melted. Place chicken on grill, skin side up. Cook for 1 hour and 15 minutes to 1 hour and 30 minutes, turning and basting with sauce every 4 minutes. 8 servings.

Mrs. D. L. Kaylor, Five Points, Alabama

MAPLE-BARBECUED BROILERS

4 broiler halves	1 tsp. salt
1/2 c. melted butter	Dash of pepper
1 clove of garlic, minced	1/4 tsp. dry mustard
3 tbsp. wine vinegar	1/4 tsp. marjoram
1 tbsp. maple syrup	

Place the broiler halves on grill, skin side up, 4 to 5 inches from coals. Combine remaining ingredients and blend well. Cook chicken for 20 minutes, then turn and brush with maple mixture. Cook for 20 minutes and turn. Cook for 15 to 20 minutes longer or until tender, brushing with sauce frequently. 4 servings.

Mrs. Albert S. Warren, Charlotte, North Carolina

EASY BARBECUED CHICKEN

1 1/2 sticks margarine, melted	2 fryers, disjointed
Garlic salt to taste	1 bottle garlic barbecue sauce

Mix the margarine and garlic salt. Place fryers on barbecue grill over low coals and brush with margarine mixture. Cook for about 1 hour or until tender, turning and brushing with margarine mixture frequently. Cook for 15 minutes longer, brushing with barbecue sauce frequently. 6-8 servings.

Mrs. Cooper Dixon, Hampton, Virginia

PRESIDENT'S BARBECUED CHICKEN

1 c. butter	2 tsp. dried leaf oregano
3/4 c. lemon juice	4 fryers, halved
2 tsp. garlic salt	3 tsp. salt
2 tbsp. paprika	1/2 tsp. pepper

Melt the butter in a small saucepan and stir in the lemon juice, garlic salt, paprika and oregano. Place the chickens in a shallow dish and sprinkle with salt and pepper. Pour marinade over chickens and cover. Marinate for 3 to 4 hours at room temperature, turning occasionally. Drain and reserve marinade. Place chicken, skin side up, on grill set 3 to 6 inches from charcoal briquets that have reached the light gray ash stage and brush generously with reserved marinade. Cook for 45 minutes to 1 hour and 15 minutes or until tender, turning and brushing with marinade occasionally. Leg should twist easily out of thigh joint and pieces should feel tender when probed with a fork when chicken is done. 8 servings.

President's Barbecued Chicken (above)

baked & braised chicken

Chicken combined with rich, well-seasoned sauces . . . crisp, brightly colored vegetables . . . the perfect blend of herbs and spices . . . all these combine to make memorable baked and braised chicken dishes. Southern women — long experts at preparing chicken in many different ways — enjoy serving their families and friends such sparkling fare.

In this section, the very best of these unusual recipes have been brought together for your cooking and dining pleasure. Every recipe has been painstakingly developed by a southern homemaker and served with pride at her table to win her fame as a great cook. Many such special recipes are yours now in the pages that follow.

On those occasions when you want to serve the very best, try Baked Chicken with Ham Stuffing. This combination of two favorite southern flavors will turn your dinner into a gourmet's delight. Another exciting flavor combination is found in Chicken Breasts with Pecan Stuffing — two flavors, two textures in an unforgettable main dish. And still another very special dish is Regal Rice and Chicken Amandine.

And you'll find recipes for Country Captain — a very southern way of preparing chicken — and other favorites like Chicken Tetrazzini and Chicken Pilaf. Browse through these pages — you'll find so many exciting new recipes, you'll want to try one tonight!

51

TWIN CHICKENS L'ORANGE

2 fryers	1/4 c. red wine vinegar
Salt	2 c. chicken stock
6 oranges	4 peppercorns
3 sprigs of tarragon	1 tbsp. cornstarch
1 garlic clove, cut in half	Watercress
1/4 c. sugar	

Sprinkle cavity of each chicken with 1/2 teaspoon salt and hook wing tips into back. Remove peel of 1 orange with vegetable peeler. Cut peel into long strips and reserve for sauce. Squeeze juice from 4 oranges and reserve juice for sauce. Cut 2 of the squeezed oranges into small chunks. Fill each chicken cavity with orange chunks and 1 sprig of tarragon. Tie legs together with strings, then tie legs and tail together. Rub each chicken with garlic and place chickens in a shallow roasting pan. Roast in 375-degree oven for 30 minutes per pound. Stir sugar and vinegar together in a saucepan and bring to boiling point, stirring until sugar is dissolved. Reduce heat and simmer for about 5 minutes or until thickened. Add the chicken stock, remaining tarragon, peppercorns and salt to taste and bring to a boil. Reduce heat and simmer for about 10 minutes. Add reserved orange juice. Strain sauce into a bowl and add reserved orange peel. Baste chickens frequently with sauce during the last 30 minutes of roasting. Remove chickens from pan onto a heated serving platter and remove string and cavity filling. Stir small amount of water into cornstarch and stir into remaining orange sauce in a saucepan. Cook, stirring constantly, until clear and thickened. Garnish chickens with slices of remaining oranges and watercress and serve with sauce. 8 servings.

ITALIAN-STYLE CHICKEN

1 fryer	Pinch of basil leaves
Salt and pepper to taste	1 sm. clove of garlic, minced
1/2 c. salad oil	Juice of 2 lemons

Remove skin from the fryer and season fryer with salt and pepper. Place in a shallow baking pan. Mix remaining ingredients and pour over fryer. Refrigerate for 1 to 24 hours. Bake at 400 degrees for about 1 hour or until done.

Mrs. C. D. Simpson, Jr., Rector, Arkansas

PINEAPPLE-BAKED CHICKEN

1 2 1/2 to 3-lb. fryer	1 tbsp. grated orange peel
1/2 tsp. poultry seasoning	6 tbsp. melted butter
1/4 tsp. salt	1/2 c. water
1 1/2 c. soft bread crumbs	1/4 c. pineapple syrup
1/3 c. flaked coconut	1/4 c. orange juice
1/4 c. finely chopped celery	2 tbsp. bottled meat sauce
1/4 c. drained crushed pineapple	

Rinse the chicken with cold water and drain. Dry inside and outside. Rub cavity with poultry seasoning and salt. Combine the bread crumbs, coconut, celery, pineapple, orange peel and 2 tablespoons butter in a bowl and toss lightly to blend. Place in cavity of chicken and truss. Brush chicken with 3 tablespoons butter. Place on rack in a roasting pan and add water. Cover. Bake in 375-degree oven for about 1 hour. Combine remaining butter with remaining ingredients. Uncover chicken and brush with half the orange mixture. Bake for about 30 minutes longer, brushing frequently with remaining orange mixture. Garnish with pineapple rings and grape clusters. 4-5 servings.

Mrs. Herbert Butcher, Dille, West Virginia

FILBERT ROAST CHICKEN WITH HONEY GLAZE

1 c. chopped filberts
2 c. herb-seasoned stuffing
   mix
1/2 c. chopped celery
1 chicken liver, finely
   chopped
1/2 c. melted butter or
   margarine

1/2 c. water
1 5-lb. roasting chicken
1/2 c. honey
2 tbsp. soy sauce
1 tsp. grated orange peel
2 tbsp. orange juice
Green grapes
Whole filberts

Spread the chopped filberts in a shallow baking pan. Bake in 400-degree oven for 10 to 15 minutes, stirring occasionally. Combine the stuffing mix with chopped filberts, celery, chicken liver, butter, and water and toss lightly. Stuff cavity of chicken with filbert mixture, then tie chicken legs and wings with string to hold close to body. Place the chicken on rack in a shallow roasting pan. Roast in 375-degree oven for 1 hour and 15 minutes. Combine the honey, soy sauce, orange peel and orange juice and brush on chicken. Roast for 1 hour longer, basting frequently with honey mixture. Place chicken on a platter and garnish with clusters of green grapes and whole filberts. 6 servings.

Filbert Roast Chicken with Honey Glaze (above)

CHICKEN A LA FRANCAISE

2 stalks celery	2 tbsp. melted butter or
2 2 1/2 to 3-lb. chickens	margarine
2 tbsp. lemon juice	1 10 1/2-oz. can chicken
2 1/2 tsp. salt	broth
1/4 tsp. ground pepper	2 tbsp. flour
1/4 tsp. garlic powder	1/4 c. water
1 c. diced onion	

Trim stem ends of celery, keeping stalks intact. Trim leaves from celery and reserve for stuffing. Cut each stalk lengthwise into 4 wedges and set aside. Brush the chickens inside and out with lemon juice. Mix the salt, pepper and garlic powder and rub in cavities and on skin of chickens. Fill cavities with celery leaves and onion and close openings with skewers. Cover lightly. Refrigerate for 2 to 4 hours to allow flavors to permeate chickens. Place chickens on rack in a roasting pan and brush with butter. Roast in a 425-degree oven for 30 minutes or until browned. Arrange celery around chickens. Add broth to pan and cover. Reduce temperature to 375 degrees and bake for 1 hour longer or until chickens and celery are tender. Remove celery leaves from chicken cavities. Place chickens on a large platter and surround with celery wedges. Pour 2 cups pan juices into a saucepan. Mix the flour with water and stir into pan juices. Cook and stir until thickened. Serve in a bowl. 6-8 servings.

Photograph for this recipe on page 5.

GLAZED ROAST CHICKEN

1 3-lb. fryer	2 tbsp. finely chopped onion
Salt to taste	1/2 tsp. salt
Melted margarine	Dash of pepper
1/2 c. sherry	1 1/2 tbsp. cornstarch
1/3 c. dark corn syrup	3/4 c. water

Rub cavity of the chicken with salt. Truss the chicken. Brush skin with melted margarine and place, breast side up, on rack in shallow baking pan. Roast in 400-degree oven for 1 hour. Combine the sherry, corn syrup, 2 tablespoons margarine, onion, salt and pepper and baste chicken with some of the sherry mixture. Roast for 30 minutes longer, basting frequently and using all the sherry mixture. Remove chicken and place on a warm platter. Blend the cornstarch and water and stir into liquid in pan. Cook over medium heat, stirring constantly, until gravy thickens and boils for 2 minutes. Serve with chicken. 4 servings.

Photograph for this recipe on page 13.

CHICKEN BREASTS WITH PECAN STUFFING

3 c. corn bread stuffing mix	3/4 c. chopped pecans
6 tbsp. melted butter	3/4 tsp. monosodium glutamate
1/3 c. chopped onion	4 sm. chicken breasts
1/2 c. chopped celery	Lemon juice
2 tsp. chopped parsley	Salt and pepper to taste

Mix the stuffing mix, half the butter, onion, celery, parsley, pecans and mono-sodium glutamate with enough hot water to moisten. Place a mound of 1/4 of the stuffing on 4 pieces of heavy-duty aluminum foil. Brush chicken breasts with lemon juice and remaining butter and sprinkle with salt and pepper. Place 1 chicken breast over each mound of stuffing. Fold foil over chicken and seal. Place on a baking sheet. Bake at 350 degrees for 40 minutes. Open foil. Increase temperature to 400 degrees and bake for 20 minutes longer or until chicken is brown.

Mrs. Thomas G. McCullough, Chamblee, Georgia

CHICKEN KIEV

4 chicken breasts, split	1 tsp. lemon juice (opt.)
1/4 lb. hard butter	1 egg
1 tbsp. minced parsley (opt.)	1 tbsp. water
1 tsp. minced chives or scallions (opt.)	1 env. seasoned coating mix for chicken

Remove skin, bones, and cartilage from chicken breasts. Place chicken between sheets of waxed paper and pound until about 1/8 inch thick, taking care not to make any holes in the chicken. Cut the butter into 8 finger shapes and place 1 on each piece of chicken near the end. Sprinkle with parsley, chives and lemon juice and roll up each piece, folding ends in so that butter is completely enclosed. Secure with wooden picks and trim off ends of picks. Beat egg slightly with water. Dip chicken rolls into egg mixture, one at a time, then coat with seasoned coating mix according to package directions. Place in ungreased shallow baking pan, seam side down. Bake at 450 degrees for about 20 minutes or until well browned, then drain on absorbent paper. 4 servings.

Chicken Kiev (above)

BAKED CHICKEN WITH HAM STUFFING

1 5-lb. hen	1 hard-cooked egg, chopped
1 lb. chopped cooked ham	Pepper to taste
1/4 tsp. salt	1/2 c. seedless raisins
Grated rind of 1 lemon	1 diced cooked potato
8 olives, chopped	Chopped cooked giblets

Cook the hen in simmering water until nearly tender. Drain and reserve stock. Combine remaining ingredients and add enough reserved stock to moisten. Mix well. Place in cavity of hen and place hen in a baking pan. Bake in 425-degree oven until tender and brown, basting occasionally with remaining stock. 5 servings.

Mrs. Almo Haak, Yorktown, Texas

BAKED CHICKEN AND DRESSING

4 c. corn bread crumbs	1 1/2 c. melted margarine
1 c. chopped celery	1 6-lb. cooked hen, sliced
1/2 c. chopped onion	1 c. flour
1 tsp. salt	4 c. broth
Pepper	2 c. milk

Combine the corn bread crumbs, celery, onion, 1/2 teaspoon salt, 1/2 teaspoon pepper and 1/2 cup margarine and mix well. Place in large casserole and place hen on top. Mix remaining margarine and flour in a saucepan. Add remaining salt, pepper to taste, broth and milk and cook, stirring constantly, until thick. Pour over the hen. Bake at 350 degrees for 1 hour. 16 servings.

Mrs. William S. Womack, McMinnville, Tennessee

CHICKEN MARENGO

1 lb. sweet Italian sausage links, sliced	1/2 c. rose wine or chicken broth
2 tbsp. butter or margarine	1/4 c. diced green pepper
2 tbsp. salad or olive oil	1 tbsp. parsley flakes
2 2 1/2 to 3-lb. fryers	1 1/2 tsp. Italian seasoning
1/2 lb. small fresh mushrooms	1 tsp. minced onion
1 1-lb. 12-oz. can tomato puree	1/2 tsp. salt
1 8-oz. can ripe olives	1/4 tsp. ground pepper
1 bay leaf	1/4 tsp. garlic powder

Brown the sausage in a Dutch oven or heavy saucepan. Remove sausage and set aside. Discard fat. Heat the butter and oil in the same Dutch oven. Cut the chickens in serving pieces and cook in the Dutch oven until browned. Remove chicken and set aside. Rinse, pat dry and trim the mushrooms and place in the Dutch oven. Add the tomato puree. Drain the olives and reserve 1/4 cup liquid. Slice the olives and place in the Dutch oven. Add the reserved liquid and remaining ingredients and bring to boiling point, stirring occasionally. Return sausage and chicken to Dutch oven and reduce heat. Cover. Simmer for 30 to 40 minutes or until chicken is tender. One 6 to 8-ounce can sliced mushrooms, drained, may be substituted for fresh mushrooms. 8 servings.

CHICKEN AND DRESSING

1 4-lb. hen	1 c. milk
2 c. bread crumbs	1 tbsp. sage
2 c. corn bread crumbs	1 chopped onion
2 c. crushed corn flakes	1 c. chopped celery
2 eggs	Salt and pepper to taste

Cook the chicken in boiling water until tender. Drain and reserve stock. Cool the chicken and remove chicken from bones. Cut in small pieces and place in a bowl. Add remaining ingredients and mix. Add enough reserved stock to moisten and place in a casserole. Bake at 450 degrees for 25 minutes. Reduce temperature to 325 degrees and bake until done. 8 servings.

Mrs. Homer Daniels, New London, North Carolina

ROAST CHICKEN WITH RAISIN-NUT STUFFING

2 broilers, quartered	1 c. light seedless raisins
Monosodium glutamate	1 c. broken walnuts
Salt and pepper	1/2 tsp. oregano
4 c. crumbled bread	1/2 tsp. poultry seasoning
Melted margarine or butter	

Sprinkle the chicken with small amount of monosodium glutamate and salt and pepper to taste. Combine the bread, 2/3 cup margarine, 1/2 teaspoon monosodium glutamate, 2 teaspoons salt, 1/4 teaspoon pepper, raisins, walnuts, oregano and poultry seasoning and mix well. Place in a baking pan. Place chicken over bread mixture and brush with margarine. Bake in 350-degree oven for 1 hour and 30 minutes or until chicken is golden brown, brushing occasionally with margarine.

Mrs. Annie Blanchard, Heth, Arkansas

Chicken Marengo (page 56)

CHICKEN BREASTS WITH POTATO STUFFING

1 lge. onion, chopped	1/4 c. chopped parsley
1 c. chopped celery	1 tsp. salt
Margarine	1/4 tsp. pepper
4 c. mashed potatoes	Paprika to taste
2 slightly beaten eggs	4 chicken breasts, boned and
1 c. herb-seasoned stuffing mix	split

Saute the onion and celery in 1/2 cup margarine in a saucepan until tender and add potatoes. Stir in remaining ingredients except chicken and place in a greased baking dish. Place chicken breasts over top. Brush with melted margarine and sprinkle with additional salt, pepper and paprika. Bake at 375 degrees for 35 to 40 minutes or until chicken is tender and brown.

Joe H. Banks, Tuscaloosa, Alabama

LADY BIRD DELUXE CHICKEN

12 prunes	1/2 c. hot water
Ground celery	1 apple, chopped
1 c. bread crumbs	1/3 c. chopped walnuts
1/4 c. cornmeal	1 onion, chopped
4 tbsp. melted butter	1 tsp. sage
1 egg	4 chicken breasts
1 tsp. salt	2 c. cider
1/2 tsp. pepper	

Cook the prunes according to package directions and remove seeds. Stuff with ground celery. Mix the bread crumbs, cornmeal, butter, egg, salt and pepper in a bowl. Add the water, apple, walnuts, onion and sage and mix well. Bone the chicken breasts and stuff with bread mixture. Secure with skewers and place in a casserole. Pour the cider over chicken breasts. Bake in 350-degree oven for 1 hour. Place 3 prunes over each chicken breast and bake for 15 minutes longer.

Mrs. Elizabeth Ann Parnell, Winston-Salem, North Carolina

CHEESY CHICKEN ROLL-UPS

1 tbsp. minced onion	1/4 tsp. salt
1 tsp. minced green pepper	1/4 tsp. pepper
1 tbsp. butter	1/2 recipe buttermilk biscuit
1 5-oz. can chicken	dough
1 1/2 c. grated Cheddar cheese	1 c. cream of chicken soup
1/2 c. sour cream	1/2 soup can milk
1/2 tsp. hot sauce (opt.)	

Saute the onion and green pepper in butter in a saucepan until tender and drain. Drain the chicken and cut in small pieces. Add 1 cup cheese, sour cream, hot sauce, onion mixture, salt and pepper and mix well. Roll biscuit dough as thin as possible. Spread chicken mixture on dough and roll as for jelly roll. Slice and place on a cookie sheet, cut side up. Bake at 450 degrees for 10 to 12 minutes. Sprinkle remaining cheese on roll-ups and broil until cheese is melted. Pour soup and milk into a saucepan and heat through. Serve with roll-ups.

Mary Lee Moyers, Hamburg, Arkansas

CHICKEN IN WINE GRAVY

3/4 c. butter or margarine	1/2 c. dry red wine
2 fryers	1/2 c. sliced pitted ripe
1 lb. fresh mushrooms, sliced	olives
2 3/4-oz. envelopes au jus	1 lb. medium egg noodles
gravy mix	1/4 c. heavy cream
2 tbsp. instant minced onion	1/4 c. grated Parmesan cheese
2 tbsp. tomato paste	1/4 c. grated Romano cheese
2 c. water	

Heat 1/4 cup butter in a large skillet. Cut the chicken in serving pieces and brown in the butter, several pieces at a time. Remove from skillet. Add the mushrooms to butter remaining in the skillet and cook over high heat, stirring frequently, until tender. Remove from skillet. Combine the gravy mix, onion, tomato paste, water and wine in the skillet and bring to a boil, stirring constantly. Add the chicken and cover. Simmer for 25 to 30 minutes or until chicken is tender, spooning sauce over chicken occasionally and adding water if sauce becomes too thick. Add the mushrooms and olives and heat through. Cook the noodles according to package directions and drain. Cream remaining butter in a bowl and stir in the cream and cheeses. Stir in the noodles and turn into a serving dish. Sprinkle with additional Parmesan and Romano cheeses and serve with chicken mixture. One 8-ounce can sliced mushrooms, drained, may be substituted for fresh mushrooms. 8 servings.

Chicken in Wine Gravy (above)

SESAME BAKED CHICKEN A L'ORANGE

1/3 c. sesame seed	1 3-lb. chicken, disjointed
Flour	1/2 c. instant non-dairy
1 tsp. paprika	coffee creamer
1 tbsp. salt	1 1/2 c. water
1/4 tsp. pepper	1/2 c. orange juice
Grated peel of 1 orange	

Combine the sesame seed, 1/2 cup flour, paprika, salt, pepper and grated peel in a paper bag. Add the chicken, 2 or 3 pieces at a time, and shake bag to coat chicken. Reserve remaining seasoned flour. Brown the chicken in small amount of fat in a skillet over low heat. Combine the coffee creamer, 2 tablespoons flour and reserved seasoned flour in a saucepan. Add the water and orange juice and cook, stirring constantly, until thickened. Place chicken in a shallow casserole. Pour off all but 1/4 cup fat from the skillet and add the orange sauce. Cook and stir over low heat, loosening browned bits, until thoroughly blended. Pour over chicken and cover. Bake at 325 degrees for 45 minutes. Remove cover and bake for 15 minutes longer or until chicken is tender. Garnish with orange slices.

Mrs. Felton Champion, Pine Mountain, Georgia

SPICED CHICKEN

1 c. orange juice	1 clove of garlic, minced
1 1/2 c. sliced peaches	1/2 c. flour
2 tbsp. brown sugar	1 tsp. salt
2 tbsp. vinegar	1/8 tsp. pepper
1 tsp. nutmeg	1 3-lb. chicken, disjointed
1 tsp. sweet basil	Oil

Combine the orange juice, peaches, sugar, vinegar, nutmeg, basil and garlic in a saucepan. Cook over low heat for 10 minutes. Mix the flour, salt and pepper and dredge chicken with flour mixture. Brown in 1/2 inch of hot oil in large frypan, then drain off oil. Pour fruit sauce over chicken and cover. Simmer for about 20 minutes. 4-6 servings.

Mrs. J. Clifford Smith, Kelso, Tennessee

CRANBERRY-GLAZED CHICKEN

1 3-lb. fryer, disjointed	2 tsp. soy sauce
Salt and pepper to taste	1 1/2 tsp. lemon juice
1 7-oz. can jellied cranberry	1/4 c. butter or margarine
sauce	

Preheat oven to 425 degrees. Sprinkle chicken with salt and pepper and place, skin side down, in 12 x 8 x 2-inch baking dish. Combine the cranberry sauce, soy sauce, lemon juice and butter in a saucepan and heat, stirring constantly, until cranberry sauce and butter are melted. Pour over chicken. Bake for 30 minutes. Turn chicken and bake for 20 minutes longer.

Judy Radford, Cadiz, Kentucky

CHICKEN BREASTS IN APPLESAUCE

2 c. applesauce	1/4 c. diced onion
1/2 tsp. allspice	4 chicken breasts, cut in half
1 1/2 tsp. salt	1/2 c. evaporated milk
1 tbsp. flour	1 c. fine cheese cracker crumbs
1 tbsp. tomato paste	1/2 tsp. paprika
1 c. chopped celery	

Mix the applesauce, allspice, 1 teaspoon salt, flour and tomato paste and stir in the celery and onion. Place in lightly greased baking dish. Bone the chicken breasts and dip in milk. Mix the cracker crumbs, paprika and remaining salt and roll chicken in crumb mixture. Place on applesauce mixture. Bake at 350 degrees for 45 minutes or until chicken is tender.

Mrs. Tommy Taylor, Guin, Alabama

ORANGE CHICKEN AND RICE

4 fryer chicken breasts	1 tbsp. minced onion
1 tsp. monosodium glutamate	1/4 tsp. rosemary
Salt	1/4 tsp. tarragon
Pepper to taste	2 c. cooked yellow rice
2 tbsp. salad oil	Orange rind, cut in thin
1/3 c. orange juice	strips

Sprinkle the chicken with monosodium glutamate, salt to taste and pepper and place in a foil-lined baking pan, skin side down. Mix the oil, orange juice, onion, rosemary, tarragon and pinch of salt in a bowl and brush on chicken. Bake at 325 degrees for 30 minutes, basting with sauce occasionally. Turn chicken and baste with sauce. Bake for 15 minutes longer or until tender. Place the rice in a serving dish and arrange chicken over rice. Pour remaining sauce over chicken and garnish with orange rind.

Orange Chicken and Rice (above)

CHICKEN SCALLOP

4 c. diced cooked chicken	3/4 tsp. poultry seasoning
3 c. fine bread crumbs	1 1/2 c. chicken broth
1 1/2 c. cooked rice	1 3/4 c. milk
3/4 c. chopped onion	4 beaten eggs
1/2 c. chopped celery	1 can mushroom soup
1 1/3 c. chopped pimento	1 c. sour cream
3/4 tsp. salt	

Combine the chicken, bread crumbs, rice, onion, celery, pimento, salt, poultry seasoning, chicken broth, 1 1/2 cups milk and eggs and mix well. Place in a greased 9 x 13-inch baking dish. Bake at 350 degrees for 50 to 55 minutes or until knife inserted in center comes out clean, then cut in squares. Combine the soup and remaining milk in a saucepan and add the sour cream. Heat through and serve with chicken mixture.

Mrs. D. H. Kirkley, Albany, Georgia

CHICKEN AND YELLOW RICE

1 onion, chopped	3 tsp. salt
1 bell pepper, chopped	Dash of paprika
4 stalks celery, chopped	3 c. water
1 chicken, disjointed	1 can peas, drained
3 c. yellow rice	1 sm. jar olives, drained
1 can tomatoes	1 can pimento strips, drained
Chopped parsley to taste	

Cook the onion, bell pepper and celery in small amount of fat in a skillet and remove from skillet. Fry the chicken in same skillet until brown, then drain. Wash the rice and place in a baking pan. Add the tomatoes, parsley, salt, paprika, water and onion mixture and stir well. Add the chicken. Bake at 350 degrees for 1 hour and 30 minutes or until rice is done. Add the peas, olives and pimentos and bake for 8 minutes longer.

Mary P. Oyaas, Sumter, South Carolina

CHICKEN LOAF WITH MUSHROOM SAUCE

1 5-lb. hen	1 tbsp. minced onion
1 carrot	5 eggs, well beaten
1 onion	1/2 c. butter
1 bay leaf	1/2 c. flour
Celery leaves	1/2 c. coffee cream or milk
2 c. soft bread crumbs	1/2 tsp. paprika
1 c. cooked rice	2 cans mushrooms
Salt	1 tbsp. lemon juice
1 sm. can pimentos, diced	1 tsp. chopped parsley

Place the chicken, carrot, onion, bay leaf and several celery leaves in a kettle and cover with water. Bring to a boil and reduce heat. Simmer until chicken is tender and cool the chicken in broth. Drain and reserve broth. Remove skin from chicken and remove chicken from bones. Chop chicken fine. Add the bread crumbs, rice, 1 1/2 teaspoons salt, pimentos, 2 cups reserved broth, minced onion and eggs and mix well. Place in a greased baking pan. Bake at 350 degrees for 1 hour. Melt the butter in top of a double boiler and stir in the flour. Add 2 cups reserved broth, coffee cream, salt to taste, paprika and mushrooms and liquid and place over boiling water. Cook, stirring, until thick, then remove from water. Stir in the lemon juice and parsley and serve with chicken mixture.

Wilma Neff, South Pittsburg, Tennessee

SAFFRONED RICE WITH CHICKEN

1 fryer	1/2 c. chopped green pepper
1 tsp. monosodium glutamate	1 1-lb. can tomatoes
1 tsp. salt	1 6-oz. package yellow
1/2 tsp. paprika	saffron rice
2 tbsp. olive oil	1/2 c. sliced black olives
1/2 c. chopped onion	2 tbsp. capers

Cut the chicken in serving pieces and sprinkle with monosodium glutamate, salt and paprika. Heat the olive oil in a skillet. Add the chicken and cook until browned. Remove chicken from skillet. Place the onion and green pepper in the skillet and cook until tender but not brown. Drain the tomatoes and reserve liquid. Add enough water to reserved liquid to make 2 1/2 cups liquid and stir into onion mixture, scraping brown particles from bottom of skillet. Add the tomatoes, yellow rice and chicken and bring to a boil. Cover tightly and reduce heat. Simmer for 20 minutes. Add olives and capers and heat through. 4-6 servings.

Saffroned Rice with Chicken (above)

63

REGAL RICE AND CHICKEN AMANDINE

1 tbsp. minced onion	2 1/2 c. diced cooked chicken
4 tbsp. butter	2 tbsp. diced pimento
1/3 c. flour	1/2 c. slivered toasted almonds
2 c. chicken bouillon	1/4 tsp. nutmeg
1 c. heavy cream	1/4 tsp. thyme
1/4 tsp. salt	1/4 tsp. marjoram
3 c. cooked rice	1 tbsp. minced parsley

Saute the onion in butter in a saucepan until tender. Add the flour and mix well. Add bouillon gradually and cook, stirring constantly, until thick. Simmer for 10 minutes. Add the cream and heat through. Do not boil. Add remaining ingredients and mix well. Pour into greased 2-quart casserole. Bake in 375-degree oven for 25 to 30 minutes. 6 servings.

Mrs. Banks Scudder, Gordonsville, Tennessee

BLUSHING CHICK

1/4 c. butter or margarine	2 tsp. parsley flakes
1 3-lb. fryer, disjointed	1 16-oz. can peeled tomatoes
Flour	1 8-oz. can tomato sauce
1/2 tsp. dillweed	1 pkg. onion soup mix
1/2 tsp. oregano	1/3 c. grated Parmesan cheese

Melt the butter in a 9 x 13 x 2-inch pan. Dredge the chicken with flour and place, skin side up, in the pan. Bake at 400 degrees for 30 to 40 minutes. Combine the dillweed, oregano, parsley, tomatoes, tomato sauce and soup mix in a saucepan and bring to a boil. Reduce heat and simmer for 15 minutes. Pour over chicken and sprinkle with cheese. Reduce temperature to 350 degrees and bake for 30 minutes longer. 4 servings.

Mrs. J. E. Golembiewski, Slidell, Louisiana

CHICKEN ROYALE AND GRAVY

8 or 9 chicken thighs	1/2 tsp. salt
1/4 c. flour	1/8 tsp. pepper
1/4 c. melted butter	1/2 tsp. Worcestershire sauce
2/3 c. evaporated milk	1 4-oz. can mushroom pieces
1 can cream of mushroom soup	2 tbsp. onion flakes
1 c. grated sharp Cheddar cheese	

Coat the chicken with flour and place in single layer in butter in 13 x 9 x 2-inch baking dish. Broil until brown. Pour off excess fat. Combine the milk, soup, cheese, salt, pepper, Worcestershire sauce, mushroom pieces and onion flakes and pour over chicken. Cover with foil. Bake at 350 degrees for 15 to 20 minutes.

Mrs. Eric G. Stone, Stillwater, Oklahoma

CURRIED BROILED CHICKEN

1/4 c. butter	1/2 tsp. curry powder
1 tsp. salt	1 clove of garlic, crushed
1 tsp. dry mustard	1 fryer, disjointed
1 tsp. paprika	

Mix the butter with remaining ingredients except chicken and rub half the mixture on chicken. Place in a baking pan, skin side down. Broil until brown. Turn and spread with remaining butter mixture. Broil until brown and tender, basting occasionally with drippings. 4 servings.

Mrs. W. G. Rohmer, Jr., Mobile, Alabama

MINI-ROLLS PARMIGIANA

8 fryer thighs	8 oz. spaghetti or linguini
1/2 tsp. salt	1 15-oz. can tomato sauce
1 tsp. instant minced onion	1/2 tsp. dried leaf basil
1 tsp. parsley flakes	1/2 tsp. dried leaf oregano
4 oz. mozzarella cheese	Grated Parmesan cheese

Cut along thinner side of thighs to the bone, slashing thigh the length of the bone. Scrape the chicken away until bone is free while holding one end of the bone, then cut off rounded piece of cartilage. Place thighs, skin side down, on a cutting board and sprinkle with salt, onion and parsley flakes. Cut mozzarella cheese into eight 2 1/2 x 1/2 x 3/4-inch pieces and place piece of cheese on each thigh. Fold sides over cheese and fasten with skewer. Place, skewered side down, in foil-lined broiling pan. Broil for about 40 minutes or until brown. Cook spaghetti according to package directions. Combine the tomato sauce with basil and oregano in a small saucepan and heat through. Place spaghetti on a serving platter and pour tomato sauce over spaghetti. Place thighs on top. Serve with Parmesan cheese. 4 servings.

Mini-Rolls Parmigiana (above)

CHICKEN CHOP SUEY

1/2 c. chopped onions	1/8 tsp. pepper
1/2 c. chopped celery	1 tsp. Chinese brown sauce
1/2 c. chopped green pepper	1 tbsp. soy sauce
4 tbsp. salad oil	2 tbsp. cold water
1/2 c. stock or water	1/2 tsp. brown sugar
3 tbsp. cornstarch	1 can bean sprouts, drained
3/4 tsp. salt	3 c. diced cooked chicken

Cook the onions, celery and green pepper in oil in a saucepan for 5 minutes. Do not brown. Add the stock and bring to boiling point. Combine the cornstarch, salt, pepper, sauces, water and sugar and blend until smooth. Add to onion mixture and bring to boiling point. Add the bean sprouts and chicken and heat through. Serve over rice with additional soy sauce if desired.

Mrs. Archie May, Moncks Corner, South Carolina

HAWAIIAN CHICKEN

2 3-lb. chickens	2 tbsp. curry powder
1 1/2 qt. boiling water	1/4 tsp. pepper
1 bay leaf	1 tsp. ginger
1 tsp. salt	1 pkg. onion soup mix
1/2 c. butter or margarine	1/4 c. flour
1 clove of garlic, minced	2/3 c. cold water
2 tart peeled apples, chopped	Milk from 1 fresh coconut
2 c. chopped celery	2 c. light cream or milk
1 tbsp. brown sugar	

Cut the chickens in serving pieces and place in a large saucepan. Add the boiling water, bay leaf and salt and simmer until chickens are tender. Drain and reserve stock. Remove chicken from bones and cut in strips. Melt the butter in a large saucepan and saute garlic, apples and celery in the butter until soft. Stir in the brown sugar, curry powder, pepper and ginger and simmer for 5 to 10 minutes. Add the reserved chicken stock and onion soup mix and cover. Simmer for 25 minutes. Mix the flour and cold water and stir into apple mixture. Stir in the coconut milk and chicken and remove from heat. Cover and let stand for 3 to 4 hours. Place over low heat and stir in the cream. Stir until thoroughly heated and serve with rice. 12 servings.

Mrs. Johnnie P. Bradshaw, Ozark, Alabama

CHICKEN IN CURRANT-ORANGE SAUCE

1/2 c. currant jelly	Dash of hot sauce
1/4 c. frozen orange juice concentrate	1/2 c. flour
2 tsp. cornstarch	1 tsp. salt
1 tsp. dry mustard	1 3-lb. fryer, disjointed

Combine the jelly, orange juice concentrate and 1/3 cup water in a saucepan and cook and stir until smooth. Mix the cornstarch, mustard and hot sauce with 1 tablespoon cold water and stir into jelly mixture. Cook and stir until thickened and set aside. Combine the flour and salt in a paper bag. Add the chicken, 2 or 3 pieces at a time, and shake until coated. Brown in fat in a skillet over medium heat. Drain off excess fat and add orange sauce. Cover and simmer for 45 minutes or until chicken is tender.

Mrs. Myra F. Sharpe, Burlington, South Carolina

CHICKEN WITH MUSHROOMS

3 sprigs of parsley	1 sm. onion, finely chopped
1 sm. stalk celery	1 tsp. flour
3 sprigs of basil	1 tsp. salt
1 bay leaf	Dash of pepper
2 tbsp. margarine	1/4 c. white wine
1 fryer, cut in serving pieces	1/4 c. light cream
1/2 lb. mushrooms, sliced	1 egg yolk

Tie the parsley, celery, basil and bay leaf together for bouquet garni. Melt the margarine in a large skillet. Add the chicken and cook over medium heat, turning as needed, until golden brown on all sides. Add the mushrooms and cook, stirring occasionally, for 5 minutes. Stir in the onion, flour, salt and pepper, then add bouquet garni and wine. Cover and simmer for about 35 minutes or until chicken is tender. Remove chicken and place in a serving dish. Discard bouquet garni. Combine the cream and egg yolk and stir in small amount of the wine mixture. Stir back into remaining wine mixture and heat until thickened, stirring constantly. Pour over chicken. One-fourth teaspoon dried basil may be substituted for sprigs of basil.

Photograph for this recipe on page 13.

COUNTRY CAPTAIN

1 fryer	2 tsp. curry powder
1 tsp. salt	1/2 tsp. leaf thyme
1/4 tsp. pepper	1 1-lb. can stewed tomatoes
1/4 c. butter or margarine	1/4 c. currants or raisins
1 med. onion, chopped	Hot cooked rice
1 sm. green pepper, chopped	Toasted blanched almonds
1 clove of garlic, crushed	Chutney

Cut the chicken in serving pieces and sprinkle with salt and pepper. Heat the butter in a large skillet. Add the chicken and brown on all sides. Remove chicken from skillet. Add the onion, green pepper, garlic, curry powder and thyme to the skillet and cook until onion is tender but not brown. Add the tomatoes, currants and chicken and cover. Cook for 20 to 30 minutes or until chicken is tender. Serve over rice with almonds and chutney. 4 servings.

Photograph for this recipe on page 50.

Oregano Chicken with Mushrooms (below)

OREGANO CHICKEN WITH MUSHROOMS

1 4-lb. fryer	1/4 tsp. pepper
1/4 c. olive oil	1/4 tsp. leaf oregano
3/4 c. chopped onion	1 1-lb. 12-oz. can solid-pack
1 green pepper, thinly sliced	tomatoes
1 clove of garlic, minced	1 6-oz. can tomato paste
1 1/2 tsp. salt	1/3 lb. fresh sliced mushrooms

Cut the chicken in serving pieces and cook in oil in a skillet until browned. Add the onion, green pepper, garlic, salt, pepper and oregano and cook for 10 minutes, stirring occasionally. Add the tomatoes and tomato paste and cover. Cook over low heat for 45 minutes or until chicken is almost tender. Add the mushrooms and cover. Cook for 15 minutes longer. One 4-ounce can sliced mushrooms may be substituted for fresh mushrooms. 4-6 servings.

CHICKEN WILLIE

1 3-lb. fryer	1/4 lb. mushrooms, sliced
1 tsp. salt	2 cloves of garlic, minced
1/4 tsp. pepper	1/4 c. butter or margarine
1/4 c. flour	1/2 c. water
1/4 c. salad oil	2 tbsp. lemon juice
3 med. onions, sliced	1 c. drained canned tomatoes

Cut the chicken in serving pieces. Combine the salt, pepper and flour in a bag and shake chicken in flour mixture until coated. Heat the oil in a skillet and fry chicken in oil until brown. Cover and cook over low heat for 40 minutes. Add the onions, mushrooms, garlic and butter and cover. Cook for 5 minutes. Add enough flour to remaining seasoned flour to make 2 tablespoons and blend with water and lemon juice. Stir into chicken mixture and cook, stirring, until thickened. Add the tomatoes and cover. Cook for 10 minutes longer. 4 servings.

Willie M. Thomas, Pocahontas, Arkansas

CHICKEN CREOLE

3 slices bacon, diced	1 med. carrot, sliced
1 2 1/2-lb. chicken, disjointed	1 1/2 c. canned tomatoes
1 tsp. salt	1 c. water
1 tsp. paprika	1 sm. can mushrooms
1 c. chopped celery	6 stuffed olives, sliced
1 onion, minced	4 tbsp. flour
	3 sprigs of parsley, chopped

Heat pressure cooker. Add the bacon and cook until partially done. Add the chicken, salt, paprika, celery, onion, carrot, tomatoes, and water and cover. Cook at 10 pounds pressure for 15 minutes. Let pressure return to normal and remove cover. Drain the mushrooms and reserve liquid. Add mushrooms and olives to chicken mixture and bring to a boil. Mix reserved liquid with flour and stir into chicken mixture. Cook until thickened and serve with rice. Garnish with parsley.

Edna McNeely, Corinth, Mississippi

CHICKEN CACCIATORE

1 3-lb. fryer, disjointed	1 clove of garlic, minced
Salt and pepper to taste	1 sm. hot red pepper
Flour	1 bay leaf
2 med. onions, chopped	1/2 tsp. celery seed
1 No. 2 can tomatoes	1/8 tsp. sage
1 8-oz. can tomato sauce	

Season the chicken with salt and pepper and dredge with flour. Brown on all sides in small amount of fat in a skillet and remove from skillet. Saute the onions in remaining fat in the skillet until golden and drain off excess fat. Add remaining ingredients and mix. Cover. Simmer for 30 to 45 minutes. Add chicken and simmer for about 1 hour longer or until chicken is tender. 4-5 servings.

Mrs. Lewis Pierce, Leakesville, Mississippi

CHICKEN SPAGHETTI

1 pkg. spaghetti	Salt to taste
1 chicken	1 1/2 c. water
1 lge. onion, chopped	1 can cream of chicken soup
2 c. chopped celery	1/4 lb. Velveeta cheese, grated

Cook the spaghetti according to package directions and drain. Place the chicken, onion, celery, salt and water in a pressure cooker and cook at 10 pounds pressure for about 15 minutes. Let pressure return to normal. Bone the chicken and cut in small pieces. Add to mixture in pressure cooker. Add the chicken soup, cheese and spaghetti and place in a casserole. Bake at 350 degrees until heated through.

Mrs. William L. Graham, Copperas Cove, Texas

POULET A LA BATTLEYANI

Butter	Salt
7 chicken breasts	Flour
Chopped green pepper to taste	Grated Parmesan cheese
2 c. cream	2 c. boiling water
Paprika	Milk

Heat small amount of butter in a saucepan until light brown. Add the chicken and green pepper and cook over low heat until chicken is lightly browned. Pour the cream into a saucepan and cook over low heat until heated through. Do not boil. Add enough paprika to tint cream pink and add salt to taste. Pour over the chicken and simmer until chicken is tender. Sift 1 cup flour with 1 teaspoon salt and mix with 1/2 cup Parmesan cheese. Stir all at once into boiling water in a saucepan, then pour onto a heavily floured surface. Shape in 1/2-inch balls. Poach for 3 to 4 minutes in boiling milk, then drain. Dip in melted butter and roll in Parmesan cheese. Place chicken on a serving platter and arrange dumplings around chicken.

Mrs. John Fennell, Macon, Georgia

CHICKEN A LA KING

1 14-oz. can mushrooms	Salt and pepper to taste
1 sm. can peas	Onion salt to taste
1 c. diced celery	2 tbsp. soy sauce
4 tbsp. butter	2 c. diced cooked chicken
4 tbsp. flour	2 tbsp. chopped pimento
Milk	6 slices crisp bacon, crumbled

Drain the mushrooms and peas and reserve liquids. Saute the mushrooms and celery in butter in a saucepan until tender and stir in flour. Add enough milk to reserved liquids to make 2 cups liquid and stir into the flour mixture. Cook, stirring constantly, until thickened. Season with salt and pepper, onion salt and soy sauce. Add the chicken, pimento and peas and heat thoroughly. Add bacon just before serving. May be served in pastry shells or over toast points.

Mrs. J. S. Polson, Forest Cottage, Kentucky

CREAMED CHICKEN IN PATTY SHELLS

1 2-oz. can sliced mushrooms	1/3 c. milk
2 tbsp. chopped green pepper	1 c. diced cooked chicken
2 tbsp. butter or margarine	2 tbsp. chopped pimento
1 can Cheddar cheese soup	4 patty shells or toast slices

Drain the mushrooms. Cook the mushrooms and green pepper in butter in a saucepan until green pepper is tender. Stir in soup and milk. Add the chicken and pimento and heat through, stirring occasionally. Serve in patty shells. 4 servings.

Catherine Wagoner, Henry, Virginia

CREAMED CHICKEN

6 tbsp. butter or margarine	1 1/2 c. hot chicken broth
1 tbsp. cornstarch	1 c. hot milk
5 tbsp. flour	1 1/2 c. diced cooked chicken
1/4 tsp. salt	1/4 c. sliced stuffed olives
1/2 tsp. celery salt	(opt.)
1/8 tsp. pepper	

Melt the butter in a saucepan and stir in the cornstarch, flour, salt, celery salt and pepper. Add the broth and milk slowly and cook, stirring constantly, until thickened. Stir in chicken and olives and heat thoroughly. Serve on waffles or toast.

Mrs. Glenn T. Wilkerson, Winchester, Tennessee

SAILOR'S RAISIN-CHICKEN SCRAMBLE

8 pieces of frying chicken	1/2 tsp. oregano
3 tbsp. shortening	1 tsp. paprika
1 med. onion, chopped	1/4 tsp. pepper
1 c. rice	1 1-lb. can stewed tomatoes
2/3 c. dark seedless raisins	2 tbsp. chicken stock base
1 tsp. garlic salt	1 1/2 c. water

Brown the chicken over low heat in hot shortening in a heavy skillet, then push pieces to one side. Add the onion and cook until soft. Add remaining ingredients, stirring to mix with chicken, and cover tightly. Simmer for about 45 minutes or until liquid is absorbed and chicken is tender. 4 servings.

Sailor's Raisin-Chicken Scramble (above)

71

Pot of Gold Chicken (below)

POT OF GOLD CHICKEN

1 1-lb. 2-oz. can sm. yams	6 serving pieces of chicken
1 10-oz. package frozen peas	3 tbsp. salad oil
1 1-lb. 13-oz. can cling	1/2 tsp. dry mustard
peach slices	1/4 c. coarsely chopped onion
1/3 c. flour	1 to 2 tsp. grated orange rind
2 tsp. salt	1/2 c. orange juice
1/8 tsp. pepper	

Drain the yams and thaw the peas. Drain the peaches and reserve 1 cup syrup. Place the flour, salt and pepper in a paper bag and shake the chicken in flour mixture to coat. Reserve remaining flour mixture. Brown the chicken in oil in a large skillet. Place reserved flour mixture and mustard in a saucepan and blend in reserved syrup gradually. Add the onion, orange rind and orange juice and heat, stirring constantly, until slightly thickened. Pour over the chicken and cover. Simmer for 20 minutes. Add the yams, peaches and peas and cover. Simmer for 10 minutes longer. 6 servings.

CHICKEN PILAF

1 2 to 3-lb. fryer, disjointed	1/3 c. margarine
2 c. rice	1 chopped onion
2 tsp. salt	1/2 c. chopped celery
1/2 tsp. pepper	1 c. raisins

Place the chicken in a large saucepan and add 2 quarts water. Cover. Simmer for 1 hour. Add the rice, salt and pepper and simmer for 30 minutes. Melt the margarine in a frypan and cook the onion and celery in margarine until tender. Add to chicken mixture and add the raisins. Cover and simmer for 30 minutes longer.

Mrs. C. M. Conlan, Jr., Burleson, Texas

CHICKEN WITH LEEKS

1 2 1/2 to 3-lb. chicken	1 2/3 c. water
1/3 c. flour	1 c. sliced leeks
1 1/2 tsp. salt	1 c. evaporated milk
1/2 tsp. paprika	2 tbsp. chopped pimento
1/2 c. shortening	1 tsp. dried parsley
1 env. cream of leek soup mix	1/4 tsp. poultry seasoning

Cut the chicken in serving pieces. Mix the flour, salt and paprika in a paper bag and shake chicken, several pieces at a time, in flour mixture. Brown in shortening in a 10-inch skillet over medium heat and drain off drippings. Mix the soup mix and water and pour over chicken. Place the leeks over chicken and cover. Cook over low heat for 35 minutes. Place chicken on a serving platter. Stir the milk, pimento, parsley and poultry seasoning into liquid remaining in skillet and cook over low heat, stirring, until thickened. Pour over chicken or serve as gravy. 4-6 servings.

Mrs. B. R. Simpson, Fort Campbell, Kentucky

CHICKEN SHORTCAKE

6 tbsp. butter or margarine	1 tbsp. chili powder
1/2 c. diced celery	1 1/2 c. chicken broth
3 tbsp. flour	2 c. diced cooked chicken
1 tsp. salt	Hot biscuits
1/2 tsp. pepper	

Melt the butter in a saucepan. Add the celery and cook until brown. Blend in flour and seasonings. Add the chicken broth gradually and cook, stirring constantly, until thickened. Add the chicken and heat thoroughly. Split the biscuits and place chicken mixture in between and on top of biscuits. Garnish with paprika.

Mrs. Louise Brown, Lanett, Oklahoma

CHICKEN CURRY

1 med. onion, minced	1/4 tsp. ginger
1 peeled apple, chopped	1 c. chicken broth
1/4 c. margarine	1 c. milk
1/3 c. flour	1/2 c. heavy cream
1 to 2 tbsp. curry powder	Juice of 1/2 lemon
1 1/2 tsp. salt	3 c. chopped cooked chicken
1/8 tsp. pepper	4 c. hot cooked rice

Cook the onion and apple in margarine in top of a double boiler over low heat until onion is tender. Stir in the flour, curry powder, salt, pepper and ginger. Add the broth, milk and cream slowly and place over boiling water. Cook, stirring constantly, until thickened. Cover and cook for 10 minutes longer. Add the lemon juice and chicken and heat thoroughly. Serve with rice.

Mrs. June W. Galford, Dunmore, West Virginia

chicken
soups & stews

Chicken can be easily transformed into utterly delicious soups and stews – and *Southern Living* homemakers are experts at making that transformation happen! They know that nothing says "welcome" to family members or guests more quickly than the appetite-arousing smell of chicken soup or stew.

And these dishes are a boon to budget-minded women. Low in cost, high in flavor and appeal – it's no wonder that thrifty homemakers throughout the Southland have developed great recipes for chicken soups and stews.

In this section, a marvelous selection of prized recipes awaits your cooking and dining pleasure. For extra-special occasions, you'll delight in Coq d'Or Soup, an enchanting dish based on the traditional French recipe. Another sure-to-please favorite is Parmesano Chicken Soup, a borrowing from Italian cuisine. And think how your family will enjoy Chicken Mulligan.

You'll find such traditional southern dishes as Chicken Gumbo – rich, delicious, and typically Creole in its hot and spicy taste – Brunswick Stew – a southern tradition from the time of the earliest colonies – and Chicken Stew with its own light-as-air dumplings.

This is a section you'll turn to again and again when you're looking for elegant soups . . . hot and hearty stews . . . and family-tested, proven recipes!

BUTTER DUMPLING SOUP

1 hen	5 oz. noodles
2 stalks celery, diced	3 chicken bouillon cubes
2 bay leaves	Dumplings
1 1/2 tbsp. salt	

Place hen in a Dutch oven and fill Dutch oven 3/4 full with water. Add celery, bay leaves and salt and bring to a boil. Simmer for 1 hour and 45 minutes. Remove chicken and cool. Remove chicken from bones. Add chicken, noodles and bouillon cubes to broth and simmer for 30 minutes. Drop in Dumplings and simmer for 15 minutes. 8-10 servings.

Dumplings

11 oz. croutons, rolled into crumbs	1/3 c. butter
6 slices day-old bread, crumbled	1 c. scalded milk
	2 eggs, beaten

Combine the croutons and bread in a bowl. Melt the butter in milk and add to crumbs. Stir in eggs and shape in 1 1/2-inch balls.

Mrs. Paul Hubert, Atlanta, Georgia

CHICKEN BOOYAH

1 stewing chicken	1 c. chopped celery
3 tbsp. rice	1 c. chopped carrots
Salt and pepper to taste	1 c. shredded cabbage
1 c. chopped onion	1 6-oz. package noodles

Cook the chicken in boiling water until tender. Remove from broth and cool. Place the rice, seasonings, vegetables and noodles in the broth and cook until vegetables are tender. Remove chicken from bones and cut in small pieces. Add to the rice mixture and simmer for 15 minutes. 10-12 servings.

Mrs. Oscar Thompson, Pascagoula, Mississippi

CHICKEN-NOODLE-PUMPKIN SOUP

1 chicken, disjointed	1 tsp. parsley leaves
1 c. egg noodles	1 tsp. salt
2 c. cooked pumpkin	

Place the chicken in a large saucepan and cover with water. Bring to a boil and reduce heat. Simmer until chicken is tender. Add the noodles and cook until tender. Mash pumpkin and press through a sieve. Add to noodle mixture. Add parsley and salt and heat through.

Mrs. Clarence Cheney, Gatlinburg, Tennessee

CHICKEN-CORN SOUP

1 sm. stewing chicken	6 ears of corn
4 tsp. salt	1/4 c. chopped parsley (opt.)
4 oz. flat noodles	

Cook the chicken in 2 quarts water with 2 teaspoons salt until tender, adding water as needed. Cook the noodles in 2 quarts water and remaining salt for 15 minutes and drain. Remove chicken from broth and reserve broth. Skin the chicken. Remove chicken from bones and cut in small pieces. Add noodles and chicken to reserved broth. Cut the corn from cobs and add to chicken mixture. Bring to a boil and cook for 5 minutes. Add parsley just before serving. One can corn or 1 box frozen corn may be substituted for fresh corn.

Mrs. Al Williams, Savannah, Georgia

COQ D'OR SOUP

1 stewing hen, disjointed	2 carrots, diced
Salt and pepper to taste	1 pt. canned tomatoes
1 sm. onion, chopped	1 tbsp. parsley
2 stalks celery, diced	2 c. noodles or rice

Place the chicken in a 4-quart saucepan and cover with water. Add salt and pepper and cook until tender. Remove chicken from broth and cool. Add remaining ingredients except noodles to broth and cook until tender. Bone the chicken. Add noodles and chicken to onion mixture and cook until noodles are done. 12 servings.

Mrs. James Blumhorst, Tomball, Texas

CHICKEN-NOODLE SOUP

1 lge. fryer, disjointed	3 peppercorns
1 med. carrot, diced	2 beef bouillon cubes
1/2 lemon, sliced	1 tbsp. salt
1 stalk celery, diced	2 qt. water
1 med. onion, diced	1 pkg. fine noodles

Combine all ingredients except noodles in a large saucepan and cook until chicken is tender. Add the noodles and cook for 15 minutes longer. 6-8 servings.

Mrs. George Essig, Paragould, Arkansas

EASY CHICKEN-NOODLE SOUP

2 cans boned chicken, diced	1 onion, chopped
1/4 tsp. salt	5 carrots, chopped
1 tsp. pepper	1/2 c. macaroni
3 c. boiling water	

Add the chicken, salt and pepper to water in a saucepan and cook for 2 to 3 minutes. Add the onion, carrots and macaroni and simmer until carrots are tender. 6 servings.

Bernice Horace, Nacogdoches, Texas

Mushroom-Chicken Soup (below)

MUSHROOM-CHICKEN SOUP

2 13 3/4-oz. cans chicken broth	2 6 or 8-oz. cans sliced mushrooms
1/2 c. rice	2 c. slivered cooked chicken
1/4 tsp. crumbled tarragon leaves	1 c. milk
3 tbsp. butter or margarine	Salt and white pepper to taste

Pour the broth into a medium saucepan and bring to boiling point. Stir in the rice and tarragon. Reduce heat and cover. Cook for 15 to 20 minutes or until rice is tender. Drain the mushrooms and reserve liquid. Heat the butter in a medium skillet. Add the mushrooms and saute until golden brown. Stir into broth. Stir in the chicken, milk and reserved mushroom liquid and heat thoroughly. Season with salt and white pepper. Serve as a main dish in mugs with crusty French bread and a tossed green salad, if desired. One pound fresh mushrooms, sliced, may be substituted for canned mushrooms. 6 servings.

CHICKEN-RICE SOUP

1 stewing chicken, disjointed	1/3 c. flour
1 med. onion, diced	3/4 c. milk
Salt and pepper to taste	4 hard-boiled eggs
3/4 c. long grain rice	

Place the chicken in a 6-quart kettle and fill kettle 3/4 full with water. Add onion, salt and pepper and bring to a boil. Cover. Simmer for 1 hour and 30 minutes to 2 hours or until chicken is tender. Remove chicken from kettle and cool. Remove chicken from bones and place in kettle. Add the rice and cook until rice is tender. Place the flour in a saucepan and stir in milk slowly. Bring to a boil, stirring constantly, and cook, stirring, until thick. Mash the eggs and stir into milk mixture. Drop into simmering soup by teaspoonfuls and simmer for 10 minutes. 12 servings.

Mrs. Eugene Roberts, Bluefield, West Virginia

AUSTRIAN EGG SOUP

1 sm. onion, chopped fine	**2 qt. water**
2 tbsp. chopped celery leaves	**1/4 c. rice**
2 tbsp. melted shortening	**Salt and pepper to taste**
1 3-lb. chicken, disjointed	**2 eggs**

Saute the onion and celery in shortening in a saucepan until tender. Add the chicken and cook for 5 minutes. Add the water, 1 cup at a time, allowing soup to come to a boil and boil for 2 minutes between each addition. Secret of soup is not adding water all at once. Add the rice and cook until chicken is tender. Add the salt and pepper. Beat eggs well, then add 2 tablespoons hot broth, beating constantly. Add to soup, 1 tablespoon at a time, and cook for 5 minutes. 6 servings.

Mrs. John Jones, Birmingham, Alabama

CHICKEN SOUP WITH DUMPLINGS

1 onion, chopped	**2 carrots, diced**
3 tbsp. melted butter	**1/2 tsp. pepper**
1 sm. chicken	**1 tbsp. salt**
1 sm. head cabbage, shredded	**1 tbsp. paprika**
Chopped parsley to taste	**8 c. water**
Chopped celery to taste	**1/2 c. rice**
1 green pepper, diced	**Dumplings**
1 tomato, diced	

Saute the onion in butter in a large saucepan until golden brown. Cut the chicken in serving pieces and add to onion. Add the vegetables, seasonings and 2 cups water and simmer for about 30 minutes or until chicken and vegetables are tender. Pour remaining water into a saucepan and bring to a boil. Add the rice slowly. Drop the Dumplings by teaspoonfuls into rice mixture and cook until rice is tender. Add the chicken mixture and heat through.

Dumplings

1 chicken liver, scraped	**1 egg**
1/2 tsp. salt	**Flour**

Mix the liver, salt and egg in a bowl and stir in enough flour to make a soft dough.

Mrs. Michael Thomas, Tyler, Texas

CHICKEN SOUP WITH VEGETABLES

1 lge. chicken	2 c. chopped rutabagas
3 onions, chopped	4 c. diced potatoes
1 bunch celery, chopped	1 can corn
3 c. chopped cabbage	1 can peas
2 c. chopped carrots	Salt and pepper to taste

Place the chicken in a kettle and cover with water. Bring to a boil and reduce heat. Simmer until tender. Remove chicken from broth and cool. Remove chicken from bones and place in broth. Add the onions, celery and cabbage and cook for 1 hour. Add the carrots and rutabagas and cook for 1 hour. Add the potatoes, corn, peas and seasonings and cook until potatoes are done.

Mrs. Adam Blanton, New Castle, Delaware

COMPANY-CORN SOUP

1 4-lb. chicken	1/2 c. chopped celery and
4 qt. water	leaves
Salt	1/2 tsp. pepper
10 ears corn	2 hard-boiled eggs,
1 onion, chopped fine	chopped fine

Place the chicken in a large saucepan and add the water and salt to taste. Bring to a boil and reduce heat. Simmer until tender. Remove chicken from broth and strain the broth. Remove chicken from bones and chop fine. Add to broth. Cut the corn from cobs and add to chicken mixture. Add onion, celery, 1 teaspoon salt and pepper and cook until the corn is tender. Add the eggs and cook for 10 minutes longer. 6 servings.

Pearl H. Wright, Hollywood, Florida

CREAMED CHICKEN-VEGETABLE SOUP

1 carrot, chopped	1 c. milk
1 sm. onion, chopped	Salt and pepper to taste
2 1/2 c. chicken stock	2 tbsp. grated American cheese
1 1/2 tbsp. butter	1 c. minced cooked chicken
1 tbsp. flour	1 tbsp. chopped parsley

Cook the carrot and onion in chicken stock in a saucepan until tender. Drain and reserve stock. Press carrot and onion through a sieve or blend in a blender. Melt the butter in a saucepan and stir in the flour. Stir in milk and reserved stock gradually and cook over low heat until thickened, stirring constantly. Add the seasonings, carrot mixture, cheese, chicken and parsley and heat, stirring until cheese is melted. 6 servings.

Mrs. Marion Everett, Fayetteville, North Carolina

PARMESANO CHICKEN SOUP

3 qt. chicken stock	2 eggs, beaten
1/2 c. chopped celery	3/4 c. grated Parmesan cheese
1/2 c. chopped onions	1 c. chopped cooked chicken
1/4 c. chopped carrots	1/2 lb. fresh endive, chopped
Pinch of oregano	Salt to taste

Pour the chicken stock into a large saucepan and bring to boiling point. Add the celery, onions, carrots and oregano and cook for 15 minutes. Mix the eggs with cheese and add to the onion mixture. Add chicken, endive and salt and simmer for 15 minutes or until done. 6 servings.

Claude W. Dodd, Durant, Mississippi

CHICKEN SPECIALTY

1/4 c. butter or margarine	2 tsp. salt
1 fryer, cut in serving pieces	1/2 tsp. paprika
2 c. sliced celery	1/4 tsp. pepper
1 lge. onion, chopped	1/4 tsp. thyme
1 green pepper, cut in	1 tbsp. Worcestershire sauce
sm. strips	1 1-lb. can tomatoes
2 c. water	1 1-lb. can whole
3 med. potatoes, quartered	kernel corn

Melt the butter in a 6-quart kettle over medium heat. Add the chicken and brown on both sides. Remove chicken. Add the celery, onion and green pepper to kettle and cook for 5 minutes, stirring frequently. Add the water, potatoes, salt, paprika, pepper, thyme, Worcestershire sauce and chicken and simmer for 30 minutes. Add the tomatoes and corn and simmer for 10 to 15 minutes or until chicken is tender. Serve with corn sticks. 4-6 servings.

Chicken Specialty (above)

PARSLIED CHICKEN SOUP

1 chicken, disjointed	2 med. onions, halved
Salt and pepper to taste	3 med. potatoes, halved
5 med. carrots, halved	10 parsley sprigs

Place the chicken in a 6-quart pressure cooker and add 4 quarts water. Add salt and pepper. Cook at 15 pounds pressure for 1 hour. Let pressure return to normal and add remaining ingredients. Cook at 15 pounds pressure for 5 minutes and cool quickly. Skim off fat and serve with noodles or rice. 6 servings.

Mrs. Emil Zalmon, Emporia, Virginia

CHICKEN-POTATO SOUP

2 tbsp. margarine	1 can boned chicken, diced
1 tbsp. minced onion	3 med. potatoes, diced
1 can chicken broth	1/4 c. evaporated milk

Melt the margarine in a deep saucepan. Add the onion and cook until tender but not brown. Add the chicken broth, chicken and potatoes and cover. Cook for about 25 minutes or until potatoes are tender. Add the milk and stir well. 3 servings.

Mrs. Beverly Welmeyer, New Orleans, Louisiana

CLARA'S CHICKEN SOUP

5 chicken backs	1 c. frozen peas
3 med. potatoes, cubed	1 No. 2 can tomatoes
2 lge. carrots, sliced	1 tsp. sugar
2 med. onions, sliced	Salt to taste
3 stalks celery, sliced	

Cook the chicken in boiling, salted water until tender. Remove chicken from broth and cool. Remove chicken from bones and chop. Return chicken to broth and add the potatoes, carrots, onions, celery, peas and tomatoes. Cook until vegetables are tender, then add sugar and salt.

Mrs. Clara Robinson, Morehead, Kentucky

CHICKEN-VEGETABLE SOUP

1 2 to 3-lb. chicken	6 potatoes, diced
Salt to taste	1 onion, diced
2 c. diced carrots	1 whole or ground peppercorn
1 c. chopped celery	

Place the chicken in a kettle and cover with water. Add salt and cook until tender. Remove chicken from kettle and cool. Add vegetables and peppercorn to broth and cook until carrots are tender. Remove chickens from bones and add to carrot mixture. Simmer until heated through, adding water, if needed.

Mrs. Don Sadler, Pikeville, Kentucky

ADRIAN'S GUMBO

6 tbsp. shortening	**6 c. water**
6 tbsp. flour	**2 tbsp. salt**
1 med. onion, finely chopped	**2 tsp. pepper**
1 green pepper, chopped	**1 tbsp. chopped parsley**
1/4 c. diced celery	**1/2 tsp. gumbo file**
1 lge. hen, disjointed	

Heat the shortening in a kettle. Add the flour and cook, stirring constantly, until flour is dark brown. Add the onion, green pepper and celery and cook, stirring, until vegetables are wilted. Add the chicken and water and mix well. Season with salt and pepper and bring to a boil. Reduce heat and cover. Simmer until chicken is tender. Add the parsley and cook for 5 minutes longer. Remove from heat and add gumbo file. Serve over hot rice in deep soup bowls.

Mrs. Lena Eudy, Crowley, Louisiana

CHICKEN GUMBO

1 6-lb. fat hen	**Chopped parsley to taste (opt.)**
4 tbsp. flour	**Salt and pepper to taste**
4 tbsp. bacon fat	**Red pepper to taste**
2 c. chopped onions	**2 tsp. gumbo file**
1 c. chopped celery	

Place the chicken in a kettle and cover with water. Cook until tender. Brown the flour in bacon fat in a skillet. Add the onions and celery and cook for 15 to 20 minutes. Add to chicken and add the parsley, salt and peppers. Simmer until celery is tender. Remove from heat and stir in gumbo file. Serve over rice.

Mrs. Hubert Lucy, Pleasant Plains, Arkansas

EGALITE' GUMBO

1 chicken, disjointed	**1 lge. onion, minced**
1 tbsp. salt	**2 tbsp. gumbo file**
1/2 c. shortening	**Pepper to taste (opt.)**

Season the chicken with salt and brown in shortening in a saucepan. Add the onion and cook over medium heat until browned. Add enough hot water to cover and simmer until tender. Remove from heat and add gumbo file and pepper.

Mrs. N. A. Carlos, Jackson, Louisiana

Cocido (below)

COCIDO

1/2 lb. pork shoulder	1 4 3/4-oz. jar stuffed
12 chicken legs or thighs	olives, drained
2 tbsp. olive or salad oil	2 med. green peppers, sliced
2 cloves of garlic, minced	1 1/2 c. sliced scallions or
1 1/2 tsp. salt	green onions
3/4 tsp. crushed oregano	1/2 cabbage, shredded
1/2 tsp. pepper	1 c. chopped celery
3 c. boiling water	2 No. 2 cans garbanzos or
1/2 lb. diced cooked ham	chick peas, drained

Cut the pork in 1-inch cubes. Brown the pork and chicken in oil in a Dutch oven or large pot. Add the garlic, salt, oregano, pepper and water and cover. Simmer for 30 minutes. Add remaining ingredients and simmer for 15 minutes longer or until vegetables are tender. Serve in soup bowls as whole meal or serve broth as first course, then meats and vegetables. 12 servings.

CHICKEN VELVET SOUP

6 tbsp. butter or margarine	3 c. chicken broth
1/3 c. all-purpose flour	1 c. chopped cooked
1/2 c. milk	chicken
1/2 c. light cream or	Dash of pepper
evaporated milk	

Melt the butter in a saucepan and stir in flour. Add the milk, cream and broth and cook until thickened, stirring constantly. Reduce heat and stir in the chicken and pepper. Bring to boiling point and serve immediately. Garnish with snipped parsley and pimento star, if desired. 4 servings.

Rachel L. Keisler, Marion, North Carolina

CHICKEN SOUP WITH FARINA DUMPLINGS

1 4-lb. chicken, disjointed	2 c. diced celery
2 qt. boiling water	2 tbsp. diced onion
2 tsp. salt	Farina Dumplings
1/4 tsp. pepper	

Place the chicken in a kettle with water, salt, pepper, celery and onion and cover. Cook until chicken is tender. Remove chicken from stock and strain stock. Remove chicken from bones and cut in small pieces. Return to stock and bring to a boil. Drop dumplings into stock from a teaspoon and cover. Cook for about 16 minutes.

Farina Dumplings

2 c. milk	1/4 tsp. nutmeg
2 tbsp. butter	1 c. farina
1 tsp. salt	4 eggs, separated

Bring the milk to a boil in a saucepan and add butter, salt, nutmeg and farina. Cook over low heat, stirring constantly, until thick. Stir in beaten egg yolks and fold in stiffly beaten egg whites.

Mrs. Stephen Farley, Mobile, Alabama

CHICKEN SOUP WITH BREAD CRUMB DUMPLINGS

1 chicken, disjointed	1/2 c. scalded milk
3 c. fine bread crumbs	1/2 c. cream
1/2 tsp. salt	3 tbsp. melted butter
1/8 tsp. pepper	1 egg, beaten
1/4 c. nutmeg	

Cook the chicken in boiling water until tender. Remove chicken from broth and cool. Remove chicken from bones and return to broth. Bring to a boil. Place crumbs and seasonings in a large bowl. Add the milk and mix. Add the cream, butter and egg and mix well. Shape into small balls and add to broth. Cover and cook for 12 minutes.

Mrs. Dennis Kearley, Miami, Florida

CRACKER STEW

1 fryer	Pinch of sage
1/2 stick margarine	1 pt. milk
Salt and pepper to taste	Crackers

Cook the chicken in boiling water until tender. Remove chicken from broth and cool. Remove chicken from bones and place in broth. Add the margarine, salt, pepper and sage and cook until liquid is reduced to 1 1/2 cups. Add the milk and bring to a boil. Pour over crackers just before serving.

Mrs. John Johnson, Durham, North Carolina

CHICKEN STEW

2 2 1/2 to 3 1/2-lb. fryers	2 c. celery, cut in
1 chicken bouillon cube	3-in. strips
2 tsp. salt	2 c. carrots, cut in
1 bay leaf	3-in. strips
1/4 tsp. thyme leaves	1/3 c. cornstarch
12 sm. white onions	

Cut the chickens in serving pieces and place in a large kettle. Add the bouillon cube, salt, bay leaf, thyme and 5 cups water and bring to a boil. Reduce heat and cover. Simmer for 30 minutes. Add the onions, celery and carrots and cover. Simmer for about 20 minutes or until vegetables are tender. Mix the cornstarch and 1 cup water and stir into chicken mixture. Bring to a boil, stirring constantly, and boil for 1 minute. Serve in soup plates. 8 servings.

Photograph for this recipe on page 13.

CHICKEN-POTATO STEW

1 fryer, disjointed	1 sm. green pepper, chopped
1 onion, chopped	4 med. potatoes, diced
1 chicken bouillon cube	Salt and pepper to taste
1 c. water	2 tbsp. flour

Place all ingredients in a pressure cooker and cover. Cook at 15 pounds pressure for 20 minutes. Remove from heat and cool until pressure is down. Garnish with parsley.

Mrs. Bettye Huhn, Vidalia, Louisiana

QUICK CHICKEN STEW

1 fryer, disjointed	2 to 3 tsp. Worcestershire
4 celery stalks, chopped	sauce
1 lge. onion, chopped	Salt and pepper to taste
1 1-lb. can tomatoes	

Place the fryer, celery, onion, tomatoes and Worcestershire sauce in a kettle and add the salt and pepper. Cover. Cook over low heat for about 45 minutes. May be served with rice, if desired.

Mrs. James Snyder, Orlando, Florida

CONVERSATION CURRY

1 4 to 5-lb. stewing chicken	3 tbsp. tomato paste
2 tsp. salt	2 tsp. cornstarch
Pepper to taste	3 avocados
1/4 c. butter or margarine	Lemon juice
1 tbsp. curry powder	1 1/2 c. rice
3 tbsp. chopped onion	Dash of saffron
1 clove of garlic, minced	

Place the chicken in a large kettle and add 1 teaspoon salt, pepper and enough water to cover. Bring to a boil and reduce heat. Cover the kettle. Simmer for about 2 hours or until chicken is tender. Cool chicken in stock. Remove chicken from stock and remove chicken from bones. Skim the fat from stock and boil the stock until reduced to 2 1/2 cups. Melt the butter in a saucepan. Add the curry powder, onion and garlic and cook over low heat until onion is tender but not browned. Stir in the tomato paste and stock and simmer for 5 minutes. Blend cornstarch with small amount of water. Stir into curry mixture and cook, stirring, until thickened and clear. Add the chicken and heat through. Cut avocados lengthwise into halves and remove seeds and skin. Brush with lemon juice. Combine the rice, 3 cups water, remaining salt and saffron in a saucepan and bring to a boil. Cover. Simmer for about 25 minutes. Place in a bowl and place avocados on rice. Serve with chicken curry.

Photograph for this recipe on page 2.

STEWED CHICKEN AND RAISIN DUMPLINGS

1 4-lb. stewing chicken	1 qt. boiling water
2 stalks celery	1/2 c. dark seedless raisins
1 carrot	2 c. biscuit mix
1 onion, chopped	1/2 c. grated American cheese
2 tsp. salt	3/4 c. milk

Cut the chicken in serving pieces and place in a large kettle with wings and breast on top. Cut the celery and carrot in 1-inch pieces and add to chicken. Add the onion, salt and boiling water and cover. Cook over low heat for 2 to 3 hours or until tender. Skim off excess fat. Combine the raisins, biscuit mix and cheese in a bowl. Add the milk and stir until mixed. Drop by spoonfuls onto chicken mixture and cook for 10 minutes. Cover and steam for 10 minutes without removing cover. Remove chicken and dumplings from stock. Thicken stock with 1/4 cup biscuit mix blended with 1/2 cup water, if desired. Serve immediately. 6-8 servings.

Stewed Chicken and Raisin Dumplings (above)

Charleston Chicken Stew (below)

CHARLESTON CHICKEN STEW

2 2-lb. broilers	1/4 c. butter
4 c. water	1/4 c. flour
1 blade of mace	1 c. cream
1 tsp. salt	2 tsp. angostura aromatic
1/4 tsp. pepper	bitters
1 sm. onion	Juice of 1 lemon

Cut the chicken in serving pieces and place in a deep kettle. Add the water, mace, salt, pepper and onion and cover. Simmer for 40 minutes. Remove chicken from broth. Remove skin and discard. Remove onion from broth and discard. Reserve broth. Melt the butter in a saucepan and stir in flour. Add reserved chicken broth and cream gradually and cook, stirring constantly, until thickened. Add the angostura aromatic bitters and mix well. Add the chicken and bring to boiling point. Add the lemon juice, being careful not to curdle the sauce, and serve at once. 6-8 servings.

BRUNSWICK STEW

1 2 1/2 to 3 1/2-lb. fryer	1 tbsp. Worcestershire sauce
1/2 c. flour	1 tsp. sugar
1/4 c. corn oil	Dash of cayenne pepper
1/2 c. chopped onion	2 c. whole kernel corn
1 1-lb. 13-oz. can tomatoes	2 c. lima beans
1 tbsp. salt	

Cut the chicken in serving pieces and coat with flour. Heat the corn oil in a heavy kettle over medium heat. Add the chicken and cook, turning occasionally, until lightly browned. Add the onion and cook, stirring occasionally, until onion is transparent. Add the tomatoes, salt, Worcestershire sauce, sugar and cayenne pepper and cover. Simmer for about 20 minutes or until chicken is almost tender. Add the corn and lima beans and cover. Cook until chicken and vegetables are tender. Remove chicken from stew. Remove skin and discard. Remove chicken from bones and return to stew. Place over low heat until heated through. 6 servings.

Photograph for this recipe on page 74.

EASY CHICKEN STEW

1 fryer, disjointed	5 carrots, cubed
Shortening	2 med. potatoes, cubed
Salt and pepper to taste	1 sm. can peas
1 med. onion, minced	Flour
3 chicken bouillon cubes	

Brown the chicken in small amount of shortening in a skillet and add the salt and pepper. Sprinkle chicken with onion and add small amount of water. Cover. Cook until chicken is partially done. Add bouillon cubes, carrots and enough water to cover chicken and cook for 15 minutes. Add the potatoes and peas and cook for 15 minutes longer. Thicken with flour mixed with water.

Mrs. William I. Moore, Live Oak, Florida

SUPREME CHICKEN HASH

1 cooked hen	1/2 lb. Cheddar cheese, grated
1 qt. canned tomatoes	1/4 c. chopped celery (opt.)
1 lge. onion, chopped	Red pepper to taste
1 qt. milk	Salt to taste
1/2 c. butter	2 doz. crackers, crumbled
1/4 c. chicken fat	

Remove chicken from bones. Chop or grind the chicken and place in a kettle. Add remaining ingredients except crackers and simmer for about 30 minutes. Remove from heat and add enough crackers to thicken.

Mrs. Bill Morrison, Alexander City, Alabama

CHICKEN MULLIGAN

1 3 to 4-lb. hen	1 tsp. paprika
3 med. onions, chopped	3 med. potatoes, diced
1 red pepper	2 bell peppers, diced
2 No. 2 cans tomatoes	2 cloves of garlic, minced
1 No. 2 can corn	Salt and pepper to taste
2 tbsp. Worcestershire sauce	4 c. cooked rice

Cook the chicken in boiling water until tender. Drain and reserve broth. Cool the chicken and remove chicken from bones. Cook remaining ingredients except rice in reserved broth in a saucepan until vegetables are tender. Add the chicken and rice and simmer for about 30 minutes. One teaspoon hot sauce may be substituted for the red pepper.

Mrs. Charley M. Shannon, Bastrop, Louisiana

fried chicken

"Southern fried chicken"... say it and immediately your mind brings forth visions of huge tables groaning with food ... picnics under the oaks ... leisurely meals featuring the most southern of all chicken dishes – fried chicken. Yes, southern fried chicken is in a class all by itself – and homemakers in the Southland take great pride in their recipes. Every woman carefully perfects her own special way of preparing fried chicken, and this recipe becomes one of her most prized possessions.

The best of such recipes, from the kitchens of *Southern Living* readers, are awaiting you in this section. As you turn the pages, you'll find a recipe for Batter Fried Chicken – with a crisp and delicious crust that typifies southern cooking at its finest. For chicken that is crunchy good on the outside and deliciously tender inside, try Crumb-Fried Chicken. There's even a recipe for the traditional Sunday and "company's-coming" fare, Southern Fried Chicken with Cream Gravy.

In this section, you'll also discover that it's as easy to fry chicken in the oven as it is on top of the stove. Recipes for oven-fried chicken include Crusty Herb Fried Chicken ... Chicken Marianne ... Chicken Tori. There's even a recipe for Beau-Catcher Chicken – and it lives up to its name!

As you turn the pages that follow, you're certain to find recipes to delight your imagination.

BEAU CATCHER FRIED CHICKEN

1 fryer, disjointed	2 tsp. paprika
1/2 c. buttermilk	1/4 tsp. leaf thyme
1 c. flour	2 tbsp. instant minced onion
2 tsp. salt	1 stick butter, melted
1/4 tsp. pepper	

Dip the chicken into buttermilk. Mix the flour, salt, pepper, paprika, thyme and onion and dip chicken into flour mixture. Pour the butter into a shallow baking pan. Place the chicken in butter and turn to coat all sides. Place chicken, skin side down, in a single layer in the pan. Bake at 400 degrees for 30 minutes. Turn chicken and bake for 30 minutes longer or until tender.

Mrs. C. R. Fricks, Fort Smith, Arkansas

CHICKEN CRUNCH

1 can mushroom soup	1 c. crushed herb-seasoned
3/4 c. milk	stuffing mix
1 tbsp. finely chopped onion	2 tbsp. melted butter or
1 tbsp. chopped parsley	margarine
2 lb. chicken pieces	

Mix 1/3 cup soup, 1/4 cup milk, onion and parsley. Dip the chicken in soup mixture and roll in stuffing mix. Place in a 12 x 8 x 2-inch baking dish and drizzle butter over chicken. Bake at 400 degrees for 1 hour. Combine remaining soup and milk in a saucepan and heat through, stirring frequently. Serve over chicken. 4-6 servings.

Jo Anna Carmack, Livingston, Tennessee

TOWN HOUSE-FRIED CHICKEN

4 c. flour	1 tsp. Worcestershire sauce
2 1/2 tsp. baking powder	3 c. buttermilk
Paprika	3 tbsp. crushed corn flakes
1/4 tsp. pepper	1 2-lb. fryer
1/4 tsp. soda	Salt to taste

Mix 2 cups flour, 1 1/2 teaspoons baking powder, 1/2 teaspoon paprika, pepper and soda in a bowl and blend in Worcestershire sauce and buttermilk. Mix remaining flour and baking powder, pinch of paprika and corn flakes in another bowl. Cut the chicken in serving pieces and season with salt. Dip in batter, then dip in corn flakes mixture. Fry in hot fat in a deep iron skillet until golden brown.

Florence L. Costello, Chattanooga, Tennessee

CHICKEN FROM THE OVEN

1 chicken, disjointed	2 eggs, beaten
Salt and pepper to taste	Potato flakes or pancake mix
Monosodium glutamate to taste	1 c. oil

Season the chicken with salt, pepper and monosodium glutamate. Dip in eggs and roll in potato flakes. Place chicken in oil in a baking pan. Bake at 350 degrees for 30 minutes. Turn chicken and bake for 30 minutes longer.

Mrs. Harold F. Wall, Blacksburg, Virginia

CHICKEN MARIANNE

1 3-lb. fryer	1 tsp. salt
1/2 c. buttermilk	1/4 tsp. poultry seasoning
1/2 c. yellow cornmeal	4 tbsp. melted butter or
1/2 c. sifted all-purpose flour	margarine

Cut the chicken in serving pieces and dip in buttermilk. Mix the cornmeal, flour, salt and poultry seasoning and dip chicken in cornmeal mixture. Place in single layer in well-greased baking pan and pour butter over chicken. Bake at 400 degrees for 1 hour or until tender. 4 servings.

Mrs. H. L. Presley, Coldwater, Mississippi

CHICKEN AND GARLIC

1 1/2 sticks margarine	1 fryer, disjointed
1/4 tsp. garlic salt	Salt and pepper to taste
1/2 c. flour	Paprika to taste
1/2 c. cornmeal	

Melt the margarine in a casserole and sprinkle with garlic salt. Sift the flour and cornmeal together into a bowl. Season the chicken with salt and pepper and dredge with flour mixture. Place, skin side down, in margarine. Cover. Bake for 20 minutes at 350 degrees. Turn chicken and sprinkle with paprika. Bake for about 20 minutes longer or until tender. 5 servings.

Sherry Skearton, Houston, Texas

CHICKEN TORI

2 sm. fryers	1 tsp. paprika
1/2 c. butter or margarine	1/2 tsp. pepper
1/4 c. flour	1 1/2 tsp. salt
2 tsp. dry mustard	

Cut the fryers in serving pieces. Melt the butter in a large, shallow baking pan. Mix the flour, mustard, paprika, pepper and salt in a paper bag. Add the chicken, several pieces at a time, and shake the bag until chicken is coated. Place in butter and turn to coat all sides. Place in single layer in pan, skin side down. Bake for 35 to 45 minutes at 350 degrees. Turn the chicken. Increase temperature to 450 degrees and bake for 10 to 15 minutes longer or until golden brown.

Mrs. George C. Brinkmann, Sr., Port Arthur, Texas

CHICKEN PAPRIKA

1/2 c. flour	2 sticks butter, softened
2 tsp. salt	1 chicken, disjointed
1 tsp. paprika	

Mix first 4 ingredients and spread on chicken. Place chicken in single layer in a baking dish. Bake at 375 degrees for 1 hour.

Wanda Louise Parrish, Morganfield, Kentucky

CHILI CHICKEN

1/2 env. chili mix	1 tsp. monosodium glutamate
3/4 c. corn flake crumbs	8 chicken thighs
1/2 tsp. salt	1/4 c. margarine

Preheat oven to 400 degrees. Combine the chili mix, corn flake crumbs, salt and monosodium glutamate and coat each chicken thigh with crumb mixture. Melt the margarine in a shallow, foil-lined baking pan and place chicken thighs in the margarine. Cover the pan with foil. Bake at 400 degrees for 30 minutes. Baste with margarine in pan, cover and bake for 15 minutes. Remove cover and bake for 15 minutes longer. Garnish with parsley.

Mrs. George Harrison, Huntington, West Virginia

CHIPPIE CHICKEN DELIGHT

1/2 c. cranberry juice	1 1/2 c. barbecue potato chips,
3 tbsp. lemon juice	crushed
1 3-lb. fryer	1/2 c. melted butter
2 eggs, beaten	1 tsp. rubbed sage

Mix the cranberry and lemon juices and set aside. Cut the chicken in serving pieces and dip in eggs. Roll in potato chips and place in baking pan containing butter. Sprinkle with sage. Bake in 375-degree oven for about 1 hour, basting frequently with juice mixture. 4 servings.

Dale Faughn, Fredonia, Kentucky

CORN-CRISPED CHICKEN

1 2 1/2 to 3-lb. fryer,	1 c. corn flake crumbs
disjointed	1 1/2 tsp. salt
1/2 c. evaporated milk	1/4 tsp. pepper

Dip the chicken in milk. Mix remaining ingredients and roll chicken in crumb mixture. Place in single layer in a shallow baking pan lined with foil. Cover loosely with foil. Bake at 350 degrees for about 1 hour or until tender. 4-5 servings.

Mrs. Jeroma Owens, Fyffe, Alabama

COUNTRY CRUSTY-FRIED CHICKEN

1/2 c. flour	1 egg, beaten
2 c. crushed corn flakes	1 1/2 c. milk
1 tbsp. salt	1 3-lb. fryer, disjointed
1/2 tsp. pepper	1/2 c. melted butter
1 tsp. paprika	

Preheat oven to 375 degrees. Combine first 5 ingredients in a paper sack. Mix the egg and milk in a bowl. Dip chicken in egg mixture. Drop into paper sack and shake in flour mixture. Place in baking pan with butter. Bake for 45 minutes, turning once.

Mrs. Woodrow Chervenka, Rogers, Texas

CRUSTY-FRIED CHICKEN

2 pkg. garlic salad dressing mix	2 tbsp. soft butter
3 tbsp. flour	3 lb. chicken breasts, thighs and legs
2 tsp. salt	1 c. milk
1/4 c. lemon juice	1 1/2 c. pancake mix

Combine the salad dressing mix, flour and salt in a small bowl. Add the lemon juice and butter and mix until smooth. Brush all sides of chicken with flour mixture. Place in a bowl and cover. Refrigerate overnight. Heat 1/2 inch fat in a large skillet or Dutch oven. Dip chicken in milk, then in pancake mix. Brown in fat and place in a single layer in a shallow baking pan. Spoon half the remaining milk over chicken and cover with aluminum foil. Bake at 375 degrees for 30 minutes. Remove foil and baste chicken with remaining milk. Bake for 20 to 30 minutes longer or until tender. 8 servings.

Shelley Chipman, Ripley, Tennessee

HERB-FRIZZLED CHICKEN

1 chicken, disjointed	Parsley flakes
1/2 c. butter or margarine	Thyme leaves
Juice of 3 lemons	Basil leaves
Salt and pepper to taste	Rosemary leaves
Oregano	

Place the chicken on foil in a shallow oblong baking dish. Melt the butter and drizzle over chicken. Sprinkle the chicken with lemon juice, salt and pepper and desired amounts of oregano, parsley, thyme, basil and rosemary. Bake at 300 degrees for 1 hour. Increase temperature to 375 degrees and bake for about 30 minutes longer or until brown. Place the chicken on a serving platter and pour herb sauce over chicken.

Mrs. John P. Larkin, Maitland, Florida

CRUSTY HERB-FRIED CHICKEN

1 3 to 3 1/2-lb. chicken	1/2 tsp. rosemary
1/2 tsp. thyme	1 tbsp. minced parsley
1/2 tsp. marjoram	1/2 tsp. salt
3/4 to 1 c. flour	1/4 tsp. pepper
3/4 c. fat or salad oil	3/4 c. water

Cut the chicken in serving pieces and sprinkle with thyme and marjoram. Let stand for 30 minutes to 1 hour. Roll in flour and fry in hot fat in a frying pan until brown. Place in a baking pan and sprinkle with rosemary, parsley, salt and pepper. Pour water into the frying pan and stir well. Pour over chicken. Bake at 375 degrees for 40 to 45 minutes. 4-5 servings.

Mrs. Richard Comtois, New Orleans, Louisiana

DEEP-SOUTH CHICKEN

1 c. prepared biscuit mix	1/2 c. finely chopped pecans
1 tsp. salt	1 fryer, disjointed
1 tsp. paprika	1/2 c. evaporated milk
1/2 tsp. poultry seasonings	1/2 c. melted butter

Combine the biscuit mix, seasonings and pecans in a bowl. Dip the chicken in milk, then coat with biscuit mixture. Place in a 13 x 9-inch shallow baking dish and pour butter over chicken. Bake in a 375-degree oven for 1 hour or until chicken is tender. 4 servings.

Mrs. Fred R. Lantz, Corpus Christi, Texas

CRISPED CHICKEN WITH CURRIED FRUIT

1 c. corn flake crumbs	1 8 1/2-oz. can pineapple
1 tsp. monosodium glutamate	slices
1 tsp. salt	4 maraschino cherries with
1/8 tsp. pepper	stems
1 fryer	1/4 c. butter
1/2 c. evaporated milk	1/2 c. (firmly packed) light
1 1-lb. can cling peach	brown sugar
halves	2 tsp. curry powder

Combine the corn flake crumbs, monosodium glutamate, salt and pepper in a bowl. Cut the chicken in serving pieces. Dip in evaporated milk, then roll in seasoned crumbs. Place, skin side up, in an aluminum foil-lined baking pan. Drain the fruits and place in a shallow baking pan. Melt the butter in a saucepan and stir in the brown sugar and curry powder. Spoon over fruits. Place fruit mixture and chicken in oven. Bake at 350 degrees for 1 hour or until chicken is tender.

GARLIC CHICKEN

2 sticks butter or margarine
2 cans grated Parmesan cheese
2 tsp. garlic powder

2 fryers, disjointed
Salt to taste

Melt the butter in a saucepan and add the cheese and garlic powder. Cool. Season the chicken with salt and roll in cheese mixture. Place in a baking pan in a single layer. Bake at 350 degrees for 1 hour.

Mrs. O. Lee Gordon, Gainesville, Florida

OVEN-FRIED CHICKEN

1 c. flour
1 tsp. salt
1/4 tsp. pepper
1 tsp. paprika
2 eggs, beaten
1 tsp. Worcestershire sauce
1/4 c. water

1 fryer, disjointed
1 c. cracker crumbs
1/2 c. shortening
1 onion, chopped fine
1 tbsp. chopped green pepper
1 c. milk

Mix the flour, salt, pepper and paprika in a bowl. Mix the eggs, Worcestershire sauce and water in another bowl. Dip the chicken in flour mixture, then dip in egg mixture. Roll in cracker crumbs. Brown lightly in hot shortening in a skillet and place in a baking dish. Sprinkle with onion and green pepper and pour the milk over top. Cover. Bake at 350 degrees for 1 hour and 30 minutes. 5-6 servings.

Hattie Ann Macik, Rosharon, Texas

Crisped Chicken with Curried Fruit (page 96)

TANGY CHICKEN

1 2 to 2 1/2-lb. fryer	2 c. crushed rice cereal
1/2 c. tangy salad dressing	Salt to taste

Cut the chicken in serving pieces and place in a deep bowl. Add the salad dressing and stir until each piece is well coated. Marinate for 1 hour. Roll chicken in cereal crumbs and place in single layer in baking pan. Season with salt. Bake at 325 degrees for 1 hour.

Mrs. A. C. Bodholdt, Steele, Alabama

LEMON-KISSED CHICKEN

1 egg, beaten	Juice of 2 lemons
1/4 c. milk	1 stick margarine
1 fryer, disjointed	Salt and pepper to taste
2 c. cornmeal	2 sm. onions

Mix the egg and milk in a bowl. Dip the chicken into milk mixture and coat with cornmeal. Place in a baking pan. Place the lemon juice and margarine in a saucepan and heat until margarine is melted. Pour over chicken and season with salt and pepper. Slice the onions and separate in rings. Place over chicken. Bake at 350 degrees for 1 hour.

Mrs. Elsie Leake, Big Cabin, Oklahoma

MAYONNAISED CHICKEN

1 2 1/2 to 3-lb. fryer	1/2 tsp. garlic salt (opt.)
1/2 c. mayonnaise	1/2 tsp. oregano
1 1/2 tbsp. lemon juice	3/4 c. corn flake crumbs
Salt and pepper to taste	

Cut the chicken in serving pieces. Mix the mayonnaise, lemon juice, salt, pepper, garlic salt and oregano in a bowl. Dip the chicken in mayonnaise mixture, coating well, then roll in crumbs. Place in a baking pan and cover. Bake in a 400-degree oven for 45 minutes or until tender.

Mrs. Phillip Gordon Arnold, Chapel Hill, North Carolina

AROMATIC-FRIED CHICKEN

1 2 1/2 to 3-lb. fryer	1/4 tsp. salt
1/2 env. garlic salad dressing mix	1/4 c. soft butter or margarine
2 tbsp. flour	1 tbsp. lemon juice

Cut the chicken in serving pieces. Combine the salad dressing mix, flour and salt in a bowl and blend in butter and lemon juice. Spread over chicken. Place the chicken, skin side up, in a single layer in a jelly roll pan. Bake at 350 degrees for 1 hour and 15 minutes or until tender. 4 servings.

Pat Dreyer, Oak Ridge, Tennessee

HARMONY CHICKEN

1 chicken, cut in serving pieces	1 c. milk
Salt to taste	2 tbsp. margarine
1/2 c. yellow grits	

Sprinkle the chicken with salt. Place the grits in a paper bag. Dip chicken in milk and place in bag, 1 piece at a time. Shake well. Melt the margarine in a baking pan and place chicken in pan. Cover with aluminum foil. Bake at 350 degrees for 45 minutes. Turn and bake for 15 minutes longer.

Mrs. Claude Keeton, Wheeler, Mississippi

EASY-FRIED CHICKEN

1 2 1/2 to 3-lb. chicken	1 tsp. paprika
1/2 c. sour cream	1 tsp. salt
1 tbsp. lemon juice	1 clove of garlic, minced
1 tsp. Worcestershire sauce	(opt.)
1 tsp. celery salt	1 c. cracker crumbs

Cut the chicken in serving pieces. Mix remaining ingredients except crumbs. Dip chicken into sour cream mixture and roll in crumbs. Place in a shallow baking pan in a single layer. Bake in 350-degree oven for 1 hour or until tender and brown.

Maggie Query, Clover, South Carolina

PARMESAN CHICKEN

2 c. dry bread crumbs	1/4 tsp. basil
3/4 c. grated Parmesan cheese	2 tbsp. salt
1/4 c. parsley flakes	1/8 tsp. pepper
1 tsp. monosodium glutamate	2 fryers, disjointed
1 tsp. paprika	1 c. melted butter
1 tsp. oregano	

Mix all 9 ingredients except chicken and butter. Dip the chicken in butter and roll in the crumb mixture. Arrange in shallow foil-lined baking pan, skin side up, and pour remaining butter over chicken. Bake at 350 degrees for 1 hour, basting occasionally with pan drippings.

Mrs. Cleo D. Bowles, Cherokee, Oklahoma

Tropical Chicken (below)

TROPICAL CHICKEN

2 fryers
2 tsp. monosodium glutamate
1 1/2 tsp. salt
1 egg, slightly beaten
1 6-oz. can frozen pineapple
  juice concentrate, thawed

1 1/3 c. fine dry bread crumbs
1/4 c. melted butter or
  margarine
1 3 1/2-oz. can flaked
  coconut

Cut the chickens in serving pieces and sprinkle monosodium glutamate and salt over both sides of chicken. Combine the egg and pineapple concentrate in a pie plate. Combine bread crumbs and butter in another pie plate. Add the coconut and mix well. Coat the chicken with pineapple mixture, then roll in coconut mixture. Place in 2 shallow foil-lined baking pans. Bake at 350 degrees for 40 minutes. Reverse pans in oven for even baking and bake for 40 minutes longer. Cover loosely with foil if chicken browns too much before end of baking time. 8 servings.

ONION-FRIED CHICKEN

1 fryer, quartered
Thyme to taste

1/2 pkg. onion soup mix
French dressing

Place the chicken in a shallow baking dish and sprinkle with thyme and soup mix. Pour the French dressing over chicken to coat and cover with foil. Bake at 350 degrees for 1 hour. Uncover and bake for 30 minutes longer or until brown.

Mrs. A. F. Partelow, Pompano Beach, Florida

TASTY CRISP CHICKEN

1 egg, beaten	2 tsp. salt
1/2 c. milk	2 tsp. paprika
1 tsp. baking powder	1/4 c. finely chopped nuts
1 c. flour	1 fryer, disjointed
1/4 tsp. pepper	1/2 c. butter or margarine
2 tbsp. sesame seed	

Mix the egg and milk in a bowl. Mix the baking powder, flour, pepper, sesame seed, salt, paprika and nuts in another bowl. Dip the chicken into egg mixture, then dip into flour mixture. Melt the butter in a shallow baking pan and place chicken in the pan in a single layer, turning to coat with butter. Bake at 400 degrees for 30 minutes. Turn and bake for 30 minutes longer or until tender.

Mrs. T. R. Thompson, Sayre, Oklahoma

BAKED-FRIED CHICKEN

1 2 1/2-lb. fryer, disjointed	3 c. round buttery cracker crumbs
3/4 c. vegetable oil	

Dip the chicken in oil and roll in cracker crumbs. Place in foil-lined cookie pan. Bake at 350 degrees for 1 hour and loosen chicken from foil while hot.

Mrs. Travis Gordon, Chicota, Texas

TENNESSEE-FRIED CHICKEN

1 fryer, disjointed	1 stick margarine, melted
Pepper to taste	1 c. cheese cracker crumbs

Season the chicken with salt and pepper and roll in butter, then in cracker crumbs. Place in a baking pan lined with foil. Cover with foil and seal edges. Bake at 350 degrees for about 1 hour or until tender.

Mildred Gates, Memphis, Tennessee

SAVORY HERBED CHICKEN

3/4 c. flour	1 fryer, disjointed
1 tsp. salt	Shortening
1/4 tsp. pepper	Chopped parsley to taste
1/2 tsp. thyme	1/2 tsp. rosemary
1/2 tsp. marjoram	1/2 can consomme

Combine the flour, salt, pepper, thyme and marjoram in a bag. Place the chicken in the bag, several pieces at a time, and shake until coated. Brown in 1/4 inch hot shortening in a frying pan, then place in a shallow baking dish. Sprinkle with parsley and rosemary. Pour the consomme into remaining shortening in the frying pan and pour over chicken. Bake at 375 degrees for about 45 minutes.

Mrs. T. B. Hames, Stafford, Virginia

PRETZEL CHICKEN A-GO-GO

3/4 c. finely crushed pretzels	1/4 tsp. onion powder
1 tsp. salt	4 chicken breasts, boned
1/8 tsp. pepper	1/2 c. buttermilk
1/3 c. grated Parmesan cheese	1/2 c. butter
1 tsp. oregano	

Combine the pretzel crumbs, salt, pepper, cheese, oregano and onion powder. Dip chicken in buttermilk, then in pretzel mixture. Heat electric skillet to 400 degrees and add butter. Brown chicken breasts in butter. Reduce heat to 320 degrees and cover skillet. Cook for about 1 hour or until tender. Remove chicken to a platter and garnish with parsley. 4 servings.

Dr. Ben Giles, Albany, Georgia

BATTER-FRIED CHICKEN

1 2 1/2 to 3-lb. fryer	1/2 tsp. baking powder
Celery salt to taste	1/2 egg
Salt	1/2 c. milk
Pepper to taste	2 tbsp. salad oil
Flour	

Cut the chicken in serving pieces and cook in a small amount of simmering water for 20 minutes. Drain and dry thoroughly. Sprinkle with celery salt, salt to taste and pepper and coat with flour. Mix 1/2 cup flour, baking powder and 1/4 teaspoon salt in a bowl. Add the egg, milk and oil and beat until smooth. Dip the chicken into batter. Fry in deep, hot fat for 5 to 7 minutes and drain.

Mrs. Kenneth Hundley, Flagstaff, New Mexico

BUTTERMILK-FRIED CHICKEN

1 1/2 c. buttermilk	1 1/2 tsp. salt
1 1/2 tsp. summer savory (opt.)	1 tsp. monosodium glutamate
1/2 tsp. pepper	1 1/2 tsp. paprika
2 1 1/2-lb. broilers,	Shortening
disjointed	Butter
3/4 to 1 c. flour	

Mix the buttermilk, summer savory and 1/4 teaspoon pepper in a large, shallow dish. Add the chicken and cover. Marinate for 1 hour, turning occasionally. Combine the flour, salt, remaining pepper, monosodium glutamate and paprika and coat chicken with the flour mixture. Place on waxed paper and let stand for 30 minutes. Place enough shortening and butter in a skillet to fill 1/2 full and heat. Fry chicken, several pieces at a time, in the shortening mixture for 10 to 15 minutes or until tender and brown. Drain on absorbent paper. 6 servings.

Mrs. W. W. Chambers, West Point, Georgia

CHICKEN FRIED IN BATTER

1   3-lb. fryer
Salt and pepper to taste
2 eggs, beaten
1/2 c. milk

1 c. sifted all-purpose flour
1 tsp. baking powder
1 tsp. salt
1 tbsp. melted shortening

Cut the chicken in serving pieces and cook in simmering water for 30 minutes. Drain and cool. Sprinkle with salt and pepper. Mix the eggs and milk. Sift the flour, baking powder and salt together and stir into milk mixture. Blend in shortening. Dip chicken into batter. Fry in deep fat at 375 degrees until golden brown and drain on absorbent paper.

Mrs. Fred Thomas, Dallas, Texas

MUSTARD CHICKEN

1 fryer, quartered
1 tsp. salt
1/8 tsp. pepper
1/4 c. prepared yellow
   mustard

1 tbsp. soy sauce
1/2 tsp. dried leaf thyme
1/8 tsp. ginger
1 tbsp. salad oil

Sprinkle the chicken on both sides with salt and pepper and place, skin side down, in foil-lined baking pan. Mix the mustard, soy sauce, thyme and ginger in a bowl and beat in the salad oil. Brush some of the sauce on chicken. Bake in 350-degree oven for 30 minutes, brushing with sauce occasionally. Turn chicken and brush with sauce. Bake for 20 to 30 minutes longer, brushing occasionally with remaining sauce. 4 servings.

Mustard Chicken (above)

PERKY PICNIC CHICKEN

1 egg	1/4 c. flour
2 tbsp. milk	2 tbsp. grated Parmesan cheese
1 1 1/2-oz. envelope	1 fryer, disjointed
spaghetti sauce mix	Oil

Combine the egg and milk in a shallow bowl and mix lightly. Place the spaghetti sauce mix, flour and Parmesan cheese in a bowl and mix well. Dip the chicken in egg mixture, then in flour mixture. Fry in hot oil in a large skillet for about 20 minutes, turning to brown evenly on all sides. Cover and cook for 20 to 30 minutes longer or until tender. Chill and serve cold. 4 servings.

Photograph for this recipe on page 90.

CRUMB-FRIED CHICKEN

Chicken pieces	2 c. corn flake crumbs
1 c. evaporated milk	Cooking oil

Dip the chicken in milk and roll in crumbs. Fry in deep, hot oil until brown and tender.

Mrs. May C. Davis, Murfreesboro, Tennessee

CHICKEN MACADAMIA

Peanut oil	1 onion, grated
2 eggs, beaten	1/4 tsp. pepper
1/2 c. flour	2 tbsp. brandy
1/4 c. cornstarch	2 tbsp. soy sauce
1/2 c. cold water	3 chicken breasts, boned
1 1-in. piece of gingerroot,	1/2 c. slivered toasted
minced	macadamia nuts

Pour 2 tablespoons peanut oil into a blender container and add remaining ingredients except chicken breasts and macadamia nuts. Blend until mixed. Cut the chicken breasts in quarters and soak in batter for 20 minutes. Fry in deep, hot peanut oil until done. Serve on rice and sprinkle with macadamia nuts.

Sweet-Sour Sauce

1 tbsp. cornstarch	1/3 c. cider vinegar
2 tsp. soy sauce	1/2 c. sugar
6 tbsp. water	1 green pepper, diced

Combine all ingredients except green pepper in a saucepan and bring to a boil. Reduce heat and simmer for 2 minutes. Add the green pepper and remove from heat. Serve with chicken.

Mrs. Robert R. Linvill, Fort Bragg, North Carolina

PRESSURE PAN-FRIED CHICKEN

1 3-lb. fryer	1 tsp. paprika
3/4 c. flour	6 tbsp. fat
2 tsp. salt	1 sm. onion, sliced
1/4 tsp. pepper	

Cut the chicken in serving pieces. Mix 1/2 cup flour, salt, pepper and paprika and dredge chicken with flour mixture. Brown in hot fat in a pressure cooker and add onion and 1 1/4 cups water. Cover. Cook at 10 pounds pressure for 20 minutes. Place pressure cooker under running water to reduce pressure quickly and uncover. Remove chicken from cooker. Mix remaining flour and 1/2 cup water and stir into liquid in cooker. Bring to a boil, stirring constantly, and remove from heat. Add chicken and heat through.

Mrs. C. W. Floyd, Stuarts Draft, Virginia

CHICKEN-LITTLE LEGS

3 lb. chicken wings	1 tsp. salt
1/2 c. salad oil	1/8 tsp. pepper
1/2 c. lemon juice	1/2 c. chopped stuffed
1 clove of garlic, crushed	olives

Cut the chicken wings at both joints and discard tips. Mix remaining ingredients in a bowl and add wing pieces. Marinate in refrigerator for several hours or overnight, stirring occasionally. Drain and reserve marinade. Strain reserved marinade. Place wing pieces on rack in a shallow baking pan. Bake in 450-degree oven for 35 to 45 minutes or until crisp and browned, basting several times with marinade.

Chicken-Little Legs (above)

LEMON-FRIED CHICKEN

1 fryer	1/4 tsp. ground marjoram
1/4 c. lemon juice	1/8 tsp. pepper
1/2 c. corn oil	1/2 tsp. grated lemon rind
1/4 tsp. garlic salt	1/2 c. flour
3/4 tsp. salt	1/2 tsp. paprika
1/4 tsp. ground thyme	

Cut the chicken in serving pieces and place in a large, shallow pan. Mix the lemon juice, 1/4 cup corn oil, garlic salt, salt, thyme, marjoram, pepper and lemon rind and pour over chicken. Marinate in refrigerator for at least 3 hours, turning occasionally, then drain chicken on absorbent paper. Mix the flour and paprika. Coat the chicken with flour mixture and shake off excess. Heat remaining corn oil in a heavy skillet over medium heat for about 3 minutes. Add chicken carefully and fry, turning once, for about 15 minutes or until golden brown. Cover and cook over low heat for 20 minutes longer. Remove cover and cook until chicken is tender. 4 servings.

Photograph for this recipe on page 13.

FRUITY-FRIED CHICKEN

1/4 c. cooking oil	1 tsp. salt
1 3-lb. chicken, disjointed	1/2 c. golden raisins
1 tsp. chili powder	1 20-oz. can pineapple chunks
1/4 tsp. pepper	2 ripe bananas
1/4 tsp. cinnamon	1 ripe avocado
2 tbsp. grated onion	1/2 lb. white grapes

Heat the oil in a large skillet and brown the chicken in oil. Sprinkle with chili powder, pepper, cinnamon, onion and salt. Add the raisins, pineapple and juice and cover. Cook over low heat for 35 to 45 minutes, adding water if needed. Slice the bananas lengthwise and slice avocado. Place the chicken in a serving dish and garnish with bananas, grapes and avocado. Pour liquid in skillet over all. Liquid may be thickened with flour before pouring over chicken, if desired. 6 servings.

Mrs. Lodus Phillips, Baldwyn, Mississippi

SOUTHERN-FRIED CHICKEN WITH CREAM GRAVY

1 2 to 3-lb. fryer	1 c. flour
1 tsp. grated lemon rind	1 tsp. salt
1/3 c. lemon juice	1 tsp. paprika
2/3 c. salad oil	1/2 c. margarine
1/4 tsp. pepper	1 1/2 c. milk
1/2 tsp. Worcestershire sauce	1 c. light cream

Cut the chicken in serving pieces and place in a shallow dish. Combine the lemon rind, lemon juice, salad oil, pepper and Worcestershire sauce and pour over chicken. Marinate for at least 2 hours and drain. Place the chicken in a paper bag with flour, salt and paprika and shake until coated. Reserve remaining flour mixture. Melt the margarine in a skillet and saute chicken for 30 minutes or until brown and tender, turning several times. Remove from skillet. Stir 1/4 cup reserved flour mixture into drippings in the skillet. Add the milk and cream and cook over medium heat until thickened, stirring constantly. Serve with chicken.

Mrs. John Hart, Van Buren, Arkansas

FRIED CHICKEN WITH KRAUT RELISH

6 c. sauerkraut
1 4-oz. jar pimento
2 med. green peppers, chopped
2 med. onions, chopped
1/4 tsp. paprika
Freshly ground pepper to taste
1 clove of garlic, minced
1/2 c. melted butter

1/4 c. wine vinegar
1/2 c. (firmly packed) dark
   brown sugar
2 tbsp. Worcestershire sauce
2 tbsp. cornstarch
1/4 c. water
12 chicken legs with thighs

Drain the sauerkraut and reserve liquid. Drain the pimento and chop. Toss sauerkraut with green peppers, pimento, half the onions, paprika and pepper in a bowl and chill. Saute remaining onion and the garlic in butter in a saucepan until golden. Add the vinegar, sugar, Worcestershire sauce, pepper and reserved sauerkraut liquid and stir until sugar is melted. Bring to a boil over medium heat. Blend the cornstarch with water and stir into onion mixture. Boil for 30 seconds, stirring constantly, then remove from heat. Place the chicken in a baking pan in a single layer and brush with sauce. Bake at 350 degrees for 10 minutes. Brush with sauce and bake for 10 minutes. Turn chicken and bake for about 25 minutes longer or until tender, brushing frequently with sauce. Serve sauerkraut mixture with chicken.

Fried Chicken with Kraut Relish (above)

107

Chicken Casserole Supreme (page 127)

chicken
casseroles

Chicken casseroles – great chunks of dark and light chicken meat . . . crisp and crunchy vegetables . . . a perfectly seasoned sauce . . . what a delight for your hungry family! And what a boon for your food budget. Smart homemakers know that casseroles are a wonderfully delicious way to serve leftovers.

Southern homemakers know that casseroles are a surefire way to satisfy the biggest appetite, and they have become experts at mixing and matching ingredients in many unusual casserole recipes. Through careful trial-and-error experimentation, these women have developed unbeatable, error-free dishes that delight family and guests.

In the pages that follow, *Southern Living* readers share their very best casserole recipes with you. For example, Country Club Chicken Scallop is as eye-pleasingly elegant as its name implies – and utterly delicious. Chicken and Brown Rice combines two long-time traditional southern foods into one dish with an unusual and palate-pleasing flavor. From Texas comes a recipe for King Ranch Trail Drive Dish, guaranteed to fill up the hungriest "cowboy" in your family!

You'll find many more chicken casserole recipes sure to bring you compliments galore. Every recipe has won the approval of a southern homemaker's family. And every recipe is sure to win your family's approval, too.

NOODLE SURPRISE

1/2 stick butter ~~2T~~	2 egg yolks, beaten
1 med. onion, sliced	1 c. sour cream
2 tbsp. flour	8 oz. noodles
1 c. seasoned chicken stock	~~3 tbsp. melted butter~~
1 3-oz. can mushrooms	~~2 tsp. poppy seed~~
Salt	1/2 c. grated Parmesan cheese
~~2 tsp. paprika~~	1 c. bread crumbs
3 c. cubed cooked chicken	1 frozen tiny tender peas

Melt the butter in a skillet. Add the onion and cook for 5 minutes or until tender. Blend in flour. Add the stock and cook, stirring constantly, until thickened. Reduce heat. Drain and slice the mushrooms and stir into sauce. Add 1/2 teaspoon salt, paprika and chicken and simmer for 5 minutes. Stir small amount of sauce into egg yolks, then stir back into chicken mixture. Cook for 2 minutes. Stir in the sour cream and heat through. Cook the noodles in boiling water for about 10 minutes or until tender and drain. Stir in the melted butter and poppy seed and add salt to taste. Fold into chicken mixture and place in a greased casserole. Mix the cheese and bread crumbs and sprinkle over casserole. Bake in 350-degree oven until brown.

Mrs. H. W. Tinson, Miami, Florida

CHICKEN RAVIOLI

1 5 to 7-lb. cooked hen	2 c. chicken broth
2 lge. onions, chopped	1 med. can pimento strips
1 green pepper, chopped	2 pkg. noodles
1 c. chopped celery	Salt and pepper to taste
2 3-oz. cans sliced mushrooms	1 c. grated mild Cheddar cheese
2 tbsp. butter or margarine	1 c. toasted croutons
2 cans cream of mushroom soup	

Remove chicken from bones and place in a large bowl. Saute the onions, green pepper, celery and mushrooms in butter in a heavy skillet for 5 minutes or until tender. Mix the soup, broth and pimento with chicken. Cook the noodles according to package directions and drain. Stir into chicken mixture. Add the onion mixture and mix well. Add salt and pepper and place in a greased large baking dish. Top with cheese and croutons. Bake at 350 degrees for 25 minutes. 10 servings.

Mrs. Louise Spears, Norphlet, Arkansas

CHICKEN STAR BAKE

1 8-oz. package lasagna	2/3 c. milk
1 can cream of mushroom soup	2 3-oz. packages cream cheese
1/2 tsp. salt	1 c. cream-style cottage cheese
1/2 tsp. poultry seasoning	1/3 c. sliced stuffed olives

1/3 c. chopped onions (opt.)	1 1/2 c. buttered soft bread
1/3 c. chopped green pepper	crumbs
1/4 c. minced parsley	2 slices pimento, cut in star
3 c. diced cooked chicken	shapes

Cook the lasagna in boiling, salted water until tender and drain. Rinse in cold water. Mix the soup, salt, poultry seasoning and milk in a saucepan and heat through. Soften the cream cheese in a bowl. Add the cottage cheese and mix well. Stir in the olives, onions, green pepper and parsley. Place half the lasagna in 11 1/2 x 7 1/2 x 1 1/2-inch baking dish and spread with half the cheese mixture. Add half the chicken, then add half the soup mixture. Repeat layers and top with bread crumbs. Bake in 375-degree oven for 30 minutes or until heated through. Garnish with pimento stars and let stand for 10 minutes before serving. 8 servings.

Mrs. F. S. Fagan, Hendersonville, North Carolina

BLUE RIBBON CHICKEN CASSEROLE

1 6 or 8-oz. can sliced	1/4 c. sherry (opt.)
mushrooms	1/2 tsp. dried leaf marjoram
1/4 c. butter or margarine	2 tbsp. chopped chives
1/4 c. flour	1 8-oz. package med. noodles
1 tsp. salt	5 c. diced cooked chicken
2 c. chicken stock	1/4 c. grated Parmesan cheese
2 c. milk	

Drain the mushrooms and reserve liquid. Melt the butter in a saucepan and blend in the flour and salt. Stir in the chicken stock, milk and reserved liquid gradually and cook, stirring constantly, until mixture thickens and comes to a boil. Add the sherry, marjoram and chives. Cook the noodles according to package directions and drain. Stir into the sauce, then stir in the chicken and mushrooms. Turn into 3-quart casserole and sprinkle with cheese. Bake in 350-degree oven for 25 to 30 minutes and garnish with additional diced chicken. May be refrigerated before baking. Increase baking time to 50 to 60 minutes. 8 servings.

Blue Ribbon Chicken Casserole (above)

Chicken-Mushroom Casserole (below)

CHICKEN-MUSHROOM CASSEROLE

Salt	1/8 tsp. pepper
5 qt. boiling water	1/2 c. dry vermouth or
12 oz. spaghetti	chicken broth
1 med. onion, chopped	3/4 c. grated Parmesan cheese
3/8 c. butter or margarine	1/2 lb. fresh mushrooms,
1/4 c. flour	sliced
1 1/2 c. chicken broth	3 lb. cooked chicken pieces
1 c. heavy cream	

Add 1 1/2 tablespoons salt to boiling water and add spaghetti gradually so that water continues to boil. Cook, stirring occasionally, until tender and drain in a colander. Saute the onion in 1/4 cup butter in a saucepan until almost tender, then stir in the flour. Add chicken broth and cream gradually and bring to a boil, stirring constantly. Add 1 teaspoon salt, pepper, vermouth and 1/4 cup cheese and set aside. Saute the mushrooms in remaining butter in a large skillet until brown. Combine the spaghetti, mushrooms and chicken in a 2 1/2-quart casserole and pour sauce over top. Sprinkle with remaining cheese. Bake in 375-degree oven for 20 minutes or until heated through. One 4-ounce can sliced mushrooms, drained, may be substituted for fresh mushrooms. 6 servings.

CHICKEN SUPREME

1 lge. cooked hen	Salad dressing
1 can cream of mushroom soup	1 sm. carton sour cream
2 lge. onions, grated	1 c. chicken broth
1 sm. jar pimento strips	1 pkg. egg noodles
Worcestershire sauce to taste	Crushed corn flakes
Salt and pepper to taste	Slivered almonds to taste
Monosodium glutamate to taste	1/4 c. melted butter
Hot sauce to taste	

Remove the chicken from bones. Cut in bite-sized pieces and place in a large bowl. Add the soup, onions, pimento, Worcestershire sauce, seasonings and enough salad dressing to moisten and mix well. Add sour cream and broth and mix well. Cook the noodles according to package directions and stir into chicken mixture. Pour into a greased casserole and cover with corn flake crumbs. Add the almonds and drizzle with butter. Bake at 375 degrees until brown.

Mrs. Glenn E. Carlson, Dawson, Georgia

CHICKEN ROYAL

1/3 lb. wide noodles	1 can ripe pitted olives,
1 c. sliced mushrooms	chopped
2 tbsp. butter	2 cans mushroom soup
1 lge. onion, chopped	1 1/2 c. water or chicken broth
1 clove of garlic, minced	Salt and pepper to taste
1/2 green pepper, chopped	Garlic salt to taste
2 c. diced cooked chicken	1/2 c. grated Parmesan cheese
1 c. chopped walnuts	

Cook the noodles according to package directions and drain. Saute the mushrooms in butter in a saucepan until tender. Add onion, garlic and green pepper and cook until onion is tender. Add the chicken, noodles, walnuts and olives and place in a greased 2-quart casserole. Combine the soup and water and pour over the chicken mixture. Add seasonings. Bake at 350 degrees for 45 minutes to 1 hour. Remove from oven and sprinkle cheese on top.

Mrs. Darrell Royall, Austin, Texas

CHICKEN MONTEGO

1/4 c. flour	1 can cream of celery soup
1 tsp. salt	1 tsp. ground marjoram
1/8 tsp. pepper	2 c. sour cream
3 chicken breasts, split	1 4-oz. package spaghetti
1/4 c. shortening	twists
1 4-oz. can button mushrooms	1 16-oz. can sm. peas, drained

Mix the flour, salt and pepper and dip the chicken breasts in flour mixture. Cook in shortening in a skillet over moderate heat until lightly browned. Remove chicken from skillet. Drain the mushrooms and add to skillet. Cook until lightly browned. Add the soup and marjoram and mix well. Add sour cream gradually and stir until blended. Cook the spaghetti according to package directions and drain. Place in a 3-quart shallow baking dish and stir in peas and half the soup mixture. Arrange chicken over spaghetti mixture and pour remaining soup mixture over chicken. Cover. Bake at 350 degrees for 45 minutes. Remove cover and bake for 15 to 20 minutes longer or until chicken is tender. Garnish with paprika. 6 servings.

Margery G. Middlebrooks, Jonesboro, Georgia

CHICKEN TETRAZZINI

1 green pepper, chopped	1/2 c. grated sharp cheese
1 med. onion, chopped	2 tbsp. chopped pimento
1 c. chopped celery	1 8-oz. package thin spaghetti
Margarine	3 c. chicken stock
3 c. chopped cooked chicken	1/2 c. grated Parmesan cheese
1 can mushroom soup	

Saute the green pepper, onion and celery in small amount of margarine in a saucepan until tender. Stir in the chicken, mushroom soup, sharp cheese and pimento. Break the spaghetti in pieces and cook in the chicken stock in a saucepan until tender. Mix half the spaghetti with chicken mixture and place in 13 x 9-inch baking pan. Top with remaining spaghetti and sprinkle with Parmesan cheese. Cover. Bake at 375 degrees for 30 minutes.

Mrs. J. Thomas Gould, Raleigh, North Carolina

CHICKEN-CURRIED SPAGHETTI

3 cans cream of chicken soup	2 to 4 tsp. curry powder
2 cans cream of mushroom soup	1 6-oz. can button mushrooms
1 c. milk	1 tbsp. bottled onion juice
1/2 c. cold water	1/2 tsp. dried thyme
1 lb. thin spaghetti	1/4 tsp. basil
6 qt. boiling water	1/4 tsp. oregano
2 tbsp. salt	1 1/2 c. cubed cooked chicken
1/4 c. warm water	1/2 c. grated Parmesan cheese

Mix the soups, milk and cold water in a large saucepan and cook over low heat for 10 minutes, stirring constantly. Cook the spaghetti in boiling water with salt until just tender and drain. Combine the warm water and curry powder and add to soup mixture. Add the mushrooms and liquid, onion juice, thyme, basil and oregano and simmer for 10 minutes, stirring. Place the spaghetti in a 3 1/2-quart casserole. Pour soup mixture over spaghetti and toss lightly. Add the chicken and cheese. Bake in a 300-degree oven for 1 hour. 12-15 servings.

Mary F. Brown, DeKalb, Mississippi

BAKED CHICKEN SPAGHETTI

1 7-oz. package spaghetti	1 pt. chicken stock
1 No. 2 can tomatoes	1 can mushrooms, chopped
3 bay leaves	1 cooked hen, cut in cubes
1 tbsp. Worcestershire sauce	3/4 lb. cheese, grated

Cook the spaghetti according to package directions and drain. Mix the tomatoes, bay leaves, Worcestershire sauce and chicken stock in a saucepan and bring to a boil. Add the spaghetti and place in a baking dish. Add the mushrooms and chicken. Bake for 1 hour in 350-degree oven. Mix in the cheese and bake for 5 minutes longer. Serve immediately. 12 servings.

Mrs. Jack Doler, Winona, Mississippi

CHICKEN AND SPAGHETTI DISH

1 4 1/2-lb. chicken	1 c. cream of mushroom soup
1 med. green pepper, chopped	1 lb. longhorn cheese, grated
3 lge. onions, chopped	2 sm. pimentos, chopped
8 stalks celery, chopped	1 7 1/2-oz. bottle stuffed
2 cloves of garlic, minced	olives
Butter	3 7-oz. boxes spaghetti
2 sm. cans mushroom pieces	Garlic salt to taste

Cook the chicken in boiling, salted water for 2 hours and 30 minutes. Drain and reserve broth. Cool the chicken. Remove chicken from bones and dice. Saute the green pepper, onions, celery and garlic in small amount of butter in a saucepan until tender. Add the chicken, mushrooms, mushroom soup, half the cheese and half the pimentos. Drain the olives and slice. Add half the olives to the chicken mixture. Cook the spaghetti in reserved chicken broth with garlic salt for 10 minutes and drain. Add the chicken mixture and mix well. Place in a large casserole and place remaining cheese, pimentos and olives on top. Bake at 350 degrees for 20 minutes. 10 servings.

Mrs. C. L. Jester, Lubbock, Texas

CHICKEN HUNTINGTON

1 c. macaroni	1 can green peas
Chicken stock	1 can mushroom soup
1 3-lb. cooked chicken, diced	1 c. bread crumbs
1 sm. jar pimento strips	1/2 c. grated Parmesan cheese

Cook the macaroni according to package directions, using chicken stock instead of water. Add remaining ingredients except bread crumbs and cheese and mix well. Place in a 2-quart casserole and sprinkle the bread crumbs and cheese on top. Bake at 325 degrees for 1 hour. 6 servings.

Elizabeth M. Clark, Chattanooga, Tennessee

CHICKEN-MACARONI CASSEROLE

2 chicken breasts	1/8 tsp. pepper
1 c. elbow macaroni	1 tsp. dried parsley flakes
1 can cream of mushroom soup	10 oz. sharp Cheddar cheese,
1 c. evaporated milk	grated
1 tsp. salt	3 tbsp. butter or margarine

Cook the chicken in small amount of boiling water until tender. Drain and cool. Remove chicken from bones and cut in cubes. Cook the macaroni according to package directions and drain. Combine soup, milk, salt, pepper, parsley flakes and cheese and mix. Add the butter, chicken and macaroni and mix well. Place in a baking dish. Bake at 350 degrees for 25 to 30 minutes. 4-6 servings.

Mrs. Gloria Lee Edwards, Jonesboro, Tennessee

MACARONI POULET

5 chicken breasts	1 No. 2 can tomatoes
5 chicken backs	1 can cream of mushroom soup
2 c. small shell macaroni	1 c. grated Cheddar cheese
1 med. onion, chopped	1 No. 2 can English peas,
1 clove of garlic, chopped	drained
1 5-oz. can mushrooms, drained	1 sm. package almonds, chopped
2 tbsp. butter	

Place the chicken in a saucepan and cover with water. Bring to a boil and reduce heat. Simmer until tender. Drain and reserve broth. Remove chicken from bones and chop. Cook the macaroni in reserved broth until tender and drain. Saute the onion, garlic and mushrooms in butter in a saucepan until tender. Add the chicken, macaroni and remaining ingredients and mix well. Place in a casserole. Bake at 350 degrees for 10 minutes. 12 servings.

Mrs. Lillie Corley, Ft. Worth, Texas

CHICKEN WITH CASHEWS

1/2 c. water	1 sm. can water chestnuts
2 cans mushroom soup	6 oz. cashews
2 c. diced cooked chicken	1 4-oz. can mushrooms
1 c. diced celery	2 sm. cans chow mein noodles
1/2 c. grated onion	

Mix the water and soup in a large bowl. Add remaining ingredients except 1 can noodles and mix well. Place in a baking dish. Bake at 325 degrees for 30 minutes. Top with remaining noodles and bake for 10 minutes longer.

Mrs. Dan T. Williams, Macon, Georgia

CHOPSTICK CHICKEN

1 3-oz. can chow mein noodles	1/4 c. chopped onion
1 can boned chicken	1/2 c. cashews or almonds
1 can cream of celery soup	1/4 tsp. Worcestershire sauce
1/4 soup can water	1 11-oz. can mandarin oranges
1/2 c. chopped celery	

Reserve 1 cup noodles. Mix remaining noodles with remaining ingredients except oranges and place in a casserole. Cover with reserved noodles. Bake at 350 degrees until heated through. Drain the oranges and place on top. 6 servings.

Mrs. Wayne Simpson, Tampkinsville, Kentucky

FIVE-CAN CASSEROLE

1 canned whole chicken	1 sm. can chow mein noodles
1 can mushroom soup	1 sm. can evaporated milk
1 can chicken and rice soup	1 c. crushed potato chips

Bone the chicken and dice. Add remaining ingredients except potato chips and mix well. Place in a 9-inch square baking dish and top with potato chips. Bake in 400-degree oven for about 15 minutes or until bubbly. 6 servings.

Mrs. Woodrow W. Patterson, Austin, Texas

CHICKEN A LA KING CASSEROLE

1 sm. onion	1/4 c. pimento strips
2 cloves	2 c. diced cooked chicken
3/4 c. chicken broth	1 tsp. salt
3/4 c. milk	1/4 tsp. pepper
5/8 c. butter	1 1/3 c. long grain rice
3 tbsp. flour	1/2 c. grated Parmesan or Swiss
1 c. sliced mushrooms	cheese
1/4 c. minced green pepper	2 egg yolks, beaten

Stud the onion with cloves and place in a saucepan. Add the chicken broth and milk and simmer for 5 minutes. Remove the onion and keep milk mixture hot. Melt 3 tablespoons butter in a saucepan and stir in flour. Add milk mixture all at once and cook over low heat, stirring constantly, until smooth and thickened. Remove from heat. Melt 4 tablespoons butter in another saucepan and cook the mushrooms and green pepper in the butter for 5 to 7 minutes, stirring frequently. Stir into sauce and stir in pimento, chicken, salt and pepper. Remove from heat. Cook the rice in boiling water until just tender and drain. Melt remaining butter and add the rice, 1/4 cup cheese and egg yolks. Mix well. Place 2/3 of the rice mixture in a 2-quart casserole and press against bottom and sides of casserole. Add the chicken mixture and spoon remaining rice over the chicken mixture. Sprinkle remaining cheese on top. Bake at 350 degrees for 1 hour.

Mrs. George R. Cowan, Milton, Florida

CHICKEN BREASTS WITH ARTICHOKES

4 chicken breasts, halved	1 can chicken broth
1 lge. onion, thinly sliced	1 can artichokes, drained
1/2 c. chopped bell pepper	Salt and pepper to taste
1/2 c. salad oil	1 4-oz. can button mushrooms
Juice of 1 lemon	12 stuffed olives
1 c. rice	

Cook the chicken breasts, onion and bell pepper in salad oil in a skillet until brown. Drizzle lemon juice over chicken breasts. Cook the rice in chicken broth in a saucepan until tender and add remaining ingredients, being careful to keep artichokes whole. Place in a greased 8 x 8 x 3-inch casserole. Place chicken breasts and sauteed vegetables on top and cover. Bake at 325 degrees for 1 hour. Toasted almonds may be sprinkled over top before serving, if desired. 6-8 servings.

Mrs. Bennie Ward, Lambert, Mississippi

Curried Raisin-Rice Ring (below)

CURRIED RAISIN-RICE RING

1 sm. onion, finely chopped	2/3 c. seedless raisins,
1 lge. stalk celery, finely	chopped
chopped	1 tsp. salt
1/2 tsp. curry powder	4 c. cooked rice
1/2 c. butter	Creamed Chicken

Cook the onion and celery with curry in butter in a saucepan over low heat until soft but not browned. Add the raisins, salt and rice and mix well. Pack into an 8-inch ring mold. Bake at 400 degrees for about 15 minutes. Unmold and fill with Creamed Chicken.

Creamed Chicken

2 tbsp. chopped green onion	1 tbsp. lemon juice
6 tbsp. butter	2 c. cubed cooked chicken
6 tbsp. flour	1/3 c. seedless raisins
1 tsp. salt	1 c. cooked peas
3 c. milk	

Cook the green onion in butter in a saucepan over low heat until soft but not browned. Blend in the flour and salt. Add the milk and cook, stirring, for 10 to 15 minutes or until smooth and thickened. Add the lemon juice, chicken, raisins and peas and heat thoroughly. 6 servings.

QUICK CHICKEN CASSEROLE

1 stick margarine	1 chicken, disjointed
1 c. cooked rice	Salt and pepper to taste
1 can onion soup	

Cut the margarine in pieces and place in a casserole. Pour the rice on margarine and add soup. Place the chicken on top and sprinkle with salt and pepper. Bake at 325 degrees for 1 hour. 5 servings.

Mrs. Billy H. Teddlie, Harden, Texas

CHICKEN ALEXANDER

4 c. diced cooked chicken	3 beaten eggs
1 c. cooked rice	1 tsp. salt
1 c. milk	1/2 tsp. pepper
1/4 c. chopped pimento	1 tsp. chopped onion
2 c. chicken broth	1 can cream of mushroom soup
2 c. bread crumbs	Crushed potato chips

Mix all ingredients except soup and potato chips and place in a 9 x 13-inch greased baking pan. Pour the soup over chicken mixture and sprinkle with potato chips. Bake in 350-degree oven for 1 hour. 8-10 servings.

Mrs. Orpha Grayson, Jefferson, Oklahoma

CHICKEN AND BROWN RICE CASSEROLE

1/2 stick butter or margarine	Chicken stock
6 med. onions, chopped	3 c. diced cooked chicken
1 c. chopped celery	1 sm. can ripe olives, chopped
Salt and pepper to taste	1/4 c. coffee cream
1 c. brown rice	

Combine the butter, onions, celery, salt and pepper in a skillet and cook over low heat until celery is tender. Cook the rice in chicken stock until tender and add to onion mixture. Add the chicken and toss lightly. Add the olives and turn into a greased large casserole. Pour the cream over top. Bake at 425 degrees for 15 to 20 minutes or until heated through. 8 servings.

Mrs. I. E. Jackson, Winder, Georgia

CHICKEN AND RICE

5 oz. packaged precooked rice	2 tbsp. chopped pimento
1/2 pkg. onion soup mix	1 chicken, disjointed
1 can cream of mushroom soup	1/2 stick butter, melted
1 1/4 c. boiling water	Salt and pepper to taste
1/4 c. dry sherry	Paprika to taste

Combine the rice, soup mix, mushroom soup, water, sherry and pimento and place in a greased baking dish. Brush the chicken with butter and place over soup mixture. Add the salt, pepper and paprika and cover. Bake at 375 degrees for 1 hour and 15 minutes. Remove cover and bake for 15 minutes longer. 4-6 servings.

Mrs. Carol Taylor, Maitland, Florida

CHICKEN CASSEROLE

2 tbsp. butter or margarine	2 c. cubed cooked chicken
1 med. onion, sliced	1 3-oz. can mushrooms
1 med. green pepper, cut in	2 tbsp. cornstarch
strips	1/2 c. chopped walnuts or
3 c. sliced celery	almonds
1 1/2 c. chicken broth	1 1/2 c. packaged precooked rice
1 tbsp. soy sauce	

Preheat oven to 400 degrees. Melt the butter in a skillet and saute onion in the butter until tender. Stir in the green pepper, celery, chicken broth, soy sauce and the chicken. Drain the mushrooms and reserve liquid. Add mushrooms to the chicken mixture and bring to a boil. Mix the cornstarch with 3 tablespoons reserved mushroom liquid and stir into chicken mixture. Add the walnuts and rice and pour into a 2-quart greased casserole. Bake for 20 minutes or until rice is tender.

Mrs. Eva Garrett, Jonesville, Virginia

CHICKEN CONTINENTAL

3 to 4 lb. fryer pieces	1 tsp. salt
1/3 c. seasoned flour	1/8 tsp. thyme
1/4 c. butter	1/2 tsp. celery flakes
1 can cream of chicken soup	1 1/3 c. water
2 1/2 tbsp. grated onion	1 1/3 c. packaged precooked rice
1 tbsp. chopped parsley	1/2 tsp. paprika

Roll the chicken in seasoned flour and cook in butter in a skillet until golden brown. Mix the soup, onion and seasonings in a saucepan and stir in water gradually. Bring to a boil, stirring constantly. Pour the rice into a shallow 2-quart casserole and stir in all except 1/3 cup soup mixture. Top with chicken and pour remaining soup mixture over chicken. Cover. Bake at 375 degrees for 30 minutes or until chicken is tender and sprinkle with paprika.

Mrs. Edward Hammond, Lancaster, South Carolina

CHICKEN-RICE-VEGETABLE LOAF

1 4 to 5-lb. chicken	1 tsp. sage
3 c. cooked rice	2 tbsp. chopped pimento
1 c. milk	1/2 c. chopped green pepper
1/2 c. evaporated milk or cream	1 c. chopped celery
Salt to taste	1 tbsp. minced onion
1/2 tsp. pepper	1/2 c. canned green peas
1/2 tsp. paprika	4 beaten eggs

Cook the chicken in boiling, salted water until tender. Drain and reserve 1 1/2 cups broth. Cool the chicken. Remove chicken from bones and dice. Add the rice and reserved broth and mix well. Add remaining ingredients in order listed and mix well. Pack in a greased loaf pan. Bake at 325 degrees for 45 to 60 minutes. Let stand for 10 minutes before serving and turn out on a platter. Garnish with parsley.

Mushroom Sauce

3 tbsp. butter	Milk
3 tbsp. flour	1/4 tsp. white pepper
3/4 tsp. salt	1/2 tsp. paprika
1 can mushroom soup	1/2 c. canned green peas

Melt the butter in a saucepan and stir in flour and salt. Mix the soup with enough milk to make 3 cups liquid and stir into the flour mixture. Add the pepper and paprika and bring to boiling point, stirring constantly. Cook for 3 minutes and add peas. Remove from heat and serve with chicken loaf.

Mrs. J. F. Dorsey, Arkadelphia, Arkansas

DUCHESS CHICKEN

4 chicken breasts	4 canned cling peach halves,
1/4 c. butter or margarine	drained
1 10 1/2-oz. can chicken	Lemon juice
consomme	Powdered ginger
1 2-oz. can mushrooms	2 1/2 tbsp. flour
1 tbsp. instant minced onion	1 lge. can evaporated milk
3/4 c. rice	Salt to taste
1/3 c. slivered blanched	Pepper to taste
almonds	

Brown the chicken breasts in butter in a skillet. Combine the chicken consomme, mushrooms and liquid and onion in a saucepan and heat to boiling point. Add the rice and boil for 5 minutes. Turn into a baking dish. Top with chicken and almonds and cover with foil. Bake at 300 degrees for 45 minutes, then remove foil. Drizzle peach halves with lemon juice and sprinkle with powdered ginger. Place in baking dish and bake for 10 minutes longer. Stir flour into drippings in the skillet. Add the milk and cook, stirring constantly, until thickened. Season with salt and pepper. Serve with chicken mixture. 4 servings.

Duchess Chicken (above)

CHICKEN-WILD RICE CASSEROLE

2 3-lb. fryers	1 lb. fresh mushrooms
1 c. water	1/4 c. butter or margarine
1 c. dry sherry	2 6-oz. packages long grain
1 1/2 tsp. salt	and wild rice
1/2 tsp. curry powder	1 c. sour cream
1 med. onion, sliced	1 can cream of mushroom soup
1/2 c. sliced celery	

Place the chickens in a deep kettle and add the water, sherry, salt, curry powder, onion and celery. Bring to a boil and reduce heat. Cover and simmer for 1 hour. Remove from heat. Remove chickens from broth and reserve broth. Cool the chickens. Remove skin and discard. Remove chicken from bones and cut in small pieces. Wash the mushrooms and drain. Saute in the butter in a saucepan until golden brown and reserve enough mushrooms to circle casserole. Cook the rice according to package directions for firm rice, using reserved broth as part of liquid. Add the chicken and remaining mushrooms and mix well. Place in a 4-quart casserole. Mix the sour cream and soup and stir into chicken mixture. Arrange reserved mushrooms on top in circle. Bake in 350-degree oven for 1 hour. May be refrigerated for 1 day before baking, if desired. 8-10 servings.

Mrs. C. Edward Gardner, Pennington Gap, Virginia

COUNTRY CHICKEN DINNER

1 lge. hen	2 onions, diced
1 c. rice	2 c. diced celery
1 can tomato soup	1 c. diced carrots
1 can cream of mushroom soup	2 tsp. salt
1 No. 2 can sm. English peas	1/2 tsp. pepper
1 No. 2 can tomatoes	1 tsp. paprika

Cook the hen in boiling water in a large kettle until tender. Drain and cool. Remove chicken from bones and cut in large pieces. Soak the rice in enough hot water to cover for 10 minutes, then drain. Combine remaining ingredients in a large bowl. Place alternate layers of chicken, rice and soup mixture in a 2 1/2-quart casserole and cover. Bake at 350 degrees until rice is tender, adding chicken stock or water, if needed. 12 servings.

Mrs. Luther Rice, Wedowee, Alabama

CASSEROLE MEXICANA

1 tbsp. flour	3/4 c. chopped onions
1 tbsp. salad oil	1 jalapeno pepper, chopped
3 cloves of garlic, minced	1 pkg. tortillas
1 tbsp. chili powder	2 1/4 c. grated Cheddar cheese
1 tbsp. comino seed	1 can cream of chicken soup
1 No. 2 can tomato juice	1 6-oz. can evaporated milk
7 lge. chicken breasts	

Combine the flour, oil, garlic, chili powder and comino seed in a saucepan. Add tomato juice gradually and cook over low heat until slightly thickened. Cook the chicken breasts in boiling water until tender. Drain and reserve 2 cups broth. Remove chicken from bones and cut in small pieces. Cook the onions in small amount of fat until tender and add jalapeno pepper. Place half the tortillas in a casserole and add half the chicken. Add half the cheese and half the onion mixture. Repeat layers. Combine the sauce with reserved broth and remaining ingredients and mix thoroughly. Pour over casserole. Refrigerate overnight. Bake for 1 hour at 350 degrees. 10 servings.

Mrs. Phyllis Watson, Corpus Christi, Texas

KING RANCH TRAIL DRIVE DISH

1 hen	1 can seasoned tomatoes
1 sm. onion	1 chopped onion
1 celery stalk	1 doz. tortillas, broken
1 can cream of mushroom soup	1/4 env. chili mix
1 can cream of chicken soup	1 c. grated Cheddar cheese

Cook the hen in boiling water with small onion and celery until tender. Drain and reserve 2 cups broth. Discard the onion and celery. Remove chicken from bones and chop. Combine the soups, tomatoes and chopped onion. Place the tortillas in a casserole. Add the chicken, then add the soup mixture. Sprinkle with chili mix. Add the reserved broth and sprinkle with cheese. Bake at 350 degrees for 45 minutes to 1 hour.

Mrs. J. J. Stephen, Robston, Texas

SPANISH CHICKEN CASSEROLE

1 onion, chopped	2 doz. tortillas
1 clove of garlic, chopped	1 lge. cooked hen, chopped
1 can tomato soup	1 lb. Monterey Jack cheese,
1 pt. chicken broth	grated
1 can green chili peppers	

Saute the onion and garlic in a small amount of fat in a saucepan until tender. Add the soup and broth. Chop the chili peppers and stir into soup mixture. Cut the tortillas in quarters and place on a cookie sheet. Bake at 250 degrees until warm. Place alternate layers of tortillas, chicken, soup mixture and cheese in a greased shallow casserole. Bake at 350 degrees for 30 minutes. 10-12 servings.

Anna Moss, Brownfield, Texas

FULL MEAL CASSEROLE

6 slices toast	2 cans cream of chicken soup
1 lge. package frozen asparagus	3 tbsp. water
3 c. diced cooked chicken	6 slices pimento cheese

Place the toast in a large shallow casserole. Cook the asparagus according to package directions. Place alternate layers of chicken and asparagus over the toast. Mix the chicken soup with water and pour over asparagus. Bake at 350 degrees for 20 minutes. Cover top with cheese and bake until cheese is melted.

Mrs. James H. Posey, Chattanooga, Tennessee

Chicken and Mushrooms with Fresh Artichokes (below)

CHICKEN AND MUSHROOMS WITH FRESH ARTICHOKES

6 med. artichokes	1/2 lb. mushrooms, sliced
2 fryers, disjointed	2 tbsp. flour
1/2 tsp. paprika	2/3 c. chicken broth
1/4 tsp. pepper	2/3 c. dry sherry
6 tbsp. butter or margarine	Salt to taste

Remove 2 or 3 layers of outer artichoke leaves. Cut off stem and trim off 2/3 from top of artichokes. Cut in half. Cook in 2 to 3 inches of boiling, salted water in a saucepan for 15 to 20 minutes or until tender. Drain and remove chokes. Sprinkle the chicken with paprika and pepper and brown in 4 tablespoons margarine in a large skillet. Arrange chicken and artichokes in a large shallow roasting pan. Add remaining margarine and mushrooms to the skillet and saute until mushrooms are browned. Stir in the flour. Add the broth and sherry gradually and bring to a boil, stirring constantly. Add the salt and pour over artichokes and chicken. Cover. Bake in 375-degree oven for 1 hour, basting occasionally. 6 servings.

CHICKEN-AVOCADO CASSEROLE

1 6-lb. chicken, quartered	1 c. light cream
1 med. onion, chopped	1/2 c. grated Cheddar cheese
1/2 c. diced celery	1/8 tsp. rosemary
Salt	1/8 tsp. basil
1 tbsp. pepper	1/8 tsp. hot sauce
1 qt. water	1/2 lb. sliced mushrooms
4 tbsp. butter	2 ripe avocados, sliced thin
3 tbsp. flour	1/2 c. toasted slivered almonds

Place the chicken, onion, celery, 1 tablespoon salt, pepper and water in a large kettle and bring to a boil. Reduce heat and simmer until the chicken is tender. Remove chicken from broth and cool. Remove chicken from bones except wings and neck. Place the wings and neck back into broth and simmer for 30 minutes. Drain and reserve 1 cup stock. Melt 2 tablespoons butter in a saucepan and stir in the flour. Stir in reserved stock and cream and cook, stirring, until thickened. Remove from heat. Add the cheese, 1/2 teaspoon salt, rosemary, basil and hot sauce and stir until cheese is melted. Place the chicken in a 3-quart casserole. Cook the mushrooms in remaining butter until tender and place over the chicken. Pour the cheese sauce over mushrooms and cover the casserole. Bake at 350 degrees for 25 minutes. Uncover and add avocados. Bake for 15 minutes longer and sprinkle with almonds just before serving. 8 servings.

Mrs. Estell Shalla, Bay City, Texas

CLASSIC CHICKEN DIVAN

2 bunches fresh broccoli	1/2 tsp. salt
1/4 c. butter or margarine	Dash of pepper
1/4 c. flour	3 cooked chicken breasts,
2 c. chicken broth	sliced
1/2 c. light cream	1/2 c. grated Parmesan cheese
3 tbsp. sherry	

Cook the broccoli in boiling, salted water until tender and drain. Melt the butter in a saucepan and blend in flour. Add the chicken broth and cook until thick, stirring constantly. Stir in the cream, sherry, salt and pepper. Place broccoli in 13 x 9 x 2-inch baking dish and pour half the sauce over broccoli. Add the chicken. Add half the Parmesan cheese to remaining sauce and pour over the chicken. Sprinkle with remaining Parmesan cheese. Bake at 350 degrees for 20 minutes or until heated through. Broil until golden brown. 8 servings.

Mrs. Carl Freund, Eustis, Florida

CORN-TAMALE LOAF

1 med. onion	1 tbsp. chili powder
1 clove of garlic, minced	1 tsp. salt
1/2 c. salad oil	1 tsp. pepper
1 1/2 c. yellow cornmeal	3 eggs, beaten
1 3/4 c. hot chicken broth	1 17-oz. can cream-style corn
1 1/2 c. diced cooked chicken	1 tbsp. butter
1 8-oz. can tomato sauce	

Saute the onion and garlic in oil in a saucepan until tender. Add remaining ingredients except corn and butter and mix well. Pour into a well-greased 9-inch loaf pan and set in pan of hot water. Bake at 375 degrees for 1 hour or until firm and brown. Mix the corn with butter in a saucepan and heat through. Place chicken loaf on a platter and pour the corn over loaf. Garnish with green onion and olive slices, if desired. 6 servings.

Mrs. Joel Weiner, Raleigh, North Carolina

Chicken Breasts Cosmopolitan (below)

CHICKEN BREASTS COSMOPOLITAN

4 boned chicken breasts	1 c. instant nonfat dry milk
2 1/2 c. water	1 1/2 tbsp. lemon juice
1 tsp. salt	2 10-oz. packages frozen
1/4 tsp. white pepper	broccoli spears
5 tbsp. butter	1/2 c. grated Parmesan cheese
5 tbsp. flour	1/2 c. grated Cheddar cheese

Place the chicken breasts in a heavy saucepan and add the water, 1/2 teaspoon salt and 1/8 teaspoon pepper. Bring to a boil and reduce heat. Cover. Simmer until chicken is tender, then drain and reserve broth. Keep chicken hot. Melt the butter in a saucepan. Add the flour and cook over low heat for 1 minute. Add enough water to reserved broth to make 2 cups liquid and stir into flour mixture. Add the milk and remaining salt and pepper and cook, stirring constantly, until thickened and smooth. Remove from heat and stir in the lemon juice. Cook the broccoli according to package directions and drain. Place in a shallow casserole and place chicken on broccoli. Pour sauce over chicken. Mix the Parmesan and Cheddar cheeses and sprinkle over casserole. Bake at 350 degrees until brown. Asparagus spears may be substituted for broccoli. 4 servings.

CHICKEN MEAL-IN-ONE

1 chicken, disjointed	1 tbsp. snipped parsley
1 10-oz. package frozen lima	1 tbsp. minced onion
beans	1 tbsp. chopped pimento
1 10-oz. package frozen whole	1 1/2 tsp. salt
kernel corn	1/4 tsp. pepper
1 can cream of chicken soup	1/4 tsp. crushed tarragon
1/3 c. milk	1/4 tsp. crushed thyme
1 clove of garlic, minced	1/2 tsp. hot sauce

Place the chicken in a 3-quart casserole and add the beans and corn. Combine the soup, milk, garlic, parsley, onion, pimento, salt, pepper, tarragon, thyme and hot sauce and mix well. Pour over chicken mixture and cover. Bake at 375 degrees for 1 hour and 30 minutes, stirring every 30 minutes. 4-5 servings.

Anna Leigh Poole, Vicksburg, Mississippi

CHICKEN CASSEROLE SUPREME

1 10-oz. package frozen peas	4 med. carrots, quartered
2 1/2 to 3 lb. chicken pieces	4 med. potatoes, quartered
1/3 c. flour	4 med. onions, quartered
1/4 c. shortening	1 tsp. salt
1 c. water	1 can Compliment for chicken

Thaw the peas enough to separate. Shake the chicken in flour in a paper bag, several pieces at a time, and brown in hot shortening in a 5-quart Dutch oven over medium heat. Drain and add the water, carrots, potatoes, onions and salt. Pour Compliment over chicken mixture and cover. Bake at 350 degrees for 1 hour and 15 minutes or until vegetables are tender. Add the peas and bake for 15 minutes longer. 4-6 servings.

Photograph for this recipe on page 108.

SPECIAL CHICKEN CASSEROLE

1 can shoestring potatoes	2 cans boned chicken
1 can asparagus	1 c. grated cheese
1 can mushroom soup	2 tbsp. chopped pimento (opt.)

Place 1/3 of the potatoes in a 1 1/2-quart casserole and add half the asparagus. Add half the soup, then add half the chicken. Add half the cheese and half the pimento. Repeat layers, ending with potatoes. Bake in a 350-degree oven for 30 minutes.

Mrs. Mary Vaughn, Hayden, Alabama

DRUMSTICK CASSEROLE

10 drumsticks	1/4 tsp. poultry seasoning
1 can cream of chicken soup	1 sm. can carrots, drained
1/2 c. milk	1 sm. can lima beans, drained
1/4 tsp. salt	1 sm. can onions, drained
1/4 tsp. pepper	

Brown the chicken in small amount of fat in a skillet and place in a casserole. Combine remaining ingredients and pour over chicken. Bake at 375 degrees for 30 minutes. 5 servings.

Mrs. R. L. Errington, State Line, Mississippi

BAKED CHICKEN CASSEROLE

1 6-oz. can boned chicken	1/4 tsp. pepper
1 can cream of chicken soup	1 tbsp. lemon juice
1 c. diced celery	3/4 c. mayonnaise
2 tsp. minced onion	3 hard-cooked eggs, thinly
1/2 c. chopped almonds or pecans	sliced
1/2 tsp. salt	2 c. crushed potato chips

Dice the chicken and place in a bowl. Add the soup and mix well. Mix remaining ingredients except potato chips and combine with chicken mixture. Place in a casserole and sprinkle with potato chips. Bake at 350 degrees for 30 minutes. 6-8 servings.

Mrs. Fred J. Frieling, Austin, Texas

CHICKEN WITH CELERY DRESSING

2 chickens	1 c. bread crumbs
2 sticks margarine	1 c. finely chopped celery
1 c. flour	1/3 c. finely chopped onions
Salt and pepper to taste	2 eggs, well beaten
2 c. milk	6 hard-cooked eggs, sliced
3 c. corn bread crumbs	

Place the chickens in a kettle and cover with water. Bring to a boil and reduce heat. Simmer until chickens are tender. Drain and reserve broth. Cool the chickens. Remove chicken from bones and cut in large pieces. Melt the margarine in a large saucepan and stir in the flour. Season with salt and pepper. Add 4 cups reserved broth and milk slowly and cook until thick, stirring constantly. Mix the corn bread crumbs, bread crumbs, celery, onions and beaten eggs in a large bowl and add salt and pepper. Place alternate layers of chicken, hard-cooked eggs and dressing in a 4-quart casserole and cover with sauce. Bake for 1 hour at 350 degrees. 16 servings.

Eva S. Ray, Lake View, South Carolina

COUNTRY CLUB CHICKEN SCALLOP

1 c. butter or margarine	1 tsp. rubbed sage
2 c. flour	1 tsp. poultry seasoning
10 c. chicken broth	12 c. chopped cooked chicken
7 c. milk	5 c. toasted dry bread crumbs
1 tsp. celery salt	1 can French-fried onion rings

Melt the butter in a large saucepan and stir in the flour. Add the broth and milk and cook, stirring constantly, until thickened. Stir in the seasonings and remove from heat. Place alternate layers of chicken, bread crumbs and sauce in 2 large baking pans and top with onion rings. Bake at 350 degrees for 30 minutes. 30 servings.

Mrs. M. I. Stutler, Clarksburg, West Virginia

CHICKEN-ALMOND CASSEROLE

3 1/2 c. noodles	2 c. diced cooked chicken
1 c. cream of chicken soup	3/4 c. sliced cooked celery
1 6-oz. can evaporated milk	1/3 c. chopped cooked green
1 tsp. salt	pepper
1/4 tsp. pepper	1/3 c. chopped pimento
1/2 tsp. dry mustard	1 c. slivered toasted almonds
1 1/2 c. shredded sharp cheese	

Cook the noodles in boiling, salted water until tender and drain. Place in a greased 2-quart casserole. Combine the soup, milk, salt, pepper and mustard in a saucepan and heat through, stirring constantly. Add cheese and stir until cheese is melted. Add the chicken, celery, green pepper, pimento and half the almonds and pour over noodles. Sprinkle with remaining almonds. Bake in 400-degree oven for 20 minutes or until heated through. 6 servings.

Mrs. K. R. Wood, Miami, Florida

CHICKEN AND MUSHROOM BAKE

1 3-lb. chicken, disjointed	3/4 c. canned mushrooms
Seasoned flour	1 can mushroom or chicken soup
1/4 c. butter	1/2 pt. sour cream

Dredge the chicken with seasoned flour. Melt the butter in a shallow baking pan and arrange the chicken in the baking pan in a single layer, skin side down. Bake at 350 degrees for 30 minutes. Remove from oven and turn. Combine the mushrooms, soup and sour cream and pour over the chicken. Bake for 40 to 45 minutes longer or until chicken is tender. Three chicken breasts, halved, may be substituted for whole chicken. 6 servings.

Chicken and Mushroom Bake (above)

CHICKEN AND DRESSING BAKE

1 7-oz. package herb-seasoned stuffing mix	2 well-beaten eggs
1 can cream of mushroom soup	2 1/2 c. diced cooked chicken
2 c. chicken broth	1/2 c. milk
	2 tbsp. chopped pimento

Combine the stuffing mix with half the soup, broth and eggs in a large bowl. Place in 11 1/2 x 7 1/2 x 1 1/2-inch baking dish and top with chicken. Combine remaining soup with milk and pimento and pour over chicken. Cover with foil. Bake at 350 degrees for 45 minutes or until set. 6-8 servings.

Mrs. Emmett Chewning, Rhoadesville, Virginia

DEVILED CHICKEN

1 cooked chicken, diced	2 cans cream of mushroom soup
6 hard-cooked eggs, diced	2 c. white sauce or chicken broth
2 c. chopped green peppers	
2 c. chopped celery	Salt and pepper to taste
2 lge. onions, chopped	Bread crumbs

Combine all ingredients except bread crumbs and place in a large, shallow baking pan. Cover with crumbs. Bake at 350 degrees for about 30 minutes or until brown. 12 servings.

Mrs. W. M. Gee, Whiteville, Tennessee

HERBED CHICKEN CASSEROLE

3 chicken breasts, cut in half	1 5-oz. can water chestnuts
Salt and pepper to taste	1 3-oz. can broiled sliced mushrooms
1/4 c. butter or margarine	
1 can cream of chicken soup	2 tbsp. chopped green peppers
3/4 c. sherry	1/4 tsp. crushed thyme

Season the chicken with salt and pepper and brown in the butter in a skillet over low heat. Place, skin side up, in a 11 1/2 x 7 1/2 x 1 1/2-inch baking dish. Add the soup to drippings in skillet and add sherry slowly, stirring constantly. Drain the water chestnuts, slice and add to soup mixture. Drain the mushrooms and add to soup mixture. Add remaining ingredients and heat to boiling point. Pour over chicken and cover with foil. Bake at 350 degrees for 25 minutes. 6 servings.

L. F. Dickson, Dallas, Texas

GREEN PEPPERS AU GRATIN CASSEROLE

6 green peppers	1 c. chopped cooked chicken
1 onion, chopped fine	1 c. whole wheat bread crumbs
3 tbsp. butter or shortening	6 hard-cooked eggs, sliced

| 1/4 lb. cheese, grated | Salt and pepper to taste |
| 2 c. pureed tomatoes | 1 tsp. Worcestershire sauce |

Slice the green peppers crosswise. Cook in small amount of water for 5 minutes and drain. Saute the green peppers and onion in butter in a saucepan until tender. Place in a baking dish and cover with chicken and crumbs. Place eggs and cheese over chicken mixture. Combine the tomatoes, salt, pepper and Worcestershire sauce and pour over cheese. Sprinkle with additional crumbs and dot with additional butter. Bake at 375 degrees for 30 minutes.

Robina C. Whitley, Majestic, Kentucky

SPAGHETTI WITH CHICKEN LIVER SAUCE

4 tbsp. margarine	1/4 tsp. crushed thyme
1 c. chopped onion	leaves
2 cloves of garlic, crushed	1 17-oz. can plum tomatoes
1/3 c. chopped parsley	1 6-oz. can tomato paste
Salt	2 beef bouillon cubes
Dash of pepper	1 lb. chicken livers, sliced
1 1/2 tsp. oregano leaves	1 lb. spaghetti
1 tsp. Worcestershire sauce	1/2 c. grated Parmesan cheese

Melt 2 tablespoons margarine in a large skillet over medium heat. Add the onion and garlic and saute until tender. Reserve 1 tablespoon parsley for garnish. Add remaining parsley, 1 teaspoon salt, pepper, oregano, Worcestershire sauce, thyme, tomatoes and tomato paste to onion mixture. Dissolve the bouillon cubes in 1 1/2 cups boiling water and stir into onion mixture. Saute the livers in remaining margarine in a saucepan over low heat for 5 minutes and add to sauce. Cover. Bake at 350 degrees for about 35 minutes or until heated through, stirring occasionally. Add 2 tablespoons salt to 6 quarts boiling water. Add the spaghetti gradually so that water continues to boil and cook, stirring occasionally, until tender. Drain in a colander. Blend half the cheese into chicken liver mixture. Serve with remaining cheese and spaghetti sprinkled with reserved parsley. 6 servings.

Spaghetti with Chicken Liver Sauce (above)

Deep-Dish Cranberry-Chicken Pie (page 134)

chicken pies

On cold and rainy winter evenings, a traditional southern supper is chicken pie. This succulent, piping hot dish can make even the coldest night seem warm.

Generations of hospitable southern women have carefully perfected their recipes for these meat-and-vegetable packed pies. Now readers of *Southern Living* share with you the choicest of such recipes.

Every recipe in these pages has passed the most important test of all: it is the favorite dish from the kitchen of a homemaker who takes pride in serving her family the very best. It is the recipe for which she is best known and for which she has earned her reputation as a fine cook.

You'll discover how to prepare Chicken and Dumpling Pot Pie and other deep-dish chicken pies that will bring appreciative compliments from your family and guests. The next time you want to serve your family something full of old-fashioned goodness, try Old-Time Chicken Pie. They'll come back for seconds and even thirds! Magic Chicken Pie and Herbed Chicken Pie are just two more of the taste treats awaiting you in this marvelous section. And what could be more typically southern than a recipe for Chicken Pie with Sweet Potato Crust!

With a section of such recipes awaiting you, shouldn't you be serving your family and friends a chicken pie — tonight?

DEEP-DISH CRANBERRY-CHICKEN PIE

1 10-oz. package frozen peas	1/4 c. butter or margarine
1 1-lb. can whole onions	1/4 c. flour
1 4-oz. can sliced mushrooms	2 tsp. gravy coloring
1 c. fresh cranberries	Salt and pepper to taste
2 c. chicken stock or bouillon	4 c. diced cooked chicken
1 med. onion, chopped	1 c. sliced cooked carrots
2 c. light cream	1 pkg. pie crust mix

Thaw the peas. Drain the whole onions and mushrooms. Combine the cranberries, chicken stock and chopped onion in a saucepan and bring to a boil. Reduce heat and simmer for 10 minutes, stirring occasionally. Remove from heat and press through a sieve. Stir in cream. Melt the butter in a saucepan and blend in the flour. Stir in strained cranberry mixture gradually and add the gravy coloring. Cook over low heat, stirring constantly, until mixture boils and thickens, then season with salt and pepper. Combine the chicken, carrots, peas, whole onions and mushrooms in a shallow 3-quart casserole and pour sauce over chicken mixture. Prepare pie crust mix according to package directions. Roll out on a lightly floured surface into a circle about 1 inch larger than top of the casserole. Place pastry over filling and seal crust to edge of casserole. Cut several slashes in the top to allow steam to escape. Bake at 400 degrees for 35 to 40 minutes or until crust is golden brown. 8-10 servings.

Photograph for this recipe on page 132.

ALABAMA CHICKEN PIE

1 4-lb. chicken	1 med. onion
1 1/2 c. hot water	4 tbsp. flour
3 celery tops	3 hard-cooked eggs, chopped
1 tbsp. salt	1/2 recipe biscuit dough

Place the chicken in a pressure cooker and add the hot water, celery tops, salt and onion. Cook at 15 pounds pressure for 40 minutes. Cool pressure cooker quickly and remove top. Remove chicken from broth and cool. Strain the broth and chill. Cut the chicken in large pieces. Remove the fat from chilled broth and melt in a saucepan. Stir in the flour. Add enough chicken broth to make a thin sauce and cook until thickened, stirring constantly. Add the eggs and chicken and pour into a casserole. Roll out the dough on a floured surface to size of casserole and place on chicken mixture. Bake at 425 degrees for 25 to 30 minutes.

Mrs. George Childs, Winter Haven, Florida

CHICKEN-CHEESE PIE

1 1/8 c. flour	1 egg, lightly beaten
1/2 tsp. salt	2 tbsp. cold water
1/3 c. shortening	1/2 c. chopped onion

2 tbsp. chopped green pepper
1/4 c. chicken fat or butter
1/2 c. chicken broth

3 c. diced cooked chicken
3/4 c. diced cooked carrots
1 c. grated cheese

Sift 1 cup flour and salt together into a bowl and cut in shortening until mixture is size of small peas. Combine 1 tablespoon egg with water and pour over flour mixture. Stir until flour is moistened, adding water, if necessary. Roll out on floured board and place in 9-inch pie pan. Bake at 425 degrees for 8 minutes or until lightly browned. Saute the onion and green pepper in fat in a saucepan until tender and stir in remaining flour. Add the broth and cook until thickened, stirring constantly. Add the chicken, carrots and remaining egg and mix well. Turn into pie crust and top with cheese. Bake in 400-degree oven for 20 to 25 minutes. 6 servings.

Mrs. Wade Huey, Marshall, North Carolina

CHICKEN SALAD PIE

1 env. unflavored gelatin
1 1/2 c. cold water
2 chicken bouillon cubes
3/4 c. mayonnaise
1 c. sour cream
1 tbsp. lemon juice
1/2 tsp. salt

3/4 tsp. dillweed
1/8 tsp. hot sauce
2 c. diced cooked chicken
1 c. chopped celery
Sliced stuffed olives
1 tbsp. finely chopped onion
1 baked 9-in. pastry shell

Soften the gelatin in water in a small saucepan. Add the bouillon cubes and stir over low heat until gelatin and bouillon cubes are dissolved. Combine the mayonnaise, sour cream, lemon juice, salt, dillweed and hot sauce in a bowl and stir in gelatin mixture slowly. Add the chicken, celery, 3/4 cup olives and onion and mix well. Chill until mixture is thick enough to mound slightly, then spoon into pastry shell. Chill until firm and garnish with overlapping olive slices. 6 servings.

Chicken Salad Pie (above)

AROMATIC CHICKEN PIE

1 4-lb. stewing chicken	1 tsp. dried parsley flakes
Salt	2 tbsp. shortening
Pepper to taste	6 tbsp. flour
1 tsp. dried onion flakes	1 recipe pie pastry
1 tsp. celery seed	

Place the chicken in a kettle and cover with water. Add the salt to taste, pepper, onion flakes, celery seed and parsley flakes. Cook until chicken is tender. Remove chicken from broth and cool. Remove chicken from bones and cut in bite-sized pieces. Place in a baking dish. Strain the broth and reserve. Melt the shortening in a saucepan. Add the flour and dash of salt and mix until smooth. Add 3 cups reserved broth and cook over low heat, stirring constantly, until thickened. Pour over chicken and top with pie crust. Bake at 350 degrees for 30 minutes or until crust is brown. 6 servings.

Mrs. Robert H. Lamey, Victoria, Texas

BAKED CHICKEN PIE

1 2-lb. chicken	Salt and pepper to taste
1 c. frozen green peas	1 can refrigerator biscuits
1 c. chopped celery	

Cook the chicken in boiling water until tender. Drain and reserve broth. Cool the chicken and remove chicken from bones. Cook the peas and celery in small amount of reserved broth in a saucepan until partially done. Do not drain. Place the chicken and celery mixture in a greased baking dish and sprinkle with salt and pepper. Place biscuits over top. Bake at 400 degrees for about 20 minutes or until done. Carrots may be added, if desired. 6 servings.

Mrs. Mayon A. Cox, Norfolk, Virginia

CHICKEN PIE WITH COACH WHEEL CRUST

3 tbsp. flour	1 tsp. salt
3 tbsp. melted butter	1 tbsp. lemon juice
1 1/2 c. milk	1 4-lb. cooked chicken
1 1/2 c. chicken broth	

Stir the flour into butter in a saucepan. Add the milk, chicken broth, salt and lemon juice and cook until thickened, stirring constantly. Remove chicken from bones and stir into sauce. Pour into a casserole.

Coach Wheel Crust

1 1/2 c. flour	1/2 c. milk
2 tsp. baking powder	3 pimentos, chopped
1/2 tsp. salt	3/4 c. grated cheese
3 tbsp. shortening	

Sift the dry ingredients together into a bowl and cut in shortening. Add the milk all at once and mix well. Roll out thin on a floured surface. Mix the pimentos and cheese and spread over pastry. Roll as for jelly roll and cut in 3/4-inch thick slices. Place on chicken mixture. Bake at 400 degrees for 30 minutes.

Mrs. E. E. Thompson, McDonough, Georgia

CHICKEN-ASPARAGUS PIE

Pastry for 2-crust pie	Chicken broth
1 14-oz. can cut asparagus	1/2 tsp. garlic salt
4 c. chopped cooked chicken	1/2 tsp. pepper
4 hard-boiled eggs, sliced	

Line a 1 1/2-quart baking dish with pastry. Drain the asparagus and reserve liquid. Place 1/3 of the chicken in the crust and add 1/2 of the eggs. Add 1/2 of the asparagus and repeat layers, ending with chicken. Mix reserved liquid with enough chicken broth to make 3 cups liquid and stir in the garlic salt and pepper. Pour over chicken and cover with pastry strips. Bake at 350 degrees for about 45 minutes.

Mrs. E. H. Kennedy, Fayetteville, Tennessee

CHICKEN POTPIE SUPREME

2 3/4 to 3 lb. chicken breasts	3 tbsp. butter
6 celery tops with leaves	3 tbsp. flour
1 med. onion, halved	3/4 c. cream
1 tbsp. salt	1 tsp. grated onion
1 1/2 qt. cold water	1/4 tsp. mace

Combine first 5 ingredients in a Dutch oven and bring to a boil. Simmer for 45 to 60 minutes and cool chicken in broth. Drain and reserve broth. Remove skin from chicken and discard. Remove chicken from bones and cut in bite-sized pieces. Melt the butter in a heavy saucepan over medium heat and stir in the flour. Stir in 2 1/4 cups reserved broth and cream and cook, stirring constantly, for about 2 minutes or until thickened. Add the onion, mace and chicken and pour into a 2-quart casserole.

Biscuit Topping

1 c. sifted flour	3 tbsp. cold butter
1 tsp. baking powder	1/3 c. (about) milk
1/2 tsp. salt	

Combine the flour, baking powder and salt in a bowl and cut in butter until mixture is size of peas. Stir in milk and mix until flour is moistened. Drop from tablespoon over chicken mixture. Bake in 375-degree oven for 45 minutes. 6 servings.

Mrs. Charles Farley, Albuquerque, New Mexico

Make-Ahead Chicken Pie (page 139)

MAGIC CHICKEN PIE

Flour	1 c. chicken stock
2 tsp. salt	3 c. milk
1 tsp. baking powder	3 tbsp. butter
1 c. shortening	3 c. cubed cooked chicken
1 egg, lightly beaten	3 hard-boiled eggs, sliced

Combine 3 cups flour, 1 teaspoon salt and baking powder in a bowl and cut in shortening. Stir in the egg and just enough ice water to form a stiff dough. Roll out 2/3 of the mixture on a floured surface and place in a deep pie pan. Pour the chicken stock and milk into a saucepan. Mix 3 tablespoons flour with small amount of milk mixture. Heat remaining milk mixture until scalded and stir in flour mixture. Add remaining salt and the butter and cook until thickened, stirring constantly. Place alternate layers of chicken and eggs in the crust and add enough sauce to cover. Roll out remaining pastry and place over chicken mixture. Bake at 425 degrees until lightly browned. Serve remaining sauce with pie.

Mrs. R. C. Bouse, Jr., Port Bolivar, Texas

CHICKEN AND DUMPLING POTPIE

1 chicken, disjointed	2 tsp. baking powder
2 1/4 c. flour	1/4 c. shortening
1 tsp. salt	Milk
Pepper to taste	

Cook the chicken in boiling water until tender. Remove chicken from broth and place in a baking dish. Mix 1/4 cup flour, 1/2 teaspoon salt and pepper with enough cold water to make a smooth paste and stir enough into boiling broth to thicken. Pour over chicken until nearly covered. Sift remaining flour, baking powder and remaining salt together 3 times and place in a bowl. Cut in shortening. Stir in enough milk to make a medium stiff dough. Drop by spoonfuls into baking dish to cover chicken. Bake at 350 degrees for about 25 minutes.

Mrs. Harvey L. Curlee, Yorktown, Virginia

MAKE-AHEAD CHICKEN PIE

2 fryers, disjointed	8 peppercorns
3 c. cold water	1/4 tsp. leaf thyme
1 med. onion, sliced	1/4 c. butter or margarine
3 celery tops	1/2 c. flour
1 bay leaf	1 c. light cream
2 tsp. monosodium glutamate	Cheese Pastry Cutouts
2 tsp. salt	

Place the chickens in a kettle. Add the water, onion, celery tops, bay leaf, monosodium glutamate, salt, peppercorns and thyme and bring to a boil. Reduce heat and cover tightly. Simmer for 45 minutes. Remove chicken from broth and strain the broth. Cool the chicken and broth. Remove chicken from bones and dice. Melt the butter in a saucepan and remove from heat. Stir in the flour. Stir in 3 cups chicken broth gradually, then add the cream. Cook over medium heat, stirring constantly, until mixture thickens and comes to a boil. Remove from heat and add the chicken. Turn into a 13 x 9 x 2-inch shallow casserole and refrigerate overnight. Bake at 375 degrees for 55 minutes. Top with Cheese Pastry Cutouts and bake for 5 minutes longer.

Cheese Pastry Cutouts

1 recipe pie pastry	8 peppercorns
1/2 c. grated Cheddar cheese	

Mix the pastry with the cheese. Roll out 1/4 inch thick on a floured surface and make 8 chicken cutouts with cookie cutter. Place peppercorns on cutouts for eyes and place on a baking sheet. Bake at 425 degrees for 12 to 15 minutes or until lightly browned. Store in covered container until ready to place on casserole.

CHICKEN PIE WITH SWEET POTATO CRUST

3 c. diced cooked chicken	1 1/2 tsp. salt
1 c. diced cooked carrots	1/8 tsp. pepper
6 sm. white onions, cooked	1 tsp. baking powder
1 tbsp. chopped parsley	1 c. cold mashed sweet potatoes
1 c. milk	1/3 c. melted butter
1 c. chicken broth	1 egg, well beaten
1 1/4 c. flour	

Place alternate layers of chicken, carrots, onions and parsley in a casserole. Combine the milk and chicken broth. Place 1/4 cup flour in a saucepan and add milk mixture slowly. Place over low heat and cook until thickened, stirring constantly. Season with salt and pepper and pour over chicken mixture. Sift remaining flour with baking powder and remaining salt into a bowl. Add the potatoes, butter and egg and mix well. Roll out on a floured surface and place over chicken mixture. Bake at 350 degrees for about 40 minutes.

Myra B. Olson, Baton Rouge, Louisiana

New England Chicken Pie (page 141)

CHICKEN-TAMALE PIE

1 3-lb. stewing hen	12 stuffed olives, sliced
1 c. cornmeal	2 tsp. salt
1 c. tomato paste	Pepper to taste
1 onion, chopped	Cayenne pepper to taste
1 green pepper, chopped	1 c. grated cheese

Cook the chicken in boiling, salted water until tender. Remove chicken from broth and cool. Remove skin and discard. Remove chicken from bones. Cook the broth until reduced to 4 cups. Add the cornmeal and cook to a mush, stirring frequently. Cool and line a baking dish with mush. Place chicken over mush. Combine remaining ingredients except cheese and place over chicken. Sprinkle with cheese. Bake for 1 hour in 325-degree oven. Increase temperature to 425 degrees and bake until brown.

Mrs. Thomas J. Craig, Petersburg, Virginia

CHICKEN WITH CHEESE SWIRLS

3 tbsp. chopped onion	2 c. milk
3 tbsp. chopped green pepper	2 c. cubed cooked chicken
1/3 c. butter	1 recipe biscuit dough
1/3 c. flour	1/2 c. grated Cheddar cheese
1 tsp. salt	1/2 c. chopped pimento
1 can cream of mushroom soup	

Preheat oven to 425 degrees. Brown the onion and green pepper in butter in a saucepan. Add flour and salt and blend thoroughly. Add the soup and milk and cook, stirring, until smooth and thickened. Add the chicken and pour into an 8 x 12-inch baking dish. Roll out dough on a floured surface 1/4 inch thick. Sprinkle cheese and pimento on dough and roll as for jelly roll. Slice 1/2 inch thick and place on chicken mixture. Bake for 25 to 30 minutes. 6-8 servings.

Mrs. W. G. Warmack, Florence, Alabama

NEW ENGLAND CHICKEN PIE

1 3-lb. chicken	1/2 tsp. dillweed
1 med. onion, sliced	1/4 tsp. coarsely ground
1 c. boiling water	pepper
2 tsp. salt	1/4 lb. mushrooms, sliced
1/4 lb. diced ham	1 c. cooked peas
2 tbsp. butter or margarine	3/4 c. vegetable shortening
Flour	1/4 c. cold water
3/4 c. milk	1 egg, slightly beaten

Place the chicken in a shallow roasting pan. Add the onion, boiling water and 1 teaspoon salt. Bake in 350-degree oven for 1 hour or until chicken is tender. Remove chicken from pan and reserve stock and onion. Cool the chicken. Remove chicken from bones and slice. Place the chicken and ham in 9-inch pie pan. Melt the butter in a saucepan and stir in 2 tablespoons flour. Add reserved stock and onion and the milk and cook over medium heat, stirring constantly, for 1 minute or until sauce thickens and boils. Stir in the dillweed, pepper and mushrooms and cover. Simmer for 5 to 7 minutes. Stir in the peas and pour over chicken mixture. Cool. Combine 2 cups sifted flour and remaining salt in a bowl. Cut in the shortening until mixture resembles coarse meal. Sprinkle with the cold water and mix with a fork. Shape into a ball. Roll out on a lightly floured surface 2 inches larger than inverted pie plate and trim edge even. Cut a strip about 1 inch wide from pastry edge. Brush rim of pie plate with water and fit pastry strip on rim, pressing to seal. Place remaining pastry on pie plate and press edge of pastry to strip to seal. Make a series of cuts in the edge of the pastry all around the pie, holding a sharp knife horizontally. Flute the edge by forming indentations between thumb and forefinger with the edge of a knife. Decorate with leaves cut from scraps of pastry, if desired. Score top to allow steam to escape and brush top with egg. Bake in 400-degree oven for 45 minutes or until crust is golden brown.

LITTLE CHICKEN PIES

1/4 c. butter	1 1/2 c. cooked peas
1/4 c. flour	1 1/2 c. cooked carrots
2 tsp. salt	1 c. sifted flour
1/4 tsp. pepper	1/3 c. shortening
2 c. chicken stock	1 tsp. celery seed
2/3 c. cream	1/2 tsp. paprika
2 c. diced cooked chicken	2 tbsp. water

Preheat oven to 425 degrees. Melt the butter in a saucepan and remove from heat. Blend in flour, 1 1/2 teaspoons salt and pepper. Stir in the chicken stock and cream and bring to a boil, stirring constantly. Cook for 1 minute. Place equal portions of chicken in 6 small casseroles. Mix the peas and carrots and place 1/2 cup pea mixture in each casserole. Pour sauce over peas and carrots. Mix the flour and remaining salt in a bowl and cut in the shortening. Add the celery seed and paprika. Sprinkle with water and mix well. Form into a smooth ball and roll out 1/4 inch thick on a floured surface. Cut into circles to cover top of casseroles and place on casseroles. Bake for 25 minutes or until brown.

Mrs. Kevin Gardner, Columbia, South Carolina

CHICKEN-CORNMEAL PIE

2 stewing chickens
2 cloves of garlic
4 or 5 Chili Pequins
1 c. butter
1 c. flour
1 lge. can tomatoes

1 can tomato sauce
1 tbsp. cumin powder
2 tbsp. Spanish seasoning
1 1/2 c. yellow cornmeal
1 pt. black pitted olives

Place the chickens in a kettle and add the garlic, Chili Pequins and enough water to cover. Bring to a boil and reduce heat. Simmer until chickens are tender. Remove chickens from broth and cool. Strain the broth and chill. Remove fat from broth and reserve broth. Remove chicken from bones. Melt the butter in a saucepan and stir in the flour. Add the tomatoes and tomato sauce and mix well. Add enough reserved broth for thick sauce and cook until thick, stirring constantly. Add the cumin powder and Spanish seasoning. Mix the cornmeal with 1 cup water in a large saucepan. Bring 4 cups reserved broth to a boil and stir into cornmeal mixture. Cook for 15 to 20 minutes or until of medium consistency, stirring frequently. Mix the chicken, olives and tomato mixture and place in a large baking pan. Place cornmeal mixture over top. Bake at 400 degrees until brown. 8 servings.

Mrs. Lucille Neville, Meridian, Mississippi

CHICKEN BISCUIT

6 tbsp. margarine
6 tbsp. flour
3 c. milk or chicken stock
3 c. cubed cooked chicken
3/4 c. cooked peas

3/4 c. diced cooked carrots
3/4 c. diced cooked celery
1 tsp. salt
1 recipe unbaked biscuits

Melt the margarine in a saucepan. Add the flour and stir until blended. Add the milk and cook until thickened. Add the chicken, vegetables and salt and pour into a greased casserole. Cover with biscuits. Bake at 400 degrees until biscuits are brown. Cheese and parsley may be added to biscuit dough.

Mrs. Albert Steffen, Cold Spring, Kentucky

COUNTRY PIE

2 tbsp. butter
2 tbsp. flour
1 c. tomato juice
Salt and pepper
1/2 c. bread crumbs
1/8 tsp. onion salt

2 c. ground cooked chicken
1 c. packaged precooked rice
1/4 c. grated mild Cheddar
  cheese
3/4 c. water

Melt the butter in a saucepan and stir in flour. Add the tomato juice slowly, then add salt and pepper to taste. Cook over low heat until thick, stirring constantly. Place half the mixture in a bowl. Add the bread crumbs, onion salt, 1 teaspoon salt, 1/8 teaspoon pepper and chicken and mix well. Press on bottom and side of greased 9-inch pie plate. Combine remaining tomato sauce with the rice, cheese,

1/2 teaspoon salt and water and place in chicken mixture. Cover with foil. Bake at 350 degrees for 1 hour or until rice is tender, adding water, if needed.

Mrs. Matthew Searl Mills, Clemmens, North Carolina

THYMELY CHICKEN PUFF

1 c. flour	2/3 c. chicken stock
1 tsp. salt	5 eggs, separated
1 tsp. dried parsley flakes	2 tbsp. lemon juice
1 tsp. ground thyme	1 1/2 c. finely chopped
1/4 tsp. pepper	cooked chicken
1 c. evaporated milk	Nippy Cheese Sauce

Preheat oven to 325 degrees. Combine the flour, salt, parsley flakes, thyme and pepper in a medium mixing bowl. Stir in the evaporated milk, chicken stock, lightly beaten egg yolks and lemon juice. Add the chicken and blend well. Beat the egg whites in a large mixing bowl until stiff but not dry. Fold in chicken mixture and turn into a well-greased 2-quart casserole. Bake for 1 hour. Serve immediately with Nippy Cheese Sauce.

Nippy Cheese Sauce

1 tbsp. butter	Dash of pepper
1 tbsp. flour	1 c. evaporated milk
1/2 tsp. dry mustard	1 c. shredded American process
1/4 tsp. salt	cheese

Melt the butter in a small saucepan and remove from heat. Blend in the flour, mustard, salt and pepper. Stir in the milk gradually and cook over medium heat, stirring constantly, until thickened. Stir in cheese until melted and serve hot.

Thymely Chicken Puff (above)

HERBED CHICKEN PIE

1/4 c. flour	1 sm. onion, minced
1 1/2 c. milk	1 tsp. salt
1 can cream of chicken soup	2 tbsp. minced pimento
1 5-oz. can boned chicken, chopped	2 tbsp. butter
	1 recipe pastry for 2-crust pie
1 sm. can peas and carrots	1/4 tsp. thyme

Place the flour in a saucepan and stir in the milk slowly. Add the soup and mix well. Add the chicken, peas and carrots, onion, salt, pimento and butter and heat to boiling point, stirring constantly. Pour into pastry-lined pie pan. Sprinkle with thyme and cover with top crust. Cut slits for steam to escape. Bake at 400 degrees for 30 to 40 minutes or until brown.

Mrs. A. F. Fanning, Tahlequah, Oklahoma

OLD-TIME CHICKEN PIE

1 8 1/2-oz. can English peas	4 tbsp. butter
1 4-oz. can sliced mushrooms	1 c. chicken broth
1 c. chopped celery	1/2 c. milk
5 tbsp. flour	2 hard-boiled eggs, chopped
1/4 tsp. pepper	1 2-oz. jar pimentos, chopped
1/2 tsp. salt	2 3/4 c. chopped cooked chicken
1/4 tsp. monosodium glutamate	

Drain the peas and mushrooms and reserve liquids. Combine reserved liquids in a saucepan and bring to a boil. Add the celery and cook until tender. Combine the flour, pepper, salt and monosodium glutamate. Melt the butter in a saucepan and stir in flour mixture. Stir in the broth and milk and cook, stirring constantly, until thickened. Add the eggs, pimentos, mushrooms, peas, chicken and celery and mix well. Pour into greased 10 1/2 x 5 1/2 x 3-inch casserole.

Cheese Crust

1/4 c. shortening	1/4 tsp. baking powder
2 tbsp. boiling water	1/4 tsp. salt
3/4 c. flour	5 tbsp. grated American cheese

Place the shortening in a bowl. Pour in the water and mix well. Cool. Sift the flour, baking powder and salt together and add cheese. Stir into shortening mixture. Shape into a ball and roll out on a floured surface. Place over chicken mixture. Bake at 350 degrees for 45 minutes or until brown. 8-10 servings.

Mrs. Lamar Ross, Monticello, Arkansas

PEPPER POT CHICKEN PIES

1/2 c. margarine or chicken fat	1/4 c. diced celery
1/3 c. flour	1/4 c. cooked peas
2 1/2 c. chicken stock	2 1/2 c. diced cooked chicken

1 1/2 tsp. salt	2 hard-boiled eggs, chopped
3/4 tsp. pepper	1 recipe unbaked biscuits
1/2 tsp. celery seed	

Preheat oven to 425 degrees. Melt the margarine in a saucepan and blend in flour. Stir in the chicken stock and cook until thickened, stirring constantly. Add the vegetables, chicken, seasonings and eggs and turn into a 2-quart casserole. Top with biscuits. Bake for 45 minutes or until done and serve at once. 6-8 servings.

Mrs. Oda Miller, Greenville, Tennessee

SING A SONG OF SIXPENCE PIE

1 2 1/2 to 3-lb. fryer	1/2 c. white wine
1 lge. onion, sliced	Salt and pepper to taste
1/4 c. margarine	Flour
1 chicken bouillon cube	1 recipe pie pastry

Remove chicken from bones and cut in large cubes. Brown with onion in margarine in a large skillet. Add the bouillon cube, enough water to cover, wine, salt and pepper and cover. Simmer for about 30 minutes or until chicken is tender. Mix small amount of flour with enough water to make a thin paste. Bring chicken mixture to a boil and stir in enough flour mixture to thicken. Place in a casserole and cover with pastry. Cut slits in center of pastry to allow steam to escape. Bake at 425 degrees for about 30 minutes or until brown. 6 servings.

Sing a Song of Sixpence Pie (above)

OMELET POTPIE

2 c. diced cooked chicken	1 baked 9-in. pastry shell
3 tbsp. hot water	1 tbsp. chili powder
1 c. celery soup	2 egg yolks
1/2 c. diced cooked carrots	

Combine the chicken, water, soup and carrots and place in pastry shell. Sprinkle with the chili powder. Bake at 375 degrees for 10 minutes. Beat the egg yolks until light and fluffy and pour over pie. Bake for 10 minutes longer.

Sally Knox, Miami, Florida

SOUR CREAM-CHICKEN PIE

Flour	1/2 (scant) c. milk
1/2 tsp. baking powder	1 hen, cooked
1/2 tsp. salt	2 1/2 c. chicken stock
3 tbsp. shortening	1 c. sour cream

Sift 1 cup flour, baking powder and salt together into a bowl and cut in shortening. Stir in the milk. Roll out 1/4 inch thick on a floured surface and cut slits in center. Remove chicken from bones and place in a casserole. Pour the chicken stock into a saucepan and bring to a boil. Mix 5 tablespoons flour with 5 tablespoons water and stir into chicken stock. Cook until thickened, then pour over chicken. Place rolled dough over casserole. Bake in 425-degree oven for 15 minutes. Reduce temperature to 350 degrees and bake for 30 minutes. Pour sour cream through slits in crust and bake for 10 minutes longer. 8 servings.

Mrs. Grady Lowrey, Del Rio, Texas

OLD-FASHIONED CHICKEN PIE

1/3 c. chicken fat	3/4 tsp. salt
1 1/2 c. flour	3/4 tsp. pepper
3 c. chicken broth	4 c. diced cooked chicken
1 c. cream	3 hard-boiled eggs, sliced
1 tbsp. minced onion	1 tbsp. milk
1/2 tsp. ground ginger	

Melt the fat in a saucepan over low heat and blend in 1/2 cup flour. Heat until bubbly. Add the broth and cream and cook until thickened, stirring constantly. Add the onion, ginger, salt and pepper and mix well. Place the chicken and eggs in a 2-quart shallow casserole and pour in sauce. Combine remaining flour and milk and roll out thin on a floured surface. Place over the casserole, and cut slits in center. Seal edges and brush top with additional milk. Bake at 425 degrees for 25 to 30 minutes or until brown. Cooked peas, carrots, potatoes, mushrooms and whole onions may be added, if desired. 6-8 servings.

Mrs. Knox E. Owen, Jackson, Mississippi

GUNTERSVILLE CHICKEN PIE

1 stick margarine	**1 chicken, disjointed**
1 sm. onion, chopped	**1 tsp. salt**
3 tbsp. flour	**1 tsp. pepper**
2 qt. water	**1 recipe biscuit dough**

Melt half the margarine in a kettle. Add onion and cook over low heat until transparent. Add the flour and cook until brown. Stir in the water. Season the chicken with salt and pepper and place in the kettle. Cook until tender. Place half the chicken and broth in a deep pie pan. Roll out half the dough on a floured surface and place on the chicken. Bake at 350 degrees until brown. Spread with half the remaining margarine. Add remaining chicken and dough and spread remaining margarine over dough. Bake until brown. 12 servings.

Roy E. Snow, Guntersville, Alabama

VENTRU CHICKEN PATE

1 5 1/2-lb. stewing chicken	**2 hard-cooked eggs,**
1 med. onion, chopped	**chopped**
Celery tops	**2 pimentos, diced**
3 tsp. salt	**1/4 c. flour**
1/2 tsp. peppercorns	**1 c. cream**
4 c. water	**1/2 c. milk**
1 10-oz. package frozen green	**Corn Bread Topping**
peas	

Place the chicken, onion, several celery tops, salt, peppercorns and water in a kettle and bring to a boil. Reduce heat and cover. Simmer for 2 hours or until chicken is tender. Remove chicken from broth and cool. Strain the broth and chill. Remove fat and reserve. Add enough water to broth to make 2 cups liquid. Remove skin from chicken and discard. Remove chicken from bones and cut in bite-sized pieces. Cook the peas according to package directions and drain. Add to chicken with eggs and pimentos and place in a 12-cup baking dish. Melt 1/4 cup reserved chicken fat in a saucepan and stir in flour. Cook until bubbly. Stir in the broth, cream and milk and cook until thickened, stirring constantly. Cook for 1 minute and stir into chicken mixture. Spread Corn Bread Topping over top. Bake in 425-degree oven for 30 minutes or until corn bread is brown.

Corn Bread Topping

3/4 c. yellow cornmeal	**1/2 tsp. salt**
1/4 c. sifted flour	**1 egg**
1 1/2 tsp. baking powder	**1/2 c. milk**
1 tsp. sugar	**1/4 c. vegetable oil**

Mix the cornmeal, flour, baking powder, sugar and salt in a large bowl. Beat the egg slightly and stir in milk and oil. Add all at once to cornmeal mixture and stir just until mixed.

Mrs. J. L. Mitchell, Richardson, Texas

Oven-Fried Quail and Brussels Sprouts (page 165)

turkey & game birds

When English settlers first ventured into the Southland, they were impressed with the abundance of turkeys and other game birds. Even today, southern forests and marshlands teem with wild turkeys, doves, geese, ducks, grouse, partridge, and other highly prized game. Living in the midst of such abundance, southern homemakers have been inspired to create some of the finest game recipes to be found.

In the section that follows, you'll discover traditional southern dishes like Maryland-Style Wild Duck from the Chesapeake Bay region, where the finest wild ducks in the country are found . . . elegant Roast Wild Goose with Baked Apples, a traditional holiday favorite . . . and Sherried Dove, an old-time southern gourmet treat. Just think how your family and guests will enjoy Dove in Sour Cream . . . Huntsman-Style Partridge . . . or any of the other great recipes you'll find here.

Turkey comes in for its share of attention in this section, too. There is a classic southern recipe for Turkey and Dressing with Gravy, a "must" at holiday time. For an unusual taste treat, enjoy Barbecued Turkey Breast — typically southern in its sharp barbecue flavor and goodness!

These are just some of the recipes you'll find in this section. Only southern homemakers could have invented them . . . and now you, too, can enjoy them.

149

BOULANGERIE TURKEY SALAD

1 1/4 c. mayonnaise	2 c. chopped celery
2 c. diced cooked turkey	2 tsp. lemon juice or vinegar
1/2 c. chopped olives	2 c. crushed potato chips
1/2 c. chopped nuts	2 c. grated cheese
1 c. chopped onions	

Combine all ingredients except potato chips and cheese and place in a casserole. Mix the potato chips and cheese and sprinkle over turkey mixture. Bake at 350 degrees for 30 minutes and serve hot.

Mrs. James F. Carter, Opelika, Alabama

CRANBERRY-TURKEY MOLD

2 tbsp. unflavored gelatin	1 1/2 c. sugar
4 tbsp. cold water	3/4 c. hot water
2 c. hot turkey broth	4 c. cranberries
1 tsp. grated onion	1 stick cinnamon
Salt and pepper to taste	6 cloves
1 c. diced celery	Grated rind of 1 orange
2 c. diced cold turkey	1/2 c. finely diced apple
2 pimentos, chopped	1/2 c. chopped nuts

Soften 1 tablespoon gelatin in 2 tablespoons cold water and dissolve in hot turkey broth. Add the onion and seasonings and chill until slightly thickened. Fold in the celery, turkey and pimentos and pour into a mold. Chill until firm. Mix the sugar and hot water in a saucepan and bring to a boil. Add cranberries, spices and orange rind and cook until cranberry skins pop. Mash through a fine sieve. Soften remaining gelatin in remaining cold water and dissolve in hot cranberry mixture. Chill until thickened and stir in apple and nuts. Pour over gelatin in the mold and chill until firm. Unmold onto lettuce and garnish with mayonnaise, if desired. 6-8 servings.

Mrs. J. B. Nash, Laurel, Mississippi

HOLIDAY BUFFET TURKEY LOAF

1 3-oz. package lime gelatin	1/4 c. chopped green pepper
1 c. boiling water	1/2 c. chopped celery
1 1/2 c. cold water	1 1/2 tbsp. unflavored gelatin
2 tsp. salt	1 c. tomato juice
3 tbsp. vinegar	1 tsp. onion juice
1 c. grated cucumber	2 c. ground cooked turkey

Dissolve the lime gelatin in boiling water in a bowl. Add 3/4 cup cold water, 1 teaspoon salt and vinegar and mix. Chill until slightly thickened. Add the cucumber, green pepper and celery and pour into a mold. Chill until firm. Soften the unflavored gelatin in remaining cold water. Heat the tomato juice in a saucepan. Add the gelatin and stir until dissolved. Chill until slightly thickened. Fold in the onion juice, remaining salt and turkey and place over cucumber layer. Chill until firm. Unmold and garnish with poinsettia flowers of pimento and green pepper.

Mrs. Katherine Brown, Pegram, Tennessee

TURKEY SALAD SANDWICH

1 sm. loaf unsliced bread	8 thick slices turkey
Paprika-Butter	2 ripe avocados
Fresh romaine or lettuce	Lemon juice
leaves	Mayonnaise

Remove crust from bread and slice loaf lengthwise in 4 parts. Spread Paprika-Butter on one side of each slice of bread and place romaine leaves on Paprika-Butter. Cover romaine with turkey. Peel the avocados and remove seeds. Slice avocados in medium-thin slices and sprinkle with lemon juice. Arrange avocado slices over turkey and spread with small amount of mayonnaise. Place each sandwich on an individual serving plate and garnish with parsley sprigs, pimento and ripe olives.

Paprika-Butter

1 1/2 sticks butter	1 1/2 tsp. paprika
2 tsp. minced onion	

Combine 1/2 stick butter, onion and paprika in a small saucepan and cook over low heat for 5 minutes, or until butter is melted, stirring constantly. Strain and discard onion. Stir in remaining butter and mix thoroughly.

Turkey Salad Sandwich (above)

151

TURKEY-GRAPE-PECAN SALAD

1 1/2 c. diced cooked turkey	1/2 c. mayonnaise
1 c. thinly sliced celery	Salt and pepper to taste
1/2 c. green seedless grapes	1/4 c. chopped pecans

Combine the turkey, celery, grapes and mayonnaise in a bowl and season with salt and pepper. Add pecans and toss lightly. Serve on greens or avocado halves brushed with lemon juice, if desired. 6 servings.

Mrs. Robert S. Phillips, Amarillo, Texas

TURKEY-HAM SALAD

2 c. diced cooked turkey	3 tbsp. mayonnaise
1 1/2 c. diced cooked ham	Salt and pepper to taste
1/2 c. sour cream	1 tbsp. capers

Combine all ingredients in a bowl and chill. Serve on salad greens. 6 servings.

Mrs. R. P. Wolfe, Winston-Salem, North Carolina

TURKEY SALAD FOR A CROWD

1 14-lb. turkey	1/4 c. vinegar
Salt to taste	1/4 c. sugar
Celery, cut in lge. pieces	2 qt. diced celery
Onions, quartered	2 qt. seedless green grapes
Parsley	18 hard-cooked eggs, diced
1 pt. heavy cream, whipped	2 c. toasted slivered almonds
1 qt. salad dressing	Lettuce leaves

Season the turkey inside and out with salt and stuff with cut celery, onions and small amount of parsley. Place in a roasting pan and cover. Bake at 325 degrees for 4 hours and 45 minutes or until tender, then cool. Remove turkey from bones and cut in small pieces. Combine the whipped cream, salad dressing, vinegar and sugar and mix well. Chill. Mix turkey with remaining ingredients except lettuce and chill for several hours. Place the turkey mixture on lettuce and serve the whipped cream mixture with the salad. 50 servings.

Mrs. K. T. Stanton, Wilmington, Delaware

TOMATOES STUFFED WITH TURKEY SALAD

6 lge. tomatoes	1 tbsp. steak sauce
1 1/2 c. diced cooked turkey	1 c. cooked whole kernel corn
1/2 c. sliced black olives	Salt to taste
1/2 c. mayonnaise	2 tbsp. butter or margarine

Cut off tomato tops and scoop out pulp. Turn tomatoes upside down and drain. Mix remaining ingredients except butter and fill tomatoes with turkey mixture.

Dot with butter. Broil about 8 inches from heat until lightly browned. 6 servings.

Patricia Williams, Jacksonville, North Carolina

GOLDEN ROAST TURKEY WITH OYSTER STUFFING

3/4 c. chopped onion	1/2 c. chopped parsley
1 c. diced celery	1 10-lb. turkey
3/4 c. butter or margarine	1 sm. onion
1 1/2 tsp. poultry seasoning	1 celery stalk
1 1/2 tsp. salt	3 peppercorns
1/4 tsp. pepper	3 whole cloves
1 pt. oysters	1 bay leaf
7 1/2 c. coarse day-old	Cornstarch
bread crumbs	Melted butter or margarine

Cook the chopped onion and diced celery in the butter in a saucepan until onion is tender. Blend in poultry seasoning, 1/2 teaspoon salt and pepper. Drain the oysters and chop. Toss onion mixture with bread crumbs, oysters and parsley. Remove giblets and neck from turkey and wash. Place in a saucepan and cover with water. Add the small onion, celery stalk, peppercorns, cloves, bay leaf and remaining salt and cover. Cook for about 15 minutes and remove liver. Cook for about 1 hour and 15 minutes longer or until giblets are tender. Drain and reserve broth. Strain reserved broth and pour into a saucepan. Cut giblets in small pieces. Bring broth to a boil and add enough cornstarch mixed with small amount of water to thicken. Add the giblets and heat through. Stuff cavity of turkey with oyster mixture. Any remaining stuffing may be placed in a casserole and baked at 400 degrees for 30 minutes. Roast turkey according to package directions, basting with melted butter. Serve on a platter and garnish with Brussels sprouts and carrots topped with cashew nuts.

Golden Roast Turkey with Oyster Stuffing (above)

153

BAKED TURKEY AND DRESSING

1 10-lb. turkey and giblets	1/2 c. chopped onion
Salt	4 c. dry bread crumbs
Celery tops	4 c. corn bread crumbs
1 1/2 sticks butter	1/2 tsp. pepper
1 c. chopped celery	

Season the turkey with salt and place in a roasting pan. Place several celery tops in cavity of the turkey. Soak large piece of cheesecloth in 1 stick melted butter and place over breast, wings and legs of turkey. Pour 1 cup water into roasting pan. Bake at 350 degrees for 2 hours and 30 minutes to 3 hours, basting occasionally. Melt remaining butter in a saucepan. Add the celery and onion and cook until wilted. Add 1 cup hot water and set aside. Cook the giblets in boiling, salted water until tender. Drain and reserve stock. Mix the bread crumbs, corn bread crumbs, celery mixture, pepper, 1 teaspoon salt and enough reserved stock to moisten. Place in a casserole. Bake in 400-degree oven until lightly browned. Remaining stock and cut-up giblets may be combined and thickened for gravy if desired.

Mrs. Hubert Hiers, West Palm Beach, Florida

TURKEY AND DRESSING WITH GRAVY

1 10 to 12-lb. frozen turkey, thawed	1 tbsp. poultry seasoning
	1 tsp. sage
Salt	1/2 c. diced celery
1 tbsp. margarine	1/2 c. diced onion
4 qt. day-old bread crumbs	1/4 c. diced green pepper
4 c. corn bread crumbs	1 sm. can oysters, drained
1/2 tsp. parsley flakes	1/2 c. melted margarine
1 tsp. pepper	

Rub the turkey with 1 teaspoon salt and margarine and place in a shallow pan. Add 2 cups water and giblets and cover turkey with foil. Bake at 325 degrees for 4 hours to 4 hours and 30 minutes. Drain and reserve 2 cups broth. Remove giblets. Mix the reserved broth, 1 tablespoon salt and remaining ingredients. Place in cavity of turkey, beneath wings and over breast. Shape remaining dressing in balls and place around turkey. Bake at 350 degrees for 1 hour.

Giblet Gravy

2 tbsp. shortening	1/4 tsp. pepper
2 tbsp. flour	2 c. water
1/2 tsp. salt	

Melt the shortening in a saucepan. Add the flour and brown. Add salt, pepper, diced giblets and water and bring to a boil. Reduce heat and simmer until thick. Serve over dressing.

Mrs. Charles R. Jackson, Hopkinsville, Kentucky

ROASTED TURKEY WITH INDIVIDUAL CRANBERRY MOLDS

1 10 to 12-lb. turkey	1/2 c. hot water
Oil or soft shortening	1/4 c. jellied cranberry sauce
1 c. butter or margarine	2 tbsp. prepared mustard

Place turkey, breast side up, on rack in a shallow baking pan and insert meat thermometer in inside thigh muscle next to body. Rub turkey with oil and cover loosely with foil. Mix 1/2 cup butter and hot water in a small saucepan. Bake turkey in 325-degree oven until thermometer reaches 190 degrees, basting every 30 minutes with butter mixture. Combine the cranberry sauce and mustard in a small saucepan. Heat over low heat until cranberry sauce is melted, stirring constantly. Blend in remaining butter. Brush over entire surface of turkey 30 minutes before end of baking time and again 15 minutes later.

Individual Cranberry Molds

1 c. fresh cranberries	3 c. ginger ale
6 naval oranges	1/3 c. sugar
2 pkg. orange gelatin	1/2 c. chopped pecans

Rinse and drain the cranberries. Cut oranges into halves crosswise and scoop out pulp. Remove orange pulp from membranes, reserving 1 1/2 cups. Notch edges of orange shells with a sharp knife. Cut a thin slice from bottom of each orange shell to allow to stand straight. Heat one cup ginger ale. Dissolve the gelatin in hot ginger ale and stir in cold ginger ale. Chill until slightly thickened. Grind the cranberries coarsely and mix with sugar. Fold in pecans and reserved orange pulp, then fold into gelatin. Spoon into twelve 1/2-cup molds and chill until firm. Unmold by dipping into lukewarm water for several seconds. Place cranberry molds in orange cups and place around roasted turkey. Garnish with parsley sprigs.

Roasted Turkey with Individual Cranberry Molds (above)

155

TURKEY PIE WITH SWEET POTATO CRUST

3 c. diced cooked turkey	1 1/8 c. flour
1 c. diced cooked carrots	1 1/2 tsp. salt
6 sm. onions, diced and cooked	1 tsp. baking powder
1 c. turkey dressing	1 c. cold mashed sweet potatoes
1 c. evaporated milk	1/3 c. melted butter
1/2 c. turkey broth	1 egg, well beaten

Place alternate layers of turkey, carrots, onions and dressing in a greased baking dish. Combine the milk and broth. Place 2 tablespoons flour in a saucepan and stir in milk mixture slowly. Cook until thickened, stirring constantly, and add 1 teaspoon salt. Pour over turkey mixture. Sift remaining flour, baking powder and remaining salt together into a bowl and stir in sweet potatoes, butter and egg. Roll out 1/4 inch thick on a floured surface and place over turkey mixture. Bake in 350-degree oven for about 40 minutes.

Martha Rodgers, Faber, Virginia

INDIVIDUAL TURKEY PIES

1/2 c. flour	3/4 c. diced celery
1 tsp. salt	2 diced cooked carrots
1 c. cold turkey stock	2 1/2 c. diced cooked turkey
1 c. hot turkey stock	Chopped onion to taste
3/4 c. cooked peas	1 recipe pie pastry

Mix the flour, salt and cold turkey stock in a saucepan until smooth. Add the hot turkey stock and cook until thickened, stirring constantly. Add the peas and celery and cook for about 10 minutes, stirring occasionally. Remove from heat. Add the carrots, turkey and onion and mix lightly. Place in individual baking dishes and top with pastry. Bake in a 425-degree oven for about 20 minutes.

Mrs. R. E. Williams, Maysville, Kentucky

SURPRISE CASSEROLE

2 c. cubed cooked turkey	1/2 c. milk
1 can cream of mushroom soup	1 5-oz. package egg noodles
1/2 sm. can pimentos, chopped	1/2 c. grated American cheese

Place the turkey in a casserole. Combine the mushroom soup, pimentos and milk and pour over turkey. Cook the noodles according to package directions and mix with turkey mixture. Sprinkle with cheese. Bake in 350-degree oven until lightly browned.

Marguerite Kuhn, Shreveport, Louisiana

SCALLOPED TURKEY

8 slices toast, crumbled	1/4 lb. melted butter or
1/2 onion, chopped	margarine
1/4 c. chopped parsley	Salt and pepper to taste

1 sm. can mushrooms   2 c. turkey stock
4 c. diced cooked turkey

Combine the toast, onion, parsley, butter, salt and pepper in a bowl for dressing. Place 1/3 of the dressing in a greased shallow baking dish and add 1/2 of the mushrooms. Add 1/2 of the turkey and repeat layers, ending with dressing. Pour stock over top. Bake in 350-degree oven until heated through and brown. Two chicken bouillon cubes dissolved in 2 cups hot water may be substituted for turkey stock.

Mrs. M. D. Watson, Edenton, North Carolina

TURKEY AU GRATIN

1 sm. turkey	Chopped parsley to taste
1 green onion, chopped fine	Salt to taste
3 tbsp. butter or margarine	3 tbsp. tomato paste
4 tbsp. flour	2 1/4 c. chicken stock
Dash of cloves	1 1/2 c. macaroni
Dash of thyme	1/2 c. grated Parmesan cheese

Cut the turkey in serving pieces. Saute the onion in 2 tablespoons butter in a skillet until tender. Sprinkle flour over onion and stir well. Add the cloves, thyme, parsley and salt. Place turkey in the skillet and add the tomato paste and chicken stock. Cover. Simmer for about 1 hour or until the turkey is tender. Cook the macaroni according to package directions and drain. Add remaining butter and mix well. Place turkey and sauce in center of a casserole and arrange the macaroni in a ring around edge. Sprinkle Parmesan cheese on the macaroni. Bake at 350 degrees until heated through.

Turkey au Gratin (above)

BREADED TURKEY LOAF

20 slices bread	1 tsp. monosodium glutamate
3 1/2 c. milk	1 can mushroom soup
1 1/2 sticks margarine, melted	3 1/2 c. broth
1 1/2 tbsp. grated onion	6 eggs, beaten
Salt and pepper to taste	1 6-lb. turkey, cooked

Soak the bread in milk in a bowl for 5 minutes, then mash. Add the margarine, onion, salt, pepper, monosodium glutamate, soup and broth and mix well. Stir in eggs. Remove turkey from bones and cut in small pieces. Stir into bread mixture and place in a large baking dish. Bake for about 1 hour in a 350-degree oven. May be served with gravy or mushroom sauce. 20 servings.

Mrs. O. B. Alston, Columbus, Georgia

TURKEY-GREEN PEPPER CASSEROLE

3 tbsp. chopped onion	1 can cream of chicken soup
1/2 c. chopped green peppers	1 c. chopped cooked turkey
3 tbsp. margarine	1 tbsp. lemon juice
1 tsp. salt	1 pkg. refrigerator biscuits
6 tbsp. flour	1/3 c. grated cheese
1 1/2 c. milk	

Preheat oven to 450 degrees. Brown the onion and green peppers in margarine in a saucepan and stir in salt and flour. Add the milk and soup and cook until thick, stirring occasionally. Add the turkey and lemon juice and pour into a greased baking dish. Roll out biscuits to form a rectangle 1/4 inch thick. Sprinkle with cheese and roll as for jelly roll. Slice 1/2 inch thick and place on casserole. Bake for 15 minutes. Reduce temperature to 425 degrees and bake until swirls are brown. 6 servings.

Mrs. Mildred Tate, Lobelville, Tennessee

TURKEY SPAGHETTI

1/2 lb. spaghetti	1/2 c. minced celery
4 c. diced cooked turkey	1 sm. onion, grated
1/2 c. minced pimento	Salt and pepper to taste
2 c. undiluted mushroom soup	3 c. grated sharp Cheddar
1 c. turkey broth or water	cheese

Break the spaghetti in 2-inch pieces and cook according to package directions. Drain well. Add remaining ingredients except 1 cup cheese and mix well. Place in a greased large casserole and sprinkle remaining cheese over top. Cover. Bake in 350-degree oven for 1 hour. Minced green pepper may be substituted for pimento.

Mrs. M. W. Sherman, Denton, Texas

TURKEY TETRAZZINI

1 c. turkey broth	4 c. diced cooked turkey
1 can cream of chicken soup	1/2 c. sliced mushrooms
1 can cream of mushroom soup	1/2 c. grated Parmesan cheese
2 c. grated process cheese	Paprika to taste
6 c. cooked spaghetti	

Mix the broth and soups and stir in process cheese. Mix with the spaghetti, turkey and mushrooms and turn into a greased 7 1/2 x 12-inch shallow baking dish. Sprinkle with Parmesan cheese and paprika. Bake in 350-degree oven for about 30 minutes or until brown and bubbly. Milk may be substituted for part of the broth. 8-10 servings.

Ann Elsie Schmetzer, Madisonville, Kentucky

ROAST TURKEY ROLL WITH STUFFING BALLS

1 4 1/2 to 5 1/2-lb. frozen boneless turkey roll	1 c. chicken broth
2 tsp. angostura aromatic bitters	1/4 c. chopped parsley
	1/2 c. minced celery
2 8-oz. packages stuffing mix	1/2 c. chopped pecans
2 eggs, well beaten	1 c. melted butter or margarine

Bake the turkey roll according to package directions. Combine remaining ingredients except 1/2 cup butter and shape in eighteen 1 1/2-inch balls. Spread half the remaining butter in a shallow baking pan. Place stuffing balls side by side in a single layer in pan and brush with remaining butter. Bake in oven at same time as turkey roll is baking. Spoon pan drippings from turkey roll over stuffing balls.

Roast Turkey Roll with Stuffing Balls (above)

OUTDOOR CHARCOAL-BARBECUED TURKEY

Barbecue salt   1 8 to 10-lb. turkey

Rub 1 to 2 tablespoons barbecue salt on inside of turkey. Tie the wings securely over breast and tie the drumsticks together or tuck in the band of skin at end of the turkey. Insert spit rod in front of tail and run diagonally through breast bone. Fasten tightly with spit forks at both ends and tie securely with twine. Test for balance and readjust until satisfactory. Rub barbecue salt over outside of the turkey as generously as the skin will hold, then insert meat thermometer into thickest part of breast or thigh. Cook over coals for 3 hours and 30 minutes to 4 hours or to 185 degrees on meat thermometer. Add flavor, if desired, by tossing orange or lemon rind, garlic buds, basil, oregano, tarragon or freshly ground pepper on coals during last 10 minutes.

Photograph for this recipe on cover.

FRIED TURKEY

1 egg, beaten   Fine cracker crumbs
1 tbsp. water   Pepper to taste (opt.)
8 to 10 slices white turkey,   Cooking oil
  1/2 in. thick

Mix the egg and water in a bowl and dip turkey slices into egg mixture. Dip in cracker crumbs and sprinkle with pepper. Fry in oil in a skillet over medium heat until lightly browned.

Mrs. Lee Day, Pine Bluff, Arkansas

SWEET AND SOUR TURKEY

1 No. 2 can pineapple chunks   1/2 tsp. salt
1/3 c. vinegar   2 1/2 c. diced cooked turkey
1/4 c. brown sugar   3/4 c. green peppers, cut in
2 tbsp. cornstarch   1 1/2-in. strips
1 tbsp. soy sauce   1/4 c. thinly sliced onion

Drain the pineapple and reserve juice. Add enough water to reserved juice to make 1 cup liquid. Combine pineapple liquid, vinegar, brown sugar, cornstarch, soy sauce and salt in a saucepan. Cook over low heat until thickened and clear, stirring constantly, then remove from heat. Add the turkey and let stand for 10 minutes. Place the green peppers in boiling water to cover and let stand for 5 minutes. Drain well. Mix the green peppers, onion and pineapple with turkey mixture and heat through. Serve over rice. 4-6 servings.

Mrs. Anita Darnell, Greenville, Texas

PINEAPPLE-GLAZED ROCK CORNISH HENS

4 Rock Cornish hens   Salt and cracked pepper
1/4 c. dry white wine   to taste

Wild Rice Stuffing
1/4 c. melted butter
2 8 1/2-oz. cans pineapple
   slices

1/2 c. chicken broth
2 tbsp. sugar
1/4 tsp. ginger
1 tsp. cornstarch

Rub cavity of hens with wine, salt and pepper and fill loosely with Wild Rice Stuffing. Skewer openings. Place remaining stuffing in a casserole and cover. Brush hens with some of the butter and place, breast side up, in a shallow baking pan. Drain the pineapple and reserve 1/2 cup syrup. Mix 1/4 cup reserved syrup with the chicken broth and pour over hens. Bake hens and stuffing at 350 degrees for about 1 hour, basting hens every 15 minutes with remaining butter and pan drippings. Top each hen with a pineapple slice. Mix the sugar, ginger and cornstarch with remaining reserved syrup and spoon over hens. Place remaining pineapple slices in baking pan. Remove casserole from oven. Increase temperature to 400 degrees and bake for about 15 minutes longer, or until hens are glazed, basting occasionally. Serve pan liquid as sauce.

Wild Rice Stuffing

1 c. washed wild rice
1/4 c. butter
1 1/2 c. chicken broth
1 tsp. salt
6 green onions, chopped

1 c. chopped celery
1/2 c. chopped toasted almonds
1 8-oz. can sliced mushrooms
1/2 tsp. marjoram
1/8 tsp. nutmeg

Soak the rice in hot water to cover for 1 hour. Drain and dry on paper towels. Saute in the butter in a saucepan until golden. Add the chicken broth and salt and cover tightly. Simmer for about 25 minutes or until tender. Add the green onions, celery, almonds, mushrooms, marjoram and nutmeg.

Pineapple-Glazed Rock Cornish Hens (page 160)

161

LIME-GLAZED CORNISH HEN

4 1 1/4-lb. frozen Rock Cornish hens	1/4 c. lime juice
1/2 c. melted butter	2 tsp. soy sauce
2 tbsp. brown sugar	2 tsp. salt

Thaw the hens according to package directions. Mix the butter, brown sugar, lime juice and soy sauce. Rub cavities of hens with salt and brush with half the butter mixture. Fasten wings to hens with skewers. Place hens, breast side up, on rack in shallow roasting pan and brush with remaining butter mixture. Roast according to package directions, basting frequently with drippings.

Mrs. H. B. Rainville, Spartanburg, South Carolina

DOVE IN SOUR CREAM

12 dove	3 or 4 slices bacon
Salt and pepper to taste	Beef or chicken stock or water
Flour	1 c. sour cream
Oil or butter	

Season the dove with salt and pepper and roll in flour. Brown lightly in oil in a skillet. Place bacon in a baking dish and place dove on bacon. Pour small amount of stock into baking dish and cover. Bake in 350-degree oven for 1 hour. Pour sour cream over dove and bake for 10 minutes longer.

Mrs. W. C. Lindley, Phoenix, Arizona

SHERRIED DOVE

6 dove	1 stick butter
Salt and pepper to taste	2 c. boiling water
Flour	1/2 c. dry sherry

Season the dove with salt and pepper and dredge with flour. Melt the butter in a heavy iron skillet. Add the dove and cook until brown. Add the boiling water and sherry and cover skillet. Bake in 350-degree oven for about 1 hour. 6 servings.

Mrs. Robert H. Dunlap, Austell, Georgia

MARYLAND-STYLE WILD DUCK

2 wild ducks	1 piece of ham fat, 4 in. square
1 lge. onion, chopped	
Salt to taste	

Place the ducks in a Dutch oven and add enough water to cover. Add the onion, salt and ham fat and cook until ducks are tender. Drain off liquid and discard onion and ham fat. Place ducks in the Dutch oven, breast side down. Bake at 450 degrees until browned.

Charlotte A. Sterling, Crisfield, Maryland

DUCK WITH POTATO DRESSING

8 c. ground potatoes	1/2 tsp. nutmeg
2 c. fresh minced parsley	2 c. water
2 c. ground celery	1 8 1/2-lb. duck
Salt and pepper to taste	

Mix first 6 ingredients in a saucepan and cover. Cook until potatoes are done, stirring frequently. Stuff duck with dressing and place in a roasting pan, breast side up. Place remaining dressing around duck. Bake at 450 degrees for 20 minutes. Reduce temperature to 350 degrees and bake until duck is done, adding hot water, if necessary. 8-10 servings.

Anna S. Harding, Houston, Texas

FLORIDA-STYLE WILD DUCK

2 2 to 2 1/2-lb. wild ducks	3/4 tsp. dry mustard
6 bacon slices	1/2 tsp. ground ginger
1 6-oz. can frozen orange	1/2 tsp. salt
juice concentrate, thawed	1 tbsp. cornstarch
1 garlic clove	1 c. water

Tie the legs and wings of the ducks close to body and place ducks in a shallow baking pan, breast side up. Place bacon over ducks. Roast in 450-degree oven for 20 to 25 minutes. Reduce temperature to 325 degrees and bake until ducks are tender. Combine undiluted orange concentrate, garlic, mustard, ginger and salt in a small saucepan and heat to boiling point. Brush over ducks generously and roast for 10 minutes longer. Mix the cornstarch with small amount of the water and stir into remaining orange sauce. Add remaining water and stir over low heat until thickened. Serve with ducks. 4 servings.

Florida-Style Wild Duck (above)

Game Birds Naranja (below)

GAME BIRDS NARANJA

6 pheasant	3 green onions, minced
Salt and pepper	3/4 tsp. dried tarragon leaves
Sliced salt pork or bacon	6 tbsp. currant jelly
6 to 8 oranges	1/4 tsp. dry mustard
3 tbsp. butter or margarine	

Tie the legs and wings close to body of each pheasant with string. Season pheasant with salt and pepper to taste. Cover breasts completely with slices of salt pork and tie in place with string. Place pheasant in a roasting pan. Roast at 425 degrees for 30 minutes. Wash the oranges. Remove very thin orange-colored top of the rind from 1 orange with a potato peeler and cut in fine pieces with scissors to make 3 tablespoons. Cut off peel of 3 or 4 oranges in circular motion, cutting deep enough to remove white membrane. Go over oranges again to remove any remaining white membrane. Cut along side of each dividing membrane from outside to middle of core and remove section by section, over bowl, to retain juice from oranges. Drain and measure 1 1/2 cups orange sections. Squeeze juice from remaining oranges and add to juice in bowl to make 1 1/4 cups juice. Melt the butter in a large skillet. Add onions and tarragon and cook for 2 to 3 minutes. Add the orange juice, shredded peel, currant jelly, mustard and 1/4 teaspoon salt and bring to a boil, stirring constantly. Remove pheasant from oven and remove salt pork. Place pheasant in the skillet with sauce and cover. Simmer for 15 to 20 minutes, then remove pheasant to a platter. Add orange sections to sauce and heat through. Serve with pheasant.

ROAST WILD GOOSE WITH BAKED APPLES

1 8-lb. goose	2 tbsp. fat
2 c. bread crumbs	1/4 tsp. sage
1 chopped onion	1 tsp. salt

Pepper to taste
8 apples

1/4 c. brown sugar
3 cooked sweet potatoes, mashed

Place the goose in a kettle of boiling water and simmer for 1 hour. Remove from kettle and wipe dry. Combine the bread crumbs, onion, fat, sage, salt and pepper in a bowl and stuff the goose. Place in a roasting pan. Roast at 500 degrees for 15 minutes. Reduce temperature to 350 degrees and roast for about 3 hours. Wash and core apples and sprinkle with brown sugar. Stuff with sweet potatoes. Place in oven with the goose and bake until tender. Serve hot with goose. 8 servings.

Mrs. E. H. Barksdale, Nashville, Tennessee

OVEN-FRIED QUAIL AND BRUSSELS SPROUTS

12 quail
1 1/2 c. sauterne
2 10-oz. packages frozen
   Brussels sprouts
4 eggs, beaten
1/2 c. milk

1 1/2 c. fine dry bread crumbs
2 tbsp. salt
1 tsp. cracked pepper
2 tbsp. chervil
2/3 c. butter or margarine

Tie legs of the quail together and place quail in a shallow dish. Pour the sauterne over quail and marinate in refrigerator for 12 hours, turning occasionally. Thaw the Brussels sprouts and cut in half. Drain the quail and dry thoroughly. Combine the eggs and milk in a bowl. Mix the bread crumbs, salt, pepper and chervil in a bowl. Dip quail in egg mixture, then in bread crumb mixture. Dip the Brussels sprouts in egg mixture, then in bread crumb mixture. Saute quail in butter in a skillet until golden brown on all sides and remove from skillet. Saute Brussels sprouts in same skillet until golden brown. Arrange quail and Brussels sprouts in a large, shallow baking dish and cover. Bake in 400-degree oven for 20 minutes or until quail are tender. 6 servings.

Photograph for this recipe on page 148.

HUNTSMAN-STYLED PARTRIDGE

2 or 3 young partridge
Seasoned flour
7 oz. brandy or rum
1 sm. onion, diced

2 carrots, cut in sticks
1 tsp. mixed seasonings
1 c. consomme
1 can mushrooms

Cut the partridge in serving pieces and dredge with seasoned flour. Brown in small amount of fat in a skillet. Pour brandy over partridge and ignite. Let flame die down, then add onion, carrot sticks and seasonings. Mix with partridge, scraping browned bits from bottom of skillet. Add the consomme and mushrooms and cover. Simmer for 45 minutes or until partridge are tender. 4-6 servings.

Mrs. R. C. Scott, Goldsboro, North Carolina

Pineapple-Chicken Teriyaki (Japan) (page 183)

poultry recipes

WITH A FOREIGN FLAVOR

Versatile poultry is a favorite, not just with southern women but with women from many lands who blend chicken with fruits, vegetables, and seasonings of their native lands to create palate-pleasing dishes. Many of these dishes feature sharply flavored sauces, the bite of herbs and spices, or other distinctive flavors which mix so well with chicken.

Especially creative *Southern Living* homemakers have gone outside their own region and explored some of these foreign dishes. As a result, many poultry recipes of European, Middle Eastern, African, and even Asian origin have found their way into southern cuisine.

From the Congo came a recipe which soon was known as Chicken Pili-pili. Sweet and Sour Chicken brings with it all the aromatic flavor of the Orient. Poulet Amandine was borrowed from France, and Chicken Nuevo Laredo is a traditional Mexican dish. Every one of these recipes has been adapted for American taste by a southern homemaker who wanted to bring variety into her family's meals. Now these recipes are gathered into one delightful section, awaiting your cooking pleasure.

As you turn through these pages, imagine your family's excited surprise as they discover an Eastern meal . . . a French one . . . or an international dinner on your dining table. Yes, this is a section you'll rely on for wonderfully different meals.

167

CHICKEN IN WINE WITH WALNUTS (ALBANIA)

1 4 to 5-lb. chicken	1 lb. shelled walnuts
1 tsp. salt	4 tbsp. butter
1/2 tsp. pepper	2 tbsp. flour
1 c. white cooking wine	Rice
1 c. water	

Season the chicken with salt and pepper and place in a large baking pan. Add the wine and water and cover. Bake at 325 degrees for 2 hours or until chicken is tender. Remove chicken from baking pan and cut into serving pieces. Reserve broth. Crush the walnuts in a blender or grind. Melt the butter in a 12-inch skillet over low heat. Stir in the flour and cook, stirring constantly, until flour is brown. Add the walnuts and 2 cups reserved chicken broth gradually and mix well. Add the chicken, coating each piece with the sauce, and cook over low heat until sauce is thick. Remove from heat and cover. Let stand for 5 to 10 minutes before serving. Serve with rice. 4 servings.

Mrs. Grady Foshee, Huntsville, Alabama

CHICKEN PILI-PILI (CONGO)

1 c. palm oil	1 sm. pili-pili, chopped
1 fryer, disjointed	2 ripe tomatoes, chopped
1/4 c. chopped onion	2 c. water
1 tsp. salt	1 c. chopped peanuts

Heat the palm oil in an iron skillet. Add the chicken and fry until golden brown. Add the onion, salt, pili-pili, tomatoes and water and cover. Cook for 1 hour or until chicken is tender. Add the peanuts and cook for 10 minutes longer. Serve with rice. Pili-pili is a hot red pepper. Salad oil may be substituted for palm oil. 4 servings.

Mrs. Frank McElroy, LaGrange, Texas

CANTONESE-FRIED CHICKEN (CHINA)

1 2 1/2 to 3 1/2-lb. fryer	6 water chestnuts, sliced
3 tbsp. brown gravy sauce	1 1/2 c. sliced fresh mushrooms
1 1/2 tsp. salt	1 c. chicken broth
1/2 tsp. pepper	1 tbsp. soy sauce
1 1/2 tsp. sugar	1 tbsp. cornstarch
3 tbsp. butter	1 tbsp. water
3 tbsp. shortening	

Cut the chicken in serving pieces and place in a saucepan. Add enough boiling water to cover, brown gravy sauce, 1 teaspoon salt, pepper and 1 teaspoon sugar. Cook over low heat for 15 minutes. Drain and pat dry. Brown chicken in butter and shortening in a skillet until golden brown. Cover and cook over low heat for 20 minutes. Remove from skillet and place on a platter. Pour off all but 3 tablespoons fat from skillet and add water chestnuts, mushrooms, broth, soy sauce and remaining salt and sugar. Cover and simmer for about 5 minutes. Combine the cornstarch and water and stir into vegetable mixture. Cook until thickened. Pour over chicken and garnish with green onions. 4-6 servings.

Ava Lynn Torrence, West Point, Virginia

BUTTON MUSHROOM CHICKEN (CHINA)

3 chicken breasts	3 tbsp. vegetable oil
1 tbsp. cornstarch	1 can button mushrooms
1 tsp. salt	1 slice ginger
1/4 tsp. white pepper	1 clove of garlic
1 tsp. soya sauce	

Remove chicken from bones and shred. Mix with 1 teaspoon cornstarch, 1/2 teaspoon salt, pepper, soya sauce and 2 tablespoons vegetable oil. Drain the mushrooms and reserve 1/4 cup liquid. Stir in remaining cornstarch and salt and pour into a saucepan. Add the mushrooms and cook until thickened, stirring constantly. Chop the ginger and garlic and fry in remaining vegetable oil in a skillet until brown. Add the chicken mixture and cook over high heat for 30 seconds. Pour in mushroom mixture and cook until chicken is just done. Do not overcook. Serve with rice. 4-6 servings.

Mrs. Elizabeth J. Pickett, Marks, Mississippi

CHICKEN AND ALMONDS (CHINA)

3 tbsp. chicken broth	1 tbsp. diced green onion
1/3 tsp. baking powder	1 tbsp. diced green pepper
1 egg white	2 tbsp. diced bamboo shoots
2 tsp. cornstarch	1/2 c. diced celery
4 tsp. sherry	1 tsp. soy sauce
1 c. boned diced chicken breast	1/2 tsp. salt
1 tbsp. shortening	1/2 tsp. sugar
1/2 c. sliced fresh mushrooms	1/2 c. chopped almonds
1 tbsp. sliced ginger	

Mix 2 tablespoons chicken broth, baking powder, egg white, 1 teaspoon cornstarch and 1 tablespoon sherry in a bowl. Add the chicken and marinate for 15 minutes. Melt the shortening in a skillet. Add the chicken mixture and cook, stirring constantly, for 2 to 3 minutes. Add the mushrooms, ginger, onion, green pepper, bamboo shoots and celery and cook for 1 to 2 minutes. Combine remaining chicken broth, cornstarch and sherry with remaining ingredients and add to chicken mixture. Cook for 1 minute longer or until heated through. Serve with fried rice or Chinese noodles. 4-6 servings.

Mrs. Sam Greeley, Macon, Georgia

CHICKEN CURRY (CHINA)

1/2 stick butter	1 tsp. lemon juice
3 to 4 tbsp. flour	1/4 tsp. ground ginger
1 sm. chopped onion	1 c. (about) milk
2 1/2 tsp. curry powder	1 cooked chicken
1/2 tsp. salt	

Melt the butter in a frying pan. Stir in the flour, onion, curry powder and salt and cook until onion is tender. Remove from heat and add the lemon juice and ginger. Place over heat and add milk, stirring constantly. Cook until thickened, stirring frequently. Remove chicken from bones and cut in small pieces. Stir into milk mixture and heat through. Serve over rice with side dishes of crisp bacon, chopped nuts, chopped green onion, bananas, raisins, boiled eggs, toasted coconut and dates.

Mrs. James I. Finley, Durant, Mississippi

CHICKEN ORIENTAL (CHINA)

1 4 to 6-lb. hen, disjointed	1/2 tsp. fresh sliced ginger
1/2 c. shoyu or soy sauce	1/2 tsp. dry mustard
1/4 c. honey	1/2 c. chopped green onion
1 clove of garlic, minced	

Place the chicken in a casserole, skin side down, and cover. Bake at 350 degrees for 2 hours. Pour off 2/3 of the drippings and turn chicken. Mix the shoyu sauce, honey, garlic, ginger and mustard and pour over chicken. Cover and bake for 40 minutes. Remove cover and bake until chicken is lightly browned. Sprinkle green onion over chicken. 10-12 servings.

Mrs. Daisy Massey, Fredericksburg, Texas

CHICKEN WITH VEGETABLES (CHINA)

1 stewing chicken	2 c. shoestring carrots
3 tbsp. bead molasses	2 c. shoestring celery
3 tbsp. soy sauce	1 lge. onion, chopped
3 tbsp. vinegar	1 No. 2 can mixed Chinese
Salt to taste	vegetables
Cornstarch	

Cook the chicken in boiling water until tender. Drain and reserve stock. Cool the chicken. Remove chicken from bones and cut in bite-sized pieces. Mix the molasses, soy sauce, vinegar and salt with reserved stock in a saucepan and bring to a boil. Add enough cornstarch mixed with small amount of water to thicken. Add the chicken, carrots, celery and onion and cook until vegetables are tender-crisp. Add mixed vegetables and heat through. Serve over noodles. 10-12 servings.

Mrs. Fred Hathorn, Crowley, Louisiana

CHICKEN-NOODLE DISH (CHINA)

1 can Chinese noodles	2 cans mushroom soup
2 c. diced cooked chicken	1 soup can milk
1 sm. can water chestnuts	1/4 c. slivered almonds
1 c. diced celery	1 sm. can broiled mushrooms
1/2 sm. onion, chopped	

Combine the first 5 ingredients in a large casserole. Mix the soup and milk in a saucepan and heat through. Pour over the casserole and sprinkle with almonds. Add the mushrooms. Bake at 350 degrees for 30 minutes. 4-6 servings.

Mrs. Jack Farmer, Niceville, Florida

CHICKEN WITH PINEAPPLE (CHINA)

1 3 1/2 lb. chicken	1 tbsp. wine or vinegar (opt.)
1 tsp. salt	1/4 c. water
1 tsp. soya sauce	1 can pineapple tidbits
1/4 tsp. pepper	1 tsp. sugar
1/2 tsp. monosodium glutamate	1 tsp. cornstarch
4 tbsp. cooking oil	1 tbsp. sesame seed
1/2 tsp. minced garlic	

Remove chicken from bones and cut in strips. Mix the salt, soya sauce, pepper, monosodium glutamate and 1 tablespoon oil in a bowl. Stir in the chicken and marinate for 10 minutes. Cook the garlic and chicken mixture in remaining oil in a heavy skillet for 3 minutes, stirring constantly. Sprinkle with wine and cook for 3 minutes, stirring constantly. Add the water and cook for 5 minutes. Drain the pineapple and reserve juice. Add reserved pineapple juice and sugar to chicken mixture and cover. Cook over low heat for 10 minutes. Add pineapple chunks and stir. Cook for 2 minutes. Mix the cornstarch with 1 tablespoon water and stir into chicken mixture. Cook until thickened. Place on lettuce-lined platter and sprinkle with sesame seed. 4-6 servings.

Mrs. William Brown, Nashville, Tennessee

CHICKEN CHOP SUEY (CHINA)

1/2 c. chopped green pepper	1/2 c. chicken broth
1/2 c. chopped onion	2 tbsp. flour
1 1/2 tbsp. butter	1/2 c. blanched slivered
1 c. shredded cooked chicken	almonds, toasted
1 c. chopped celery with leaves	2 tbsp. soy sauce
1 c. canned bean sprouts	1/2 c. sauteed mushrooms

Saute the green pepper and onion in butter in a saucepan for 3 minutes. Add the chicken and cook for 3 minutes longer. Add the celery, bean sprouts and 1/4 cup broth. Mix remaining broth and flour and stir into chicken mixture. Bring to a boil, stirring constantly, then stir in almonds, soy sauce and mushrooms. Serve hot with rice. 8 servings.

Mrs. Doris Starkey, Spur, Texas

GREEN PEPPER AND TOMATO CHICKEN (CHINA)

5 to 6 lb. chicken breasts	4 tbsp. cornstarch
Cooking oil	2 tbsp. soy sauce
2 green peppers, cut in strips	3 or 4 tomatoes
Salt and pepper to taste	1 1/2 c. long grain rice

Cook the chicken breasts in boiling, salted water until tender. Drain and reserve 2 cups broth. Cool chicken. Remove chicken from bones and cut in thin strips. Heat small amount of oil in a frying pan. Add green peppers and cover. Cook over low heat until green peppers are tender. Add the salt, pepper and chicken. Dissolve the cornstarch in small amount of reserved chicken broth. Add remaining broth to the chicken mixture and bring to boiling point. Blend in cornstarch and soy sauce and cook, stirring, until thickened. Cut the tomatoes in wedges and add to chicken mixture. Cook until heated through and serve over rice. 10 servings.

Maude Haynes, Tupelo, Mississippi

ORIENTAL CHICKEN (CHINA)

1/3 c. cornstarch	1 green pepper, cut in strips
2 tsp. paprika	2 tbsp. brown sugar
1 2 1/2-lb. fryer, disjointed	2 tbsp. soy sauce
1/4 c. cooking oil	1/3 c. broken walnuts
1 1-lb. 4-oz. can pineapple	1/4 c. seedless raisins
chunks	3 c. hot cooked rice
1 c. sliced celery	

Mix the cornstarch and paprika in a bag. Add the chicken, 2 or 3 pieces at a time, and shake until coated. Reserve remaining cornstarch mixture. Brown the chicken in hot oil in a skillet over low heat. Cover tightly and cook for about 20 minutes or until almost tender. Drain the pineapple and reserve syrup. Add pineapple, celery and green pepper to chicken mixture and cover. Cook for 5 minutes. Combine 1 tablespoon reserved cornstarch mixture with the brown sugar, soy sauce and 1/4 cup reserved pineapple syrup and stir into chicken mixture. Cover and cook for 10 minutes longer. Stir walnuts and raisins into rice and serve with the chicken mixture. 4-5 servings.

Mrs. Joe Hendrix, Durham, North Carolina

SWEET AND SOUR CHICKEN (CHINA)

1 1 1/2-lb. fryer	2 med. peeled tomatoes, cut in
Salt and pepper to taste	wedges
Flour	1 c. sugar
1 egg, beaten	1 c. distilled vinegar
1 sm. can pineapple chunks	Kitchen Bouquet
1 lge. bell pepper, cut in squares	Sesame seed
Grated rind of 1/4 lemon	

Remove chicken from bones and cut in 3/4-inch chunks. Season with salt and pepper and roll in flour. Mix the egg and 1/4 cup water and dip the chicken in egg mixture. Roll in flour. Fry in deep fat at 350 degrees until light brown. Combine 1 cup water with remaining ingredients except Kitchen Bouquet and sesame seed in a saucepan and bring to a boil. Cook until slightly thickened and add enough Kitchen Bouquet to color brown. Garnish with sesame seed and serve over rice. 4 servings.

Mrs. Dorothy E. Perryman, Alpine, Texas

ROAST DUCK (CHINA)

1 4 to 5-lb. duck	1/8 tsp. whole aniseed
Salt	Soy sauce
2 tbsp. instant minced onion	2 tbsp. honey
1 tbsp. celery flakes	2 tbsp. cider vinegar
1 1/2 tsp. sugar	1 tsp. cornstarch
1/4 tsp. ground cinnamon	

Preheat oven to 325 degrees. Remove excess fat from body and neck cavities of duck and rub inside with salt. Combine the onion, celery flakes, sugar, cinnamon, aniseed, 1/3 cup soy sauce and 1 cup water in a saucepan and bring to boiling point. Tie the duck's neck tightly with string. Rub outside of duck with small amount of soy sauce mixture. Pour remaining soy sauce mixture in cavity of duck and sew opening tightly. Place duck on a rack, breast side up, in a roasting pan. Bake for 20 minutes. Mix 1 cup water, honey, vinegar, 1 1/2 teaspoons soy sauce and 3 1/2 teaspoons salt and brush over duck. Bake for 1 hour and 30 minutes or until duck is tender, basting every 20 minutes with the vinegar mixture. Remove from oven and drain sauce into a saucepan. Heat to boiling point. Mix the cornstarch with small amount of water and stir into sauce. Cook until slightly thickened and serve with duck. 4 servings.

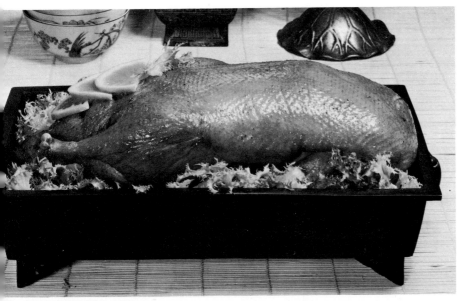

Roast Duck (China) (above)

173

YORKSHIRE CHICKEN (ENGLAND)

1 1/3 c. flour	1 tsp. baking powder
3 tsp. salt	1 1/2 c. milk
1 1/2 tsp. sage	1/4 c. melted butter
1/4 tsp. pepper	3 eggs, well beaten
1 fryer, disjointed	1/4 c. chopped parsley (opt.)
1/4 c. oil	

Combine 1/3 cup flour, 2 teaspoons salt, sage and pepper in a bag and shake chicken in flour mixture. Brown in the oil in a skillet, then place in a casserole. Combine remaining flour and salt and the baking powder and sift into a bowl. Add the milk, butter and eggs and blend well. Add the parsley and blend until smooth. Pour over the chicken. Bake for 1 hour at 350 degrees. 6 servings.

Mrs. Jesse Norman, Greenville, South Carolina

CHICKEN WITH HOT SAUCE (ETHIOPIA)

1 2 1/2-lb. fryer, disjointed	2 tbsp. chili powder
3 c. boiling water	2 tbsp. tomato paste
Juice of 1 lemon	4 tbsp. red wine
1 tsp. salt	1/2 tsp. ginger
6 med. onions, chopped	1/2 tsp. pepper
4 tbsp. fat	6 hard-cooked eggs

Place the chicken in a saucepan and cover with boiling water. Add the lemon juice and salt and cover. Simmer for 10 minutes. Drain and reserve 2 cups broth. Brown the onions lightly in fat in a saucepan, stirring constantly. Add 1 cup reserved chicken broth, chili powder and tomato paste and blend well. Simmer for 4 minutes. Add the wine, ginger, pepper, remaining broth and chicken and simmer for 30 to 40 minutes or until chicken is tender. Pierce each egg several times and add to chicken mixture. Cook for 3 minutes longer. Serve hot with rice or Ethiopian bread. 4-6 servings.

Mrs. Gladys Blake, Louisville, Kentucky

POULET AMANDINE (FRANCE)

3 chicken bouillon cubes	1/2 c. minced celery and
2 c. hot water	leaves
3/4 c. flour	1/4 c. minced parsley
1 1/2 tsp. salt	4 green onions, minced
1 tsp. pepper	1 sm. can mushrooms
1/2 tsp. paprika	1/2 c. slivered almonds
1 fryer, disjointed	Onion powder to taste
1/4 c. salad oil	Garlic powder to taste

Dissolve the bouillon cubes in hot water. Mix the flour, salt, pepper and paprika and dredge chicken with flour mixture. Heat the oil in a large casserole and place the chicken in oil, skin side down. Sprinkle remaining flour mixture over chicken and cover with celery, parsley, onions, mushrooms and almonds. Sprinkle with onion powder and garlic powder and pour bouillon over top. Bake in 400-degree oven for about 15 minutes. Reduce temperature to 350 degrees and bake for 1 hour longer. Serve with rice. 4-6 servings.

Dean L. Eidson, Corpus Christi, Texas

CHICKEN BREASTS VERONIQUE (FRANCE)

3 chicken breasts, halved	1 tbsp. minced carrot
Salt and pepper to taste	1/2 bay leaf
Flour	1 c. meat stock
Butter	1 c. sherry
Oil	1 No. 2 can muscatel grapes
1 tbsp. minced onion	

Season the chicken with salt and pepper and dredge with flour. Saute in skillet in equal quantities of butter and oil until brown, then place in a shallow casserole. Melt 2 tablespoons butter in a saucepan. Add the onion, carrot and bay leaf and cook over low heat until butter is brown. Stir in 2 tablespoons flour and cook until bubbly. Add the stock and cook until thick and smooth. Strain and season with salt and pepper. Swirl the saucepan with sherry and reduce heat. Add the brown sauce and grapes and pour over chicken. 6 servings.

Mrs. Norman Sands, Waycross, Georgia

TURKEY SAUCE PIQUANTE (FRANCE)

1 5 to 6-lb. turkey	3/4 tsp. salt
1/4 c. chopped onion	1/4 tsp. cayenne pepper
1/4 c. chopped celery	2 tbsp. chopped green onion
2 tbsp. chopped green pepper	2 tbsp. chopped parsley
1 8-oz. can tomato sauce	1 1/2 tsp. piccalilli

Cut the turkey in serving pieces. Place the back and neck in a saucepan and add 2 cups boiling water. Simmer until liquid is reduced to 1 cup. Drain and reserve stock. Discard back and neck. Fry remaining turkey in fat in a large skillet until golden brown. Remove from skillet and set aside. Saute the onion, celery and green pepper in small amount of fat in same skillet until tender. Add the tomato sauce, salt and cayenne pepper and simmer for 30 minutes. Add reserved turkey stock and turkey and cover. Simmer for about 1 hour and 30 minutes or until turkey is tender. Remove from heat and add green onion, parsley and piccalilli. Serve the turkey over spaghetti or steamed rice with sauce.

Sybil A. Roy, Baton Rouge, Louisiana

CHICKEN WITH SAUERKRAUT (GERMANY)

1 1/2 c. flour	2 cans potatoes
2 tsp. salt	2 to 3 cans
2 tsp. pepper	sauerkraut
2 tsp. dry mustard	1 1/2 c. cooking
1 2 1/2 to 3-lb. fryer,	sherry
disjointed	

Mix the flour, salt, pepper and mustard and dredge the chicken with flour mixture. Brown in a small amount of fat in a skillet. Layer the chicken, potatoes and sauerkraut in a large saucepan and pour the sherry over the top. Cover. Cook over low heat for 1 hour and 30 minutes to 2 hours. 6 servings.

Mrs. Marian L. Carpenter, Farmersville, Texas

CHICKEN WITH RICE (GERMANY)

1 4-lb. chicken, disjointed	1/2 bay leaf
2 qt. boiling water	1 sm. onion, chopped
1 tbsp. salt	3 carrots, chopped
2 sprigs of parsley	1/2 lb. rice

Place the chicken in a kettle and add the water and salt. Cook over low heat until tender. Add the parsley, bay leaf, onion and carrots and cook over low heat until vegetables are tender. Cook the rice according to package directions and drain. Add to the chicken mixture and bring to a boil. Serve hot. Chicken may be removed from kettle before adding rice and browned in butter, if desired. 8-10 servings.

Mrs. Paul Tupper, Louisville, Kentucky

EPICUREAN CHICKEN LIVERS (GREECE)

4 tbsp. butter or margarine	1 4-oz. can sliced mushrooms
1 lb. chicken livers	1 10 1/2-oz. can giblet
1/2 c. chopped celery	gravy
1/2 c. chopped onion	1/4 tsp. salt
1/2 tsp. rubbed sage	Curried rice

Melt the butter in a 10-inch skillet over low heat. Cut the livers in bite-sized pieces. Add the livers, celery, onion and sage to skillet and cook until vegetables are tender but not brown. Drain the mushrooms and stir into the liver mixture. Stir in the gravy and salt. Cook over medium heat, stirring occasionally, until heated through. Serve over curried rice. 4 servings.

Mrs. Matthew Dobson, Marietta, Georgia

CHICKEN PAPRIKA (HUNGARY)

4 chicken breasts, halved	1 tbsp. paprika
6 tbsp. butter	3/8 c. flour

1 tsp. salt	3/4 c. finely diced celery
2 tbsp. shortening	2/3 c. water
1 med. onion, minced	1/2 c. sour cream or cream

Remove chicken from bones and brown in 4 tablespoons butter in a frying pan. Cream remaining butter in a bowl and stir in paprika, 1/4 cup flour and salt. Spread over chicken and cover. Cook over low heat for 30 minutes. Melt the shortening in a saucepan. Add the onion and cook until lightly browned. Add celery and water and cover. Cook for 8 to 10 minutes. Pour over the chicken and cover. Cook for 15 minutes. Stir remaining flour into sour cream and stir into pan juices. Cover and cook for 5 to 6 minutes longer. 4 servings.

Elizabeth Heard, Jackson, Mississippi

TURKEY PAPRIKASH (HUNGARY)

1/4 c. butter	1 tsp. sugar
1/2 c. finely chopped onion	1 1/2 c. milk
1 6-oz. can sliced mushrooms	1 c. sour cream
1/4 c. flour	2 1/2 c. diced cooked turkey
2 tsp. paprika	Buttered noodles
1 tsp. salt	

Melt the butter in a heavy saucepan and add the onion. Drain the mushrooms and add to onion. Cook and stir until the onion is transparent. Blend in the flour, paprika, salt and sugar. Add the milk and cook, stirring constantly, until smooth and thickened. Remove from heat and stir in the sour cream. Add the turkey and heat through. Serve on noodles. 6 servings.

Turkey Paprikash (Hungary) (above)

CHICKEN AND ONIONS (HUNGARY)

1   2 to 3-lb. fryer
Salt to taste
1 stick margarine

4 c. onion rings
1 lge. can evaporated milk

Cut the chicken in serving pieces and season with salt. Cook in the margarine in a large skillet over medium heat until tender. Remove chicken from skillet and cool slightly. Remove chicken from bones. Add the onion rings to margarine in the skillet and cook until tender. Add milk and cook over low heat until thickened. Add the chicken and heat through. Serve over noodles or rice and garnish with parsley or tomato wedges.

Mrs. C. M. Conlan, Jr., Burleson, Texas

GINGER CHICKEN (INDIA)

3 tbsp. butter
3 tbsp. flour
1 1/2 tsp. salt
1 1/2 tsp. curry powder
3/4 tsp. ginger
Dash of pepper

3 c. milk
2 c. cooked chicken, cut in
   chunks
3 hard-cooked eggs, sliced
4 c. hot buttered rice

Melt the butter in a saucepan and blend in the flour, salt, curry powder, ginger and pepper. Add the milk and cook over medium heat, stirring constantly, until thickened. Add the chicken and eggs and heat through. Serve over rice. 6-8 servings.

Ginger Chicken (India) (above)

CHICKEN CURRY (INDIA)

1/2 c. butter	1 tsp. salt
2 onions, minced	1/2 tsp. pepper
1 fryer, disjointed	1/2 tsp. cayenne pepper
2 c. canned tomatoes	1 c. light cream
1 to 2 tbsp. curry powder	Hot cooked rice

Melt the butter in a deep saucepan. Add the onions and cook over low heat until tender. Add the chicken and stir well. Add the tomatoes and seasonings and cover tightly. Simmer for 1 hour or until chicken is tender, stirring occasionally. Add the cream and bring to a boil. Make a border of rice on a platter and place chicken mixture in center. 6 servings.

Gussie Mae Beard, Pelican, Louisiana

CHICKEN DELHI (INDIA)

1 1/2 tsp. ginger	1 c. grated onion
1/8 tsp. coriander	1 tbsp. turmeric
1/8 tsp. pepper	1 1/2 tsp. salt
1 2 to 3-lb. fryer,	1/2 pt. yogurt
disjointed	1/2 pt. light cream
1/4 c. melted butter	1 sm. onion, sliced in rings

Preheat oven to 350 degrees. Combine the ginger, coriander and pepper and rub on chicken. Place the chicken in a shallow roasting pan. Combine the butter, grated onion, turmeric, salt, yogurt and light cream and pour half the mixture over chicken. Roast for 1 hour, basting frequently with remaining yogurt mixture. Top chicken with onion rings and roast for 1 hour longer or until chicken is tender. Arrange chicken on a platter. Remove excess fat from gravy and pour some of the gravy over chicken. Serve remaining gravy with chicken. 8 servings.

Hazel Kirk, Lakeland, Florida

CHICKEN MADRAS (INDIA)

1/4 c. butter or margarine	1/2 tsp. dry mustard
1 tart apple, pared and diced	1/8 tsp. sage
1 c. diced cooked carrots	1 1/2 c. chicken broth
1 stalk celery, diced	1 bay leaf
2 sm. onions, chopped	3 c. diced cooked chicken
1 clove of garlic, minced	1/2 c. light cream
2 tbsp. flour	2 tbsp. chopped chutney
1 tsp. curry powder	Rice ring
1 tsp. salt	

Melt the butter in a large saucepan. Add the apple, carrots, celery, onions and garlic and cook, stirring frequently, for 5 minutes. Remove from heat. Mix the flour, curry powder, salt, mustard and sage and stir into butter mixture. Cook, stirring, until bubbly. Stir in the chicken broth and add bay leaf. Bring to boiling point, stirring constantly, and boil for 1 minute. Stir in the chicken, cream and chutney and heat through. Remove bay leaf and serve chicken mixture in rice ring. 4-6 servings.

Mrs. Val C. Manley, Bristol, Virginia

CHICKEN AND VEGETABLES (ITALY)

6 chicken breasts	1 tsp. salt
1 lge. onion, sliced	1 lge. can tomatoes
3 med. green peppers	1 6-oz. can sliced mushrooms
3 stalks celery	2 tbsp. lemon juice

Brown the chicken in small amount of fat in a large skillet. Pour off all except 3 tablespoons fat. Place the onion over chicken. Cut the green peppers in 1-inch chunks and place over onion. Slice the celery in 1-inch pieces and place over green peppers. Add the salt and pour tomatoes over top. Bring to a boil and cover. Reduce heat and simmer for 30 minutes. Add the mushrooms and lemon juice and simmer for 10 minutes longer. 6 servings.

Brenda Joyce McKinley, Cedar Grove, West Virginia

CHICKEN RAVIOLI (ITALY)

1 chicken	1/4 c. parsley flakes
6 eggs	1 c. bread crumbs
1 tsp. nutmeg	5 c. flour
1/2 lge. can grated Parmesan cheese	1 onion
	2 tbsp. tomato paste
Salt to taste	Pepper to taste

Place the chicken in a kettle and cover with boiling water. Cook until chicken is tender. Remove chicken from broth and cool. Remove chicken from bones, grind and place in a bowl. Add 2 eggs, nutmeg, cheese, salt, parsley and bread crumbs and mix well. Beat remaining eggs and mix in the flour, salt and enough water for a stiff dough. Roll out on a floured surface and cut in 3-inch squares. Place 1 heaping teaspoon chicken mixture on each square. Fold and press edges together. Add the onion, tomato paste, salt and pepper to chicken broth and bring to a boil. Reduce heat and simmer for 25 minutes. Remove onion and add the chicken squares. Cook for 20 minutes.

Dorotha Danel, Coyle, Oklahoma

CHICKEN TETRAZZINI (ITALY)

1 4 1/2-lb. hen, disjointed	1 tbsp. lemon juice
Salt	2 tbsp. flour
1 tsp. onion salt	Paprika to taste
1/2 tsp. celery salt	1/4 tsp. pepper
1/2 lb. spaghetti	1/8 tsp. nutmeg
6 tbsp. butter or margarine	1 c. heavy cream
1/2 lb. sliced mushrooms	2/3 c. grated Parmesan cheese

Place the chicken in a deep kettle and add 3 cups boiling water, 2 teaspoons salt, onion salt and celery salt. Cover. Simmer until chicken is tender. Remove chicken from broth and cool. Remove chicken from bones and cut in large pieces. Drain 2 1/2 cups broth from the kettle and reserve. Add 3 quarts water and 2 tablespoons salt to remaining broth and bring to a boil. Add spaghetti slowly and cook, stirring occasionally, for 6 minutes. Drain and place in a 12 x 8 x 2-inch baking dish. Beat 3 tablespoons butter in a medium skillet. Add the mushrooms and sprinkle with lemon juice and 1/2 teaspoon salt. Saute the mushrooms, stirring occasionally, until soft but not brown. Mix the mushrooms, remaining butter and chicken with spaghetti. Mix small amount of reserved broth with the flour. Stir into remaining reserved broth in a saucepan. Add remaining ingredients except cheese and cook, stirring constantly, until thickened. Stir into spaghetti mixture and sprinkle with cheese. Bake at 350 degrees for 30 minutes. May be refrigerated overnight before baking. One-half cup cooking sherry may be substituted for 1/2 cup reserved broth. 8 servings.

Mrs. Theresa F. Pearson, Millers Creek, North Carolina

EGG NOODLES WITH CHICKEN CACCIATORE (ITALY)

1 2 1/2 to 3-lb. fryer	1/4 c. dry sherry
3 tbsp. olive or salad oil	Salt
1 sm. onion, chopped	1/4 tsp. pepper
1 clove of garlic, minced	1/4 tsp. marjoram
1/2 lb. mushrooms, sliced	3 qt. boiling water
1 1-lb. 3-oz. can tomatoes	8 oz. medium egg noodles
1 6-oz. can tomato paste	

Cut the chicken in serving pieces and brown in oil in a large skillet. Drain the chicken on paper towels and discard drippings. Mix the onion, garlic, mushrooms, tomatoes, tomato paste, sherry, 1 1/4 teaspoons salt, pepper and marjoram in the skillet and bring to a boil. Reduce heat and cover. Simmer for 30 minutes. Add the chicken and cover. Simmer for 20 minutes longer or until chicken is tender. Add 1 tablespoon salt to boiling water. Add the noodles gradually so that water continues to boil and cook, stirring occasionally, until tender. Drain in a colander and serve with chicken. 4 servings.

Egg Noodles with Chicken Cacciatore (Italy) (above)

CHICKEN AND NOODLES (ITALY)

1 c. chopped onion	1/4 tsp. powdered oregano
1 clove of garlic, minced	Salt and pepper to taste
1/2 c. chopped green pepper	1 1/2 c. chicken broth
2 tbsp. butter or margarine	5 c. cubed cooked chicken
2 cans tomato soup	1 8-oz. package noodles or
1 3-oz. can pimento, chopped	spaghetti
1 or 2 bay leaves	Paprika to taste
1/2 tsp. chili powder	Grated Parmesan cheese to taste
1/2 tsp. sugar	

Saute the onion, garlic and green pepper in butter in a 10-inch skillet over medium heat until tender. Add the tomato soup, pimento, bay leaves, chili powder, sugar, oregano, salt and pepper and simmer for 5 minutes. Add the chicken broth and chicken and simmer for 5 minutes. Cook the noodles according to package directions and stir into chicken mixture. Top with paprika and Parmesan cheese. May be refrigerated for several hours to blend flavors. Heat and serve. 6-8 servings.

Mrs. L. S. Coers, Mathis, Texas

CHICKEN IN FOIL (ITALY)

1 lge. fryer	1 tsp. salt
4 tbsp. olive oil	Pepper to taste
1 onion, chopped	1/2 tsp. oregano
1 stalk celery with leaves,	1 c. tomato sauce
chopped	2 tbsp. onion soup mix

Cut the chicken in serving pieces and brush with oil. Place in a broiler pan and broil until light brown on both sides. Place large sheet of heavy-duty foil in a shallow baking pan and sprinkle half the onion and celery on foil. Place chicken on onion mixture, cut side up, and sprinkle with salt, pepper and oregano. Spread tomato sauce over chicken and sprinkle with soup mix. Add remaining onion and celery and close foil tightly. Bake at 350 degrees for 1 hour and 30 minutes. 4 servings.

Mrs. Frances L. Dover, Spartanburg, South Carolina

OVEN-FRIED CHICKEN (ITALY)

1 1/2 c. fine dry bread crumbs	2 tsp. salt
3/4 c. grated Parmesan cheese	1/4 tsp. pepper
1/4 c. chopped parsley	1 3-lb. fryer, disjointed
1 clove of garlic, minced	1 c. melted butter

Combine first 6 ingredients. Dip chicken in butter and roll in crumb mixture. Place in single layer in a shallow baking pan and drizzle with remaining butter and crumb mixture. Bake in 375-degree oven for about 45 minutes. 4 servings.

Mrs. Mildred Bigby, Talpa, Texas

TRUFFLED ROAST CAPON (ITALY)

2 walnut-sized canned white truffles, sliced	1/2 tsp. poultry seasoning
	4 tbsp. melted butter
1 5-lb. capon	Salt to taste
Pepper to taste	1/2 c. Marsala or port

Insert half the truffle slices under skin of the breast of the capon, then rub capon with pepper and poultry seasoning. Place remaining truffle slices in cavity of the capon and truss. Wrap in aluminum foil and refrigerate for 24 hours. Brush capon with melted butter and place on rack in a shallow baking pan. Pour remaining butter over capon and cover with aluminum foil. Roast in 300-degree oven for 1 hour. Season with salt and roast for 1 hour, basting frequently with Marsala and pan juices. Remove foil and roast for 30 minutes longer or until light brown. 4-6 servings.

Sister Mary Louise, Clarksburg, West Virginia

PINEAPPLE-CHICKEN TERIYAKI (JAPAN)

1 1-lb. 4 1/2-oz. can pineapple slices	1/4 c. cooking oil
	2 tbsp. cider vinegar
1/2 c. soy sauce	1 sm. clove of garlic, minced
1 tbsp. molasses	1/4 c. sauterne
2 tbsp. brown sugar	5 chicken breasts

Drain the pineapple and reserve 1/4 cup syrup. Mix the reserved syrup, soy sauce, molasses, brown sugar, oil, vinegar, garlic and sauterne. Bone and skin the chicken breasts and place in a shallow dish. Add the pineapple. Pour the molasses mixture over chicken mixture and cover. Marinate in refrigerator for several hours. Drain and reserve marinade. Grill chicken over hot coals, turning and basting frequently with reserved marinade, until tender and browned. Grill pineapple on both sides and serve 2 slices with each chicken breast. 5 servings.

Photograph for this recipe on page 166.

PINEAPPLE CHICKEN (JAPAN)

2 1/2 lb. chicken breasts	2 tbsp. red wine vinegar
1 tsp. powdered ginger	1/2 c. water
Seasoned flour	1/4 c. brown sugar
4 tbsp. butter or margarine	1 4 1/2-oz. can crushed pineapple
1/4 c. soy sauce	

Sprinkle the chicken with ginger on both sides and dredge with seasoned flour. Brown in butter in a skillet. Mix the soy sauce, vinegar, water and brown sugar in a bowl and pour over chicken. Spoon pineapple over chicken and cover. Simmer for 50 minutes, basting occasionally with soy sauce mixture. Serve hot. Two teaspoons minced gingerroot may be substituted for powdered ginger. 4 servings.

Mrs. Wendy Wilson, Silver Spring, Maryland

Chicken-Lettuce Oriental (Laos) (below)

CHICKEN-LETTUCE ORIENTAL (LAOS)

1 med. head iceberg lettuce	1 2 1/2-lb. fryer, disjointed
1/3 c. soy sauce	1/4 c. blanched whole almonds
1/4 c. white wine	2 tbsp. oil
1 tbsp. sugar	1 13 1/2-oz. can pineapple
1 tsp. ground ginger	chunks
1 clove of garlic, minced	1 tbsp. cornstarch

Core, rinse and drain the lettuce and chill in a plastic bag. Combine the soy sauce, wine, sugar, ginger and garlic in a shallow dish. Place the chicken in wine mixture and marinate for 1 hour, turning and basting occasionally. Remove chicken to a baking pan. Bake at 325 degrees for 1 hour, basting twice with marinade. Brown the almonds in oil in a skillet. Remove and drain on paper towels. Place the undrained pineapple in the skillet and heat. Mix the cornstarch with remaining marinade and add to pineapple. Cook and stir until sauce comes to a boil and is thickened, then add the chicken and almonds. Cut the lettuce crosswise in slices. Place slices, cut side down, on a board and cut crosswise and lengthwise in bite-sized chunks. Line platter with lettuce and spoon the chicken and sauce over lettuce. Serve immediately. Three tablespoons lemon juice and 1 tablespoon water may be substituted for wine. 4-5 servings.

CHICKEN WITH MINT (LAOS)

1 2 1/2 to 3-lb. fryer	1 bell pepper, sliced
2 tsp. salt	2 tsp. soy sauce
1 tsp. monosodium glutamate	1 tsp. sugar
3 tbsp. olive oil	1 5-oz. can water chestnuts
1 white onion, sliced	2 tbsp. fresh chopped mint

Cut the chicken in serving pieces and season with salt and monosodium gluta-mate. Brown in olive oil in a heavy skillet. Add the onion and bell pepper and cover. Simmer until chicken is tender. Add the soy sauce and sugar. Slice the water chestnuts and add to chicken mixture. Cook for 5 minutes. Add the mint and cook for 3 minutes longer. Serve on rice. One tablespoon dried mint may be substituted for fresh mint. 4 servings.

Jack Anderson, Plaquemine, Louisiana

HACIENDA CHICKEN (SPAIN)

3 tbsp. butter or margarine	1 tbsp. chopped parsley
1/2 c. chopped onion	1 tsp. paprika
1 16-oz. can tomatoes	1 tbsp. salt
1 c. water	1/4 tsp. pepper
1/2 c. chopped green pepper	1 stewing chicken
1 2 1/2-oz. can sliced	1 c. rice
mushrooms	1/2 c. sliced green olives
1 whole clove	

Melt the butter in a heavy skillet. Add the onion and cook until lightly browned. Add the tomatoes, water, green pepper, mushrooms and liquid, clove, parsley, paprika, salt and pepper. Cut the chicken in serving pieces and add to tomato mixture. Bring to a boil and cover. Reduce heat and simmer for 1 hour. Add the rice and olives and cook for 1 hour or until rice is done and chicken is tender. 6 servings.

Naomi M. Vaught, Bradenton, Florida

CHILI CHICKEN (MEXICO)

2 lge. stewing hens	1 tsp. cumin
2 eggs, beaten	1 tsp. chili powder
2 c. seasoned flour	1 tsp. pepper
Shortening	2 lge. cans chili salsa
1 tsp. oregano	

Cut the chickens in serving pieces. Dip in eggs and dredge with flour mixture. Fry in shortening in a skillet until brown, then place in a casserole. Mix remaining ingredients and pour over chicken. Bake at 350 degrees for 2 hours or until chicken is tender. 10 servings.

Mrs. Patricia Bryant, Greenville, Kentucky

CHICKEN NUEVO LAREDO (MEXICO)

1 3-lb. chicken	1 tsp. parsley flakes
2 lge. limes	Butter
Salt to taste	1 sm. can mushrooms

Cut the chicken in quarters or halves and soak in salted water for 1 hour. Line a baking pan with large piece of foil and place chicken on foil. Squeeze juice of limes over chicken and place lime peel around chicken. Sprinkle the chicken with salt and parsley flakes. Dot with butter and add the mushrooms. Wrap foil around chicken mixture. Bake at 350 degrees for 30 to 45 minutes. Turn back foil and bake until chicken is brown. 3-4 servings.

Alicia Hampton, Naples-Omaha, Texas

Turkey Mole (Mexico) (below)

TURKEY MOLE (MEXICO)

2 green peppers, cut in chunks
2 sm. onions, peeled
2   1-lb. cans tomatoes
1   4-oz. can pimento, drained
1/2 c. blanched almonds (opt.)
1/4 c. salad oil
1 tbsp. chili powder
1 1/4 tsp. salt

1/2 tsp. hot sauce
1/8 tsp. cinnamon
1/8 tsp. ground cloves
2 bouillon cubes
1/4 c. fine dry bread crumbs
1 sq. unsweetened chocolate
8 cooked turkey slices

Place the green peppers, onions, tomatoes, pimento and almonds in a blender container and cover. Blend for 1 minute or until smooth. Heat the oil in a skillet. Add the tomato mixture, seasonings, spices and bouillon cubes and bring to a boil. Reduce heat and cover. Simmer for 30 minutes. Uncover and stir in bread crumbs and chocolate. Heat, stirring occasionally, until chocolate is melted. Layer the sauce with turkey slices in a 2 1/2-quart casserole or on a large oven-proof platter. Bake in 350-degree oven for about 20 minutes and serve with rice. 8 servings.

CHICKEN IN CREAM (RUSSIA)

1 fryer
Flour
3 1/2 c. heavy cream
1/4 tsp. salt

1/8 tsp. pepper
1/2 tsp. finely chopped dill
1 med. onion, chopped

Remove chicken from bones and cut in small pieces. Dredge with flour. Brown in small amount of fat in a skillet and drain. Place in a shallow roaster. Add the cream, salt, pepper, dill and onion and cover. Bake at 350 degrees for 35 to 45 minutes. 4-6 servings.

Mrs. Daniel Grisholm, Charlottsville, Virginia

STUFFED CHICKEN (PAKISTAN)

1 sm. onion
1 med. green gingerroot
1 tbsp. pepper
1 tsp. salt
1 c. yogurt or sour cream
1 3 1/2 to 4-lb. chicken
4 sm. boiled potatoes

2 hard-cooked eggs
Juice of 1 lemon
2 tbsp. chopped blanched
   almonds
1/4 c. seedless raisins
1/4 c. butter

Chop the onion and gingerroot together. Add the pepper, salt and yogurt and mix well. Spread over chicken and pierce chicken all over with a fork. Let stand for 1 hour or longer. Dice the potatoes and eggs and place in a bowl. Sprinkle with lemon juice. Add the almonds and raisins and mix well. Place in cavity of chicken and truss the chicken. Melt the butter in a Dutch oven and place chicken in butter. Cover. Cook over low heat for about 2 hours or until chicken is tender, turning frequently. 4-5 servings.

Ruth Dantzler, Columbia, South Carolina

PEACH CHICKEN (PERSIA)

1 16-oz. can peach halves
1/4 c. lemon juice
2 tbsp. melted butter
3 lge. chicken breasts, halved

Salt and pepper to taste
1 10 1/2-oz. can mandarin
   oranges

Press peaches and syrup through a sieve. Add the lemon juice and butter and mix well. Sprinkle chicken with salt and pepper and place, skin side down, on rack in a broiling pan. Broil 6 inches from heat for about 15 minutes, brushing with peach mixture every 5 minutes. Turn chicken and broil for 15 minutes longer, brushing with peach mixture every 5 minutes. Mix remaining peach mixture with oranges and syrup in a saucepan and heat to boiling point. Spoon over chicken and serve with rice, if desired. One 16-ounce can pitted sweet cherries may be substituted for oranges. 6 servings.

Mrs. Margie Gilchrist, Borger, Texas

SMOTHERED CHICKEN (RUMANIA)

2 tbsp. butter or margarine
1 2 1/2 to 3-lb. fryer
2 tbsp. all-purpose flour
1 c. sour cream
2 tsp. seasoned salt

1/4 tsp. pepper
2 tbsp. snipped parsley
1 tbsp. poppy seed
2 c. water
2 tsp. lemon juice

Melt the butter in a large skillet. Cut the chicken in serving pieces and brown in the butter. Remove from skillet. Stir the flour into drippings remaining in skillet, scraping bottom of skillet well. Blend in the sour cream, seasoned salt, pepper, parsley, poppy seed and water and bring to a boil, stirring constantly. Place the chicken in the skillet and cover. Simmer for 45 minutes or until chicken is tender, then stir in the lemon juice. 4 servings.

Mrs. Carl Phillips, Raleigh, North Carolina

RICE AND CHICKEN (SYRIA)

1 fryer, disjointed	Pepper and cinnamon to taste
Butter	2 c. rice
3 tsp. salt	3 or 4 med. onions, sliced
1 sm. onion	2 No. 300 cans chick peas

Cook the chicken in small amount of butter in a large skillet until partially done. Add enough water to cover, 2 teaspoons salt, small onion, pepper and cinnamon and bring to a boil. Reduce heat and simmer until chicken is just tender. Remove chicken from skillet and set aside. Strain and reserve broth. Soak the rice in hot, salted water. Melt 1/4 cup butter in the skillet. Add the sliced onions and remaining salt and saute until light brown. Set aside. Place the chicken in a 4-quart saucepan and add the peas. Add the onions, pepper and cinnamon. Drain the rice and place on onions. Add enough water to reserved broth to make 4 cups liquid and pour over rice. Bring to a boil and reduce heat. Cover. Cook until rice is done and liquid has evaporated. Turn upside down on large, round platter. 8 servings.

Billie Sebert, Clinton, Oklahoma

CHICKEN POLYNESIAN (TAHITI)

2 chicken breasts, split	1/3 c. water
2 tbsp. shortening	2 tsp. lemon juice
1/2 c. slivered green pepper	2 pineapple slices
1/4 c. sliced onion	2 c. hot cooked rice
1 tsp. curry powder	1/4 c. toasted coconut
1 can tomato soup	

Brown the chicken breasts in shortening in a skillet. Add the green pepper and onion and brown lightly. Pour off fat. Add the curry powder, soup, water and lemon juice and cover. Cook over low heat for 40 minutes. Drain the pineapple and cut in half. Place 1/2 pineapple slice on each chicken breast and cover. Cook for 5 minutes longer or until chicken is tender. Uncover and cook to desired consistency. Toss the rice with coconut and serve with chicken. 4 servings.

Chicken Polynesian (Tahiti) (above)

INDEX

PHOTOGRAPHY CREDITS: Florida Citrus Commission; National Broiler Council; The R. T. French Company; Accent-International; California Avocado Advisory Board; Florida Fresh Fruit and Vegetable Association; American Mushroom Institute; American Spice Trade Association; Best Foods: A Division of Corn Products Company, International; John Oster Manufacturing Company; The Apple Pantry; Angostura-Wuppermann Corporation; Pet Milk Company; Brussels Sprouts Marketing Program; National Macaroni Institute; Filbert/Hazelnut Institute; Spanish Green Olive Commission; California Strawberry Advisory Board; National Kraut Packers Association; General Foods Kitchens: Shake 'n Bake; Ocean Spray Cranberries, Incorporated; Diamond Walnut Kitchen; Carnation Company; Artichoke Advisory Board; R. C. Bigelow Tea Company; Procter and Gamble Company: Crisco Division; Knox Gelatine, Incorporated; McIlhenny Company; Evaporated Milk Association; Sugar Information, Incorporated; California Raisin Advisory Board; Cling Peach Advisory Board; National Dairy Council; American Dry Milk Institute; Pineapple Growers Association; Keith Thomas Company; Campbell Soup Company.

Printed in the United States of America.